son of the city

DANTE ROSS
son of the city

RARE BIRD
LOS ANGELES, CALIF.

RARE BIRD

THIS IS A GENUINE RARE BIRD BOOK

Rare Bird Books
6044 North Figueroa Street
Los Angeles, CA 90042
rarebirdbooks.com

Set in Dante
Printed in the United States

10 9 8 7 6 5 4 3 2 1

Library of Congress Cataloging-in-Publication Data

Names: Ross, Dante, author.
Title: Son of the city : a memoir / by Dante Ross.
Description: Los Angeles : Rare Bird Books, 2023.
Identifiers: LCCN 2019052616 | ISBN 9781947856943 (hardback)
Subjects: LCSH: Ross, Dante. | Sound recording executives and
producers—United States—Biography. | LCGFT: Autobiographies.
Classification: LCC ML429.R72 A3 2020 | DDC 781.64092 [B]—dc23

LC record available at https://lccn.loc.gov/2019052616

DEDICATION

I dedicate this to all my friends and family who are no longer here. I try to take a part of every one of you with me everywhere I go. Thank you for sharing your beings with me and making my life a better one.

John Ross, Norma Ross, Geeby Dajani, John Gamble, Daniel Dumile, Dingilizwe Dumile, Ason Unique, Andy Kessler, Yves Brewer, Uncle QR Hand, Uncle Sidney Dominitz, Adam Yauch, Chris Lighty, John Berry, Dave Parsons, Gabby Mejia, and Sean "The Captain" Carasov.

CONTENTS

PROLOGUE

My dad first mentioned writing a book with me in 2009, in passing, after his second round of chemotherapy. He thought a dual biography chronicling our separate upbringings in New York and our combined fascination with music and culture would be the common thread. I was intimidated by the idea, but also intrigued. My father was an accomplished writer and journalist, having published eleven books in his illustrious career. It would be, for my dad, quite possibly his last published work, and for me it would be my first. This full circle-of-life metaphor was not lost on either of us.

As his inevitable passing drew closer daily, I undertook the task of documenting my life, my complicated relationship with him, my career in the music industry, my highly dysfunctional childhood, and the oft-strained relationship I maintained with the world at large. I have spent more than thirty years involved in making music in one form or another—often knee-deep in the trenches, as a conduit for some incredible talent. On some levels, it is what validates me to many people, my father included. It is perhaps the most important part of my journey.

By the grace of God, I choose this path.

My main concern with attempting to write this book was that I didn't know if I was ready to explore the good and bad things in my past, to find out whether the experience would open up some old wounds. (I still might not be, in all honesty.) Lucky for me, my pops, if nothing else, was a persistent person. He stayed on me about writing, and for that I am once again thankful.

If you ever encountered my father, chances are you remember it. He was a rebel of the highest order, very honest, direct, and irreverent. He resembled a Bohemian pirate, looking like a cross between Dr. John and a retired biker, minus the ink. He was a true character and a man of conviction. Truly, he was unforgettable. And, like me, he was a flawed person. All of the people I truly love are, and my father was no exception. He was also my best friend and my kindred spirit. I dedicate this book to him.

He was beyond worth it.

My dad suggested when writing this book that we explore our unique stories individually, as he felt they were connected via lineage regardless of the separate yarns we would spin. He felt there was also a lot of common ground for us to meet on and explore together. We bonded deeply over our mutual love of sports, particularly basketball. Even if we hadn't seen each other for a long time, we would jump right into a debate about my Knicks and his Lakers, along with music, pop culture, and politics. My pops loved art, and we spent lots of time going to museums and galleries together. Even though he was such a dominant influence in my life, my pops didn't raise me—my mother did. Nonetheless, I feel the transference of personality traits, likes, rhythms, and overall aesthetic was hereditary.

Unfortunately, he passed before we were able to complete our intertwining stories, which led me down a different path than I initially intended. I think he would have ordained the end result of our project, albeit with a sarcastic remark or three—that was just his way.

This is my story.

JUST BEGUN

The music bug bit me at an early age. My mom constantly played music in the pad; she dug singer-songwriters like Bob Dylan, Van Morrison, Joni Mitchell; folk pioneers like Woody Guthrie; and, most of all, soul singers like Otis Redding, Bill Withers, Aretha Franklin, and Wilson Pickett. Her favorite artist, though, was Janis Joplin.

My dad, on the other hand, had a more esoteric taste in music, which was borderline avant-garde and ran the gamut from free jazz to Sam Cooke. He wasn't into rock 'n' roll—for the most part, he thought it was corny. He couldn't stand the Led Zeppelins of the day. He was a beatnik, a jazzbo, a bohemian, and I thought that was pretty cool. Besides jazz, he appreciated Marvin Gaye, Tower of Power, Stevie Wonder, Chaka Khan, and Rufus. But his soundtrack of choice was more Coltrane, Mingus, and Miles—artists I couldn't grasp as a kid but whom I grew to love over time.

My first love was Black music. It began while watching *Soul Train* with my older sis and imitating dance steps at her urging. Then came my fixation with *The Jackson 5ive* cartoon. I was a full-on Michael Jackson fanatic. On my seventh birthday, I walked to Delancey Street with my sister, Dylan, and bought a cutout copy of *ABC* for $1.99 with the fiver my friend Bobby Rivera's grandfather had slipped me. (Cutouts were records where the corner of the album cover was literally "cut out," allowing a discounted price for the retail store and the customer. This was a common thing in the seventies.) I played *ABC* nonstop for the next three months while my friends and I tried to mimic the Jackson 5's dance steps, always arguing over who was going to be Michael. I usually ended up being Tito or Randy or some shit. That's what happens when you're one of the only white kids in the crew.

A few years later, I got into the Stones, Elton John, and the Beatles. As a teenager, I moved on to the Clash, the Bad Brains, and a plethora of obscure punk bands that I still love to this day. Then, in 1986, I heard Run-DMC and everything changed for me. But I'm going to start from the beginning because I have come to realize that music isn't the only thing that has influenced my career in music.

Norma's (My Mom's) Playlist

Janis Joplin—"Me and Bobby McGee"
Van Morrison—"Moondance"
Bill Withers—"Lean on Me"
Aretha Franklin—"I Say a Little Prayer"
Bob Dylan—"The Times They are A-Changin'"
Wilson Pickett—"Mustang Sally"
Ann Peebles—"I Can't Stand the Rain"
Otis Redding—"(Sittin' on) the Dock of the Bay"
Joni Mitchell—"Coyote"
Woody Guthrie—"Tear the Fascists Down"

My New York story begins in San Francisco. I was born at San Francisco General Hospital, smack dab in the middle of the 1960s. I'd imagine San Francisco was a pretty dope place to be during that time, but I couldn't tell you. My parents' marriage quickly went from the Summer of Love to Altamont. My mom took me and my older sister, who was twelve at the time, back to New York, where both my parents were born.

The story my mom always told me about meeting my dad sounded like a Hallmark card framed in Bohemian folklore. It was 1957. As the 1960s approached, there was panic over fallout shelters, Communism, and race; American military advisers suffered their first casualties in Vietnam; and the FDA had just held its first hearings on the birth control pill. Change was in the air, and New York was the most hip and progressive city in the world.

Allen Ginsberg gave a reading in front of a crowd of fifteen hundred at Columbia, much to the chagrin of the uptight faculty. Fidel Castro lunched with Wall Street bankers, fed a Bengal tiger at the Bronx Zoo, and spoke to thirty thousand people in Central Park. The Frank Lloyd Wright–designed Solomon R. Guggenheim Museum opened, looking like nothing else. Amos Vogel's Cinema 16 club screened John Cassavetes's *Shadows*, arguably the first independent film. New Yorkers lined up in the cold outside the Five Spot, a tiny jazz club in the Bowery, to hear an alto saxophonist who had been hyped for months as the next Charlie Parker—a twenty-nine-year-old named Ornette Coleman, who happened to be an acquaintance of my dad's. This was a year before he would invent the term "Free Jazz."

My mom first spotted my dad and his wiry bespectacled self in Washington Square Park one afternoon as bongo-playing beatniks gathered near the fountain. They exchanged looks, and a few days later she saw him again in the San Remo Café, the legendary artists' hangout on Bleecker Street. Smitten, my dad kicked the Willie Bobo to my mom, and next thing you know they were an item. After a few weeks of dating, my mother and father moved in together. This in itself is pretty wild, being that mom was a single parent back when it was still quite taboo. She had given birth to my sister in 1955. I don't know much about her father except he was half Japanese, which I always thought was interesting.

My mom and dad lived on Houston off Orchard, in the building that now houses the Mercury Lounge. They ate at Katz's Deli and hung out at places like Kettle of Fish and the Minetta Tavern in the West Village. Caught in the whirlwind of beat culture and following the trail of Kerouac and Ginsberg, they moved with my older sister to Mexico to live amongst the people.

It is almost inconceivable to me that they would leave New York during such a stimulating time. But when I think about my parents' background, it makes sense. My dad was from the Upper West Side and raised on

West Broadway way before it became SoHo. He was a Jewish kid from a semi-privileged background. I remember him saying that when he lived on Central Park West as a kid, he had a doorman, something I couldn't fathom. But his father and grandfather both attended Communist meetings at a time when that was a dangerous thing to do. (I'm not sure if either were actually party members, but it wouldn't surprise me.)

My mom was an Italian from Sag Harbor, a suburb in Long Island. Her childhood is something of a mystery to me. She had a brother and a sister, both of whom I never met. I do know she was sent to boarding school at an early age after her mother passed. She wasn't close with her family, and I had no relationship with them my entire life. I never met her father, either, as he passed away prior to my birth. Mom did her best to shy away from anything associated with her family and where she was reared. My mom was a true rebel, a tough woman who had no interest in fitting into the box that society wanted to put her in. She was a feminist years before it became fashionable, and I imagine my dad loved her for it.

They stayed in Mexico for almost six years. They spoke basic Spanish when they started their journey and learned to adapt, becoming fluent over time. My sister quickly picked up Spanish, as children do, and fit in with the locals from day one. They lived in Zihuatanejo and later Michoacán, seemingly in a happy environment, when tragedy struck. My mother became pregnant with my older brother, Tristan. It was an easy birth, but Tristan was burdened with health problems and passed a few weeks later due to crib death. My mother had a nervous breakdown, and my father went on a long, hard drinking binge.

My mother needed psychiatric and medical attention. Against my father's will, they landed in San Francisco where she and my dad had a community of friends from New York and Mexico who had blazed a similar trail of Bohemia. San Francisco in the early sixties was another step on the beat trail of life. My mother recovered slowly, and my father joined her there and took a job working at the city dump.

My folks got involved in local politics and became members of the Progressive Labor Party, a Communist Party offshoot. My dad helped organize a successful welfare strike before running for mayor, which attracted the ire of the local police who in turn beat him brutally at a demonstration at City Hall, injuring his left eye permanently. His activism was legendary. He was drafted to the US Army in 1963 and refused to serve, making him the second person in America to do so. He was sentenced to five years in Terminal Island. My mom was left to fend for herself, which I would imagine was a rough time for her. A year into his sentence, my dad won an appeal.

Legend has it that upon my father's release from prison, the warden told him he never learned to be a prisoner. My dad said, "Thanks, that's the biggest compliment I have ever been given."

It's a cool story, and I have heard many about my dad, so it would be easy to glorify his exploits. Yes, he was a man of principle, and he was willing to suffer the consequences for his beliefs regardless of what it would inflict upon him and his family. He enjoyed being a martyr, and at times we suffered for it.

I was born after my father got out of jail in October of 1965. I was a last-ditch effort to save my parents' marriage after the loss of their son and my father's spell in prison. I was supposed to help heal the wounds. That's a lot to ask of a newborn. They tried for about a year and a half, but by the spring of 1967, my mom had had enough.

Our first New York City abode was a railroad apartment located on East Ninth Street between Avenues B and C. One of my earliest recollections is coming home from a walk with my sister. My mom was on her knees in the middle of our living room, crying hysterically. We had been robbed. All our shit had been gone through, and they stole what little we had, including our TV and my mom's beloved stereo. We then moved to 171 East Second Street, between Avenues A and B, which turned out to be the spot where I would spend most of my childhood.

Moving to New York and growing up there is what defines much of who I am and how I look at the world, however skewed that may be. I've traveled a lot in my life and still love my city and my neighborhood, though I now reside—for the time being—in Los Angeles. I was raised on the Lower East Side, and I intend to be buried there someday. They can spread my ashes around the hood like they did for the fallen poet Miguel Piñero, another LES original.

As I look back on my childhood, I realize that the crazy shit I was exposed to was not the norm. Everywhere I turned there were drugs, single parents, alcoholism, physical abuse, or some combination thereof. We just dealt with it because we had no choice. I used to hear out-of-towners comment how nothing seemed to surprise New Yorkers. I wonder why.

I could tell a-thousand-and-one tragic stories, but none of that is unique to me. Each and every one of us has a story, some more tragic than others. If we are lucky, we experience emotional growth from our struggles. It took me a long time to look at my childhood through that lens. For a good deal of my life, I was pissed off that I grew up the way I did. I hated my father for caring more about his activism than his family; I hated my mother for being so screwed up; and I hated my sister for bullying me. I probably hated myself for hating them. I wasn't thinking about making lemonade out of lemons; I was trying to figure out how to squirt that lemon into your eye.

I came to realize that growing up how I did on the Lower East Side exposed me to a lot of different cultures as a shorty, which turned out to be a real blessing for me. It's one thing to study multiculturalism in college, it's another to live it. And back when I was growing up, there was nowhere more diverse than downtown Manhattan.

My sister taught me how to swim with the sharks pretty early on. Dylan was pretty gully, a tough chick who never took any shit from anyone—least of all her kid brother. We both learned to be tough from our mom, who was tough on the outside yet quite fragile on the inside. Dylan was a real looker. She had porcelain white skin, light freckles, slightly slanted clear blue eyes, and long, straight black hair with a bad attitude to match. She attracted a lot of attention. She dug Latin dudes and had no shortage of dates throughout high school. She was a serious dancer and got into salsa dancing when we were young. She was constantly working on a sewing pattern for a new dress and learning some exotic dance steps. She used to enter dance contests with her boyfriend, Omar, a cool-ass Puerto Rican cat with an Afro—and it wasn't surprising when they'd win.

I clearly remember hearing Latin music for the first time around age five. My sister and her friends were listening to Willie Colón and learning the latest Latin dances, and I was freaked out by the sounds. From then on, I tuned into Latin rhythms whenever I heard them in the street—coming out of a bodega, playing from passing cars, or trickling down from my upstairs neighbors. It sounded both majestic and athletic to me. To this day, my knowledge of the art form is limited, but great salsa and boogaloo grooves still move me. I loved me some Willie Colón and Eddie Palmieri; that's just the Lower East Side in me.

When I was about five, my dad came to stay with us for a few weeks to try to kick the dope and speed habits he'd developed in San Francisco. His condition and behavior stirred up serious dysfunction in our house. I vividly remember the bloody, speed-induced hospital diorama he gave my mom for Christmas and how it made her bawl like a baby. I had a sense that something was very wrong with my family dynamic, but I didn't comprehend the gravity of the situation and wasn't able to truly understand the seriousness of my dad's state. In retrospect, it lets me know that my mom still had feelings for my father. It was unnerving to witness the emotional effect he was having on her.

As much as my dad's visit wreaked havoc in our house, there was a special moment we shared with my upstairs neighbors. We wrote get-well cards to Willis Reed, our fallen Knick hero, who was injured in the 1973 championship series. A week later, we received Willis Reed autographs. I don't know if they were real or not, but it was a catalyst for my dad's and my endless basketball-related exchanges. The Knicks had won the NBA title in 1970, and my lifelong love affair with basketball had begun. I thought it was cool of my dad since he was a diehard Lakers fan.

My pop's visit to New York also encouraged the FBI to show up at our house one morning while my mom and I were going off to work and school, respectively. Two of the corniest, whitest guys I had ever seen were standing at the bottom of our stoop. They had bad haircuts and wore cheap gray suits with white socks and ties.

Who the hell wore ties around here? I thought.

"Excuse me, miss," one of them said. "Are you Norma Ross?"

"Who's asking?" my mom blurted back.

"The FBI, Miss Ross," the other said. "We're looking for John Ross and believe you know where he is."

"Do you have a warrant?"

"No, but we can get one if need be," he said. "Now, will you answer a few questions for us?"

"Get a warrant then," she said. "I don't talk to cops. Excuse me. I have to get my son to school, if it's okay with you."

"You could get in a lot of trouble speaking to us like that, Norma."

My mom looked stunned, pissed, and worried all at once as soon as he referred to her by her first name. She took a moment and regained her composure. "I have to go. My son's gonna be late for school. Next time, get a warrant."

The FBI flunky said, "Next time we will, don't worry. Have a nice day, Norma."

"You'll need one, asshole," she said, as she grabbed me by the hand and dragged me off to school, leaving the stunned FBI men on our stoop. I remember thinking my mom had big *cajones* that day.

Before we got to school, I asked her, "Mom, who were those guys?"

"The FBI. Never talk to the FBI or any cop unless you have to," she said. "Understand?"

"But I thought cops were good, Ma?"

"Not usually, and definitely not those clowns."

She then went on to explain that being a fink was the worst thing a person could be. My dad had been upstairs in the house, trying to kick dope, and my mom wasn't about to tell the FBI about it. We didn't know exactly why the FBI was sweating my dad at the time, but we came to learn they had had an eye on him since he ran for mayor on the San Francisco Progressive Labor Party ticket in 1967.

I learned a valuable lesson that day from my mom: never snitch. My mom followed her own advice even when it came to dealing with me. My mom had merely said that my dad was "sick." I wouldn't learn that he was kicking both heroin and speed until my father hipped me to it almost three decades later. He confessed that after that month ended, he took a Greyhound back to San Francisco where he didn't waste a moment scoring a bag of dope right at the bus terminal.

After he crawled back to SF, he started to fade out of our lives. His great, cartoon-laden letters arrived less and less frequently. I missed him, never more so than when my New York Knicks played his Los Angeles Lakers in the 1973 NBA Championship. He hadn't called in a few months, so I almost hit the ceiling when my mom said he was on the phone after the first game, which the Lakers had won. The Knicks would go on to take the next four games and win their last championship to date.

My dad must have been a sore loser. I didn't hear from him again until I was thirteen.

"Who the fuck is you, white boy?"

It was the first time I had ever been called a white boy. Debbie Bonilla had called me a honky in kindergarten, which I figured was the same thing.

I couldn't tell if the dude in question was Puerto Rican or mixed race, but I knew he was a prick. He had a tall, evil-looking sidekick with him and a mangy German Shepherd riding shotgun. They must have been about nine, placing them a couple years older and a combined fifty pounds heavier than me. Shit, the dog probably had me by thirty on its own.

This was the first time I had been stepped to. I was scared shitless, so I squawked some shit about living up the block. The lanky dirt bag one didn't give a shit and raised his hands to me, ready to steal my mom's and my lunch.

He said, "I don't give a fuck where you from."

I was terrified and did what I have done several times since in my life when I knew I wasn't catching any wins—I ran like the wind. I scrambled like Fran Tarkenton, making it all the way back to my building, but unfortunately, I didn't have keys because my mom didn't trust me with them yet.

I started screaming, "Mom, Mom, help!" at the top of my lungs as I ran toward the pad. She opened the window and started yelling at the two kids and the dog, who were nearing their prey. They fell back, still threatening me. I knew I was going see them again, and I wasn't thrilled. My mom rang the buzzer and started screaming at me the second I hit the hallway. Head hanging, I shuttled back upstairs, where Mom explained some cold hard facts to her seven-year-old son.

"Dante, you're going to have to stand up to those boys, you know that?"

I was baffled. I was raised on love and hippie shit, and now I had to stand up—whatever the hell that meant.

She laid it down. "When people try to pick on you, you have to fight back."

"But fighting is bad, isn't it?"

"Not if you have to protect yourself," she said. "If you don't hit back, you're going to get hit forever. You don't want that, right?"

In retrospect, my mom was a G.

"I don't like getting hit," I said. "Can I hit back first?"

"No," she said. "You can only hit people back in self-defense."

Even then, I knew it was a crock of shit. "Okay, Mom."

She gave me a kiss on the forehead and told me to go clean my room.

As predicted, my problems on the block didn't end, and a few days later I ran into them on my way home from school. This time they were with a few other mongrel-looking kids and that evil fucking dog. I was hoping they wouldn't notice me as I ducked into the bodega. The problem was I didn't have a dime on me, and the owner kicked me to the curb.

They were waiting outside. The kid who had called me white boy stepped in front of me. "You think you're tough?"

"Ah, nah," I stuttered, which was definitely the wrong answer. The mongrels and the lanky kid started laughing their asses off. Even the dog snickered. The leader, whose name I would soon learn was Ricardo Ortiz, pushed me against the wall. I put up my hands but didn't know what the hell to do. I had seen cats catch beatings before, and it never looked like much fun for the guy getting beat up. Now it was my turn. He put up his fist and let it linger in front of my face, menacingly. I braced myself when, all of a sudden, God intervened.

Actually, it was my sister. By now Dylan was sixteen. She stood all of 5' 7" in her bellbottoms and her corky platforms. She had spit curls glued down her forehead Latina-style and milk white skin. They didn't call her Casper around the way for nothing. I have to say, she had style. And more importantly for me at that moment, she had mettle. She grabbed the main kid by the neck.

"Get away from my brother," she said. Then she turned to his homeboy. "Now take your boyfriend and get. And don't let me see you near my brother again or you're gonna have to deal with me." Cats didn't want to fuck with her. She also had a string of thuggish boyfriends for backup.

My sister wasn't always around, though, and I caught my share of beatings—more than my share, probably. It was almost as though there were a contest on the LES that ran from 1972–1977 called "Who can jump the white boy the most times?" After catching a few dozen ass whippings, I learned how to handle myself a little and eventually graduated to handing out a few beatings myself. The only way you learn to fight is by losing a bunch. Anyone who tells you differently definitely didn't grow up in the streets.

After a year and change at the local public grade school, my mom decided I should change schools because the local school wasn't cutting it. In retrospect, she was right. Starting in second grade, I got bussed with a bunch of Black and Spanish kids to a predominately white alternative school called P.S. 3 in Greenwich Village. Even though P.S. 3 was only about a mile from my house, it might as well have been on the other side of the universe.

We called P.S. 3 the "Hippie School." We got to call our teachers and principal by their first names. We were allowed to learn at our own pace, which worked well for me. I ended up pushing myself and created a self-motivated accelerated program by the time I turned eight. By third grade, I was doing fifth grade work and testing at the top of my class, but it wasn't because I was motivated or brilliant. Since it was an open classroom with kids from grades three to five, I wanted to hang with the older kids, and the only way I could do that was to do the same work they were doing.

As a result, I got pegged early on as a brain. I really liked school as a kid. After elementary school, though, I kind of lost interest. It seemed like corporate bullshit to me; there were just too many rules. For most of my life, if I wanted to learn something, I found a book on that topic and read it. Reading kids' books never really appealed to me either. By the time I was in sixth grade, I was reading J. D. Salinger. In junior high, my literary taste expanded to include the likes of Jim Carroll and Charles Bukowski. Besides Jack London, Orwell, Homer, and a few other exceptions, most of the books I had to read in school were corny.

I ended up getting into Brooklyn Tech, a nine-story high school home to seven thousand students. Tech was a good school, one of the three specialized academic high schools in New York at the time, which meant you had to test to get in. By the time I started Tech, I was bored by the curriculum, so I didn't bother to try to get good grades. I had also discovered weed, skateboarding, and girls by then. I guess you could say I was preoccupied.

That wasn't the case, however, at P.S. 3. It's safe to say I peaked academically there. The most important benefit of going there was it exposed me to a life out of the hood. I'm not gonna front, I liked it. The kids from the Village lived in cool apartments. Their parents were nice; they asked me my name and how I liked school and things like that. They would give us hot chocolate with little marshmallows in it. That kind of stuff didn't happen on my block. There was none of the stress that came with living on the LES. We got to play records, read comic books, and walk around the West Village, which had trees and a notable lack of anybody trying to rob my lunch money, call me a white boy, or kick my ass.

Probably the dopest thing about P.S. 3 was that on Fridays we got to play records and have dance contests. That was where I first started honing my selector skills. I was into KC and the Sunshine Band, Average White Band,

Paul Simon, and novelty records, like Dickie Goodman's "Mr. Jaws." I really liked dancing to the Ohio Players's "Love Rollercoaster," which to this day I still dig, especially that killer guitar riff. I also dug Elton John. In fact, the second album I ever bought was *Madman Across the Water* at age eight. I didn't purchase too many albums at the time because albums were more expensive, so I ended up buying mostly 45s, which I could cop for a buck a piece. I got to show them off on Fridays, and I still have several of those records in my collection.

Fifth Grade Playlist

Dickie Goodman—"Mr. Jaws"
Ohio Players—"Love Rollercoaster"
Wild Cherry—"Play that Funky Music"
KC and the Sunshine Band—"(Shake, Shake, Shake) Shake Your Booty"
Starland Vocal Band—"Afternoon Delight"
Boz Scaggs—"Lowdown"
Rhythm Heritage—"Theme from *S.W.A.T.*"
Captain & Tennille—"Love Will Keep Us Together"
The Jackson 5—"I am Love"
Average White Band—"Pick Up the Pieces"
Foster Sylvers—"Misdemeanor"
Thin Lizzy—"The Boys are Back in Town"
Earth, Wind & Fire—"Shining Star"

I was leading a double life, and I was digging it. My friends from P.S. 3 were curious about where I came from. Most of them weren't allowed to go past 1st Avenue, so they had no idea what was really up. The one time I remember a kid coming to visit me, it ended up going bad. My homie Ricardo Ortiz beat him up.

Yeah, that same kid Ricardo who used to terrorize me with his German Shepherd, the first kid to ever step to me, ended up becoming my ace. He and his brothers had my back more times than I could count. That's how it was in my hood. It was almost like a rite of passage. The new kid on the block got his ass kicked, and when the new kid was a tall, lanky white boy, maybe he got a couple extra for GP.

The craziest thing was that Ricardo was a smart kid, but nobody knew it and they put him in the dummy classes. After we became friends, my mom started tutoring him and teaching him how to read. She eventually diagnosed him with dyslexia and got him enrolled in a specialized after-school program. But he was still always getting into trouble. I wonder what would have happened to Ricardo had he gone to P.S. 3 with me. Maybe his life would have turned out differently.

As it was, Ricardo didn't have a shot. His home life was a disaster of epic proportions. It made my family situation seem like *The Brady Bunch*. He had five brothers, all from different fathers. When we linked up, he was living with his latest stepfather, an abusive asshole, a mother that hardly spoke English, and five insane brothers. One of his brothers was named Pito, a.k.a. *Pito the Pato*, which is a less than politically correct Spanish term for homosexual. We all knew he was gay since he came out the womb, so his nickname, as painful as it may have been, stuck. Sometimes it's just like that growing up. For the record, had anyone from another block called him a *pato*, every single one of us would have fucked that guy up. Ricardo had another brother named Pee Wee, who wasn't too small, and two shorties, Manny and Danny. There was also a newborn, Junior, who I never got to see blossom.

When Ricardo got older, he ended up becoming a full-time thug. He has the distinction of being the first person busted in *Operation Pressure Point*, a ramped-up effort by the NYPD to squash drug dealing on the Lower East Side. He got popped with a deck of dope (a hundred bags of heroin) that he tried to sell to an undercover. At seventeen, he caught a ten-year-plus bid. I heard he eventually came home, but I never saw him again.

In the summer there was no school, so there was no escaping the hood. Luckily, the summer between first and second grades I made a friend, probably my first real friend on the block, a kid in my building called Bobby Rivera. Bobby, a year older than me, was a fly-guy way before he hit puberty. Always fresh, he was the first kid I ever remember rocking the PRO-Keds 69ers.

Bobby had a weird home life. First off, he lived with both parents in the same house. They had a color TV that got all the stations. And get this, his pops owned a car that actually worked, unlike the buckets that were junked all over New York at the time. On my block, the Rivera's were paid.

The Rivera's house turned out to be a sanctuary for me. They always had some rice and beans for the kid, and his father, Louie, loved the Knicks. He also had a dynamite record collection and taught Bobby and me how to do the "Funky Chicken" and the "Funky Penguin." We would dance for his parents and whomever else they might have over. It was super fun, and even back then I had some boogie in me. Zenata, Bobby's mom, used to say to Louie, "He don't dance like a white boy, look."

That was, at that point in my life, outside of my house, the highest compliment I had ever been paid.

Louie had good taste in music and some of his mojo rubbed off on me. He put me up on James Brown and Kool & the Gang. The best thing about the Riveras is that they didn't hold it against me that I was white. They just treated me as Bobby's friend. They weren't stupid; they knew my mom was an alcoholic, and there were many a night I ate at their house while my mom was passed out on the couch muttering in her drunken stupor. Zenata even helped my mom keep it together a few times, putting her to bed or plying her with black coffee so she could get to work.

One of the highlights of my childhood was when Louie and Zeneta took Bobby and me to Harlem in their gold-colored station wagon. Harlem held an almost mythical place in my mind, and this was the first time I remember going uptown. We ate at Sylvia's, the legendary soul food restaurant, and went to see *Wattstax*, the documentary about the 1972 Watts Summer Music Festival, which had been organized by Stax Records to remember the Watts Riots from seven years earlier.

It was something else. I remember Rufus Thomas mainly because he looked old and funny and The Bar-Kays, because they dressed far out.

Richard Pryor also stood out in my mind because he said the word "pussy" on screen. I had never seen or heard anything like that in my whole short existence. I had been to the movies before, but this was some next-level shit. The audience was participating with the movie, shouting jokes at the screen and clapping along with the tunes. Even if I didn't understand it, I thought it was really cool.

One day, Bobby and I were playing with a basketball next to our building. Bobby had the OG red, white, and blue ABA ball, the one Dr. J helped make famous. We were dribbling, just messing around, when we instantly got set upon by an omnipresent mob of young thugs. This was before I became friends with Ricardo. He had stopped beating me up at this point, but he hated Bobby and I happened to be with him. My future friend and the toughest eight-year-old on the block seemed as if he was already sporting a baby mustache and sideburns. He was backed by two of his five brothers. Rounding out the posse was a light-skinned, treacherous-looking Latino named Lefty, and, of course, that damn dog. I wasn't psyched on this. They rolled on us and tried to take the ball from Bobby. He wasn't having it, and he quickly got mopped up. I tried to get the dudes off of him and got a little beating myself. Bobby, on the other hand, caught a bad one.

Just as they were about to rip off Bobby's PRO-Keds, some older folks on the street yelled and the boys scattered like roaches. I didn't know what to do, so I took Bobby upstairs to his house. Zeneta dragged Bobby over to the sink and began to treat his wounds and his father, who was the closest thing that I had to a father in those days, started flipping on me.

"What the fuck happened to Bobby?"

"They tried to take our ball and then they jumped us," I said.

"Then how come he got an eye jack if y'all got jumped?"

"They jumped him, and I tried to break it up," I said, almost crying. "I got them to stop."

It must have looked like I had punked out on his son. I hadn't, but maybe I could have been more proactive when Bobby was getting lumped up. I did get clocked in the side of the head, but Bobby had caught a beating. I felt shitty. I walked the four flights downstairs to my house and wondered if Louie hated me. I realized later that he didn't, and although he didn't come out and say it, I think he loved me. His wife Zeneta did, too.

They moved when I was ten. I only saw Bobby once or twice after that, even though he only moved to Grand Street less than a mile away. Back then, you didn't venture too far from your block. I've always wanted to thank him and his family for being so kind to my mom and me.

In the 1970s, looking out my window could be more exciting than watching TV. Shit, we only had a handful of stations anyway. I witnessed dope deals, junkies OD'ing, cats getting taken off, and the police chasing grimy motherfuckers up and down the street.

I spent a lot of time looking out my window, and eventually I got pretty good at figuring out when it was safe enough to sit on my stoop. By age nine, I got to know who was doing what on the block and what the ebb and flow was looking like. All the craziness on the streets made my mom's behavior a little easier to handle. When she got drunk and wasn't able to perform her motherly duties, it seemed to make sense given the movie I was watching play out on East Second Street.

The soundtrack that accompanied my movie was just as varied as the mayhem that was unfolding. We were rocking heavy to Stevie Wonder back then, as *Songs in the Key of Life* may have been the most popular record ever up to that point. I was really digging "Fame" by David Bowie, as well as anything by Rufus. Chaka Khan was baaaad, and I have to say, I was smitten by the cover of one of their early records.

It was around midnight on a sweaty summer night when I spotted Curtis, a dope fiend friend of my family, and his homie, JoJo, practically carrying a young, long-haired Latino doper who was knee deep in a bag of Duji. The Latino cat was a novice fiend around eighteen years old or so and about to OD. Curtis and JoJo, who were in their mid-to-late twenties, were struggling to keep him awake and alive.

Curtis looked up at me in the window and yelled up, "Lil bro, throw me your wrench." At first I didn't know what the hell was up. But I wanted to help Curtis, who a year before had gotten my bike back from some other dope fiend fuck who stole it from in front of the bodega. "We gotta get my boy here under some water or he ain't gonna make it," Curtis said.

Much to my own liking, on my block, I was the master of the Johnny Pump—or as pedestrians would call it, the fire hydrant. It functioned for us ghetto kids as a local swimming pool in the summer months. I was the kid who opened the pump and led the barrage of scrappy youngin's on the block to get busy under the hydrant's ice-cold water on many a hot day. For kids like us, this was like a trip to the beach right on our own block. Who needed Coney Island, right?

"Yeah, man, let me climb on down. I got you," I said.

I guess I was always an adrenalin junkie. I could have just thrown Curtis the wrench, but I wanted in on the adventure. I climbed down my fire escape so I wouldn't risk the wrath of waking up my mom. I quickly opened the pump and had it on full blast. Curtis and JoJo pulled the young Latin brother's pants down, tighty-whities and all, and put his balls under the ice-cold water.

"Damn, Curtis, that's got to hurt, man," I said.

He barked back, "Not as much as dying."

"Shit," was all I could say.

"He ain't gonna croak. Don't worry, young blood," JoJo said.

JoJo was right. Slowly but surely the kid gained back a bit of his faculties. Though still high as a kite, the ice-cold water on his nut sack had brought him back to Earth. It was a heavy little scene that lasted all of ten minutes. Curtis thanked me and kept it moving, half-dead dope fiend in tow. I climbed back up my fire escape and thought to myself, *Why the fuck would anyone want to do drugs?* I also thought about Curtis. He was a good guy, but also a stone-cold dope fiend and thief. I had to respect the man even if he was a doper. I went to sleep with a smile on my face. I had helped save a life that night.

It was about this time that I began to realize how prevalent gangs were in New York. They weren't as structured and organized as the Crips and the Bloods were on the West Coast, but nonetheless we had them. In my hood, it was mostly Latino cats inspired by a Hispanic political offshoot of the Black Panthers called the Young Lords. We had cliques like the Dynamite Brothers, the Katos, and the Centurion Dragons raising hell and giving out free nightmares. They dressed like bikers without bikes, cutoff jean jackets with colors, military jackboots, and floppy army hats. It was a look to say the least.

I was never in a gang because my mom would have killed me. My friends and I were inspired by Bruce Lee, who shot to fame right after he died in 1973. By 1975, the Kung Fu movement was sweeping New York. Since we were from the neighborhood right around the corner from Chinatown, we had access to Chinese slippers and Kung Fu pants and throwing stars, all of which we rocked with our white wife beaters. Bruce Lee was hands down the first Asian hood superstar, holding a cultural cache only rivaled at the time by the likes of Superfly and Mohammed Ali.

One day I was chillin' out on my block. I was seven going on eight and by then the bum-rushes weren't happening that often. I saw this kid who apparently had just moved onto my block. We had an instant commonality. Like me, he was a white boy.

His name was Russell Lauricella, and we quickly became a duo of sorts. His mom was mentally unstable, and Russell got kicked out of the house a bunch, so he was always on the stoop. We bonded playing stickball and started hanging with Ricardo and two of his brothers, a mixed-race kid named Harry Blackwell, and the aforementioned Lefty, who was two years older than us and, in addition to being an all-out mad man, was the greatest shoplifter the LES had ever seen. The kid had hand skills and a lot of heart. He wasn't stupid and, more importantly, he was one of the toughest kids I ever knew. He functioned as the de facto leader of our clique.

We did a lot of crazy stuff like climb around abandoned buildings, rooftops, and backyards risking our lives for cheap thrills. Years later, my boys graduated to a few burglary sprees, which I was always too chickenshit to get involved with. Our block was tight knit, but my boy Russell was taken out of the mix periodically because his mom wasn't so keen on the Ortiz brothers. She was crazy as a bed bug but smart enough to know those guys were up to no good.

It was his loss. For us, shoplifting became a sport, and Lefty was the captain of the squad. Our favorite heists were baseball cards and yo-yos. Later on, a Black kid named William Dickerson joined the crew along with his little brother, Booshawn. The Dickersons were the only Black kids in our clique besides Harry Blackwell, who looked Spanish. On our block, you were what you looked like, and me, I looked like a white boy.

Harry was an interesting kid. His pops was Ed Blackwell, a famous jazz drummer who worked with Ornette Coleman, Don Cherry, and the wonderful Eric Dolphy, among others. He was a gruff guy who took a shine to me when he caught me slapping his conga drums one afternoon after I'd wandered into his rehearsal room. He was the first person I ever knew who was a professional musician. They lived in a two-story loft, complete with a makeshift recording studio and a small backyard.

I never got beat into a real gang, but that crew was close enough. In retrospect, I can see the allure of gang culture. Your boys became your family, and no one would ever fuck with you when you were together. And if someone was dumb enough to fuck with you when you were alone, you'd come back with your crew and beat their asses. Those of us who grew up with dysfunction in our houses created our tribes based on love and loyalty, and that was our dynamic as kids on East Second Street. It's beautiful when you think about it.

East Second Street Playlist

War—"The Cisco Kid"
James Brown—"The Payback"
Stevie Wonder—"Sir Duke"
Héctor Lavoe and Willie Colón—"Abuelita"
Héctor Lavoe and Willie Colón—"El Malo"
Queen—"Bohemian Rhapsody"

David Bowie—"Fame"
Rufus—"Tell Me Something Good"
Gladys Knight & the Pips—"Midnight Train to Georgia"
George McCrae—"Rock Your Baby"
Carl Douglas—"Kung Fu Fighting"
The Spinners—"The Rubberband Man"
Elton John—"Crocodile Rock"

The summer of 1977 in New York City was one for the ages. The city was on the verge of going bankrupt. Garbage piled up on the sidewalks as rats brazenly strolled down the street, as if they were on their way to dinner and a show. And there was a serial killer on the loose. David Berkowitz, a.k.a. the Son of Sam, shot eight young people over the course of the summer, killing six. He would taunt the authorities and all of New York by sending letters to Jimmy Breslin, the legendary New York scribe, and the *Daily News* would then blast them on their front pages.

As much as New York was shook, I'm not sure how much my hood even noticed. The block had gotten super sketchy, becoming more or less an open-air heroin market. There were several dope spots on the street and, as a result, there was a bunch of violence. There was a spate of shootings that summer. It got so heated that the NYPD SWAT unit descended upon my house and used our adjacent balcony to apprehend a cat holding people hostage at the gas station on Houston Street behind us after an armed robbery gone awry. It was classic shit, cops with bulletproof vests and guns drawn rolling though my house to get on our little roof that looked over the gas station. I was elated because it was some shit right out of a movie. My mom, on the other hand, was pissed. She called it a police state.

Then we had the blackout. The lights in New York turned off on July 13 and stayed off for two days. It wasn't fun, but I learned a valuable lesson.

While the Ortiz brothers were allowed to wreak havoc during the blackout, my mom forced me to stay in the crib. I looked out my window only to find our family friend, Willie, and his crew patrolling the fire escapes and hallways. See, he was the block's biggest dope dealer, and he was making sure his rivals weren't about to run up and try to rob his stash. The sight of cats running up and down the fire escape with guns drawn was bananas. When the lights came back on and Wille and his crew went back to their regular routine, I went to visit Ricardo and Jose, and I was pleasantly surprised to find out they had gone looting. It seemed as if they had enough gear to outfit an entire baseball team—baseballs, gloves, helmets, sneakers, bats. They gave me a bat, a glove, a pair of sneakers, and a few baseballs. I was jazzed, even though I knew it came from the sporting goods store around the corner. Although I knew the owner, Moe, I took the shit anyway.

I mean, I didn't actually steal it, right?

As soon as I got home, my mom asked where I got the gear. I told her Ricardo and Jose gave it to me. My mom was no dummy—she knew they stole the shit. She grabbed my loot with one hand and the back of my ear with the other and marched me down to the store.

Moe was inside, looking at the wreckage of his once thriving business. He saw us and smiled weakly. He had just lost his business, the one he had run for more than twenty years. The once thriving store was now just a shell.

My mom walked me in, garbage bag in tow, and told Moe I had something for him. She handed me the garbage bag full of loot and shoved me in front of Moe. I will never forget the amount of shame I felt in that second. I knew I had fucked up. Head down, full of remorse, I handed Moe back his looted baseballs, glove, bat, and sneakers.

My mom then made it worse—she demanded that I apologize.

"Moe, I'm really sorry," I said. "I didn't mean to take this stuff; my friends gave me it."

My mom, God bless her, smacked me upside my head, saying, "Dante, you look that man in his eyes when you speak to him, you understand?"

Moe looked at me and my mother and said, "Don't worry, Norma, he's a good boy. He doesn't know any better."

"Any child of mine knows better," she said. "Ain't that right, Dante?"

"Yes, Mom."

She smacked me again and said, "Dante, you're better than this. We don't steal in our house."

I looked at Moe and his destroyed store and realized this was really fucked up. He didn't deserve this. My mom demanded I explain myself to Moe.

"Moe, I'm really sorry this happened to your store," I said. "You gave us tickets to basketball camp, and I met Dr. J that day because of you. I'm really sorry your store got robbed." It was true. He had blessed the whole block with tickets to a basketball clinic sponsored by Converse and the New York Nets at Fordham University. It was a big thrill getting to shoot foul shots with Dr J. and Larry Kenon. I even got Dr. J's autograph.

Moe looked at me and put his hand on my shoulder and told me it was okay.

I asked him when the store would be open again.

He said, "Kiddo, it won't be. This was all I had. Now I'm going to retire to Long Island, like I should have years ago."

I didn't really understand. I just knew that day that you don't steal from hardworking people. Moe was a good man. My mom had taught me a life lesson I keep with me to this day.

Even though the lights were back on, the block was still going insane, and my friends and their families started to bounce. As I said, Bobby Rivera was the first to go, but by the time he moved, I had already shifted gears and was hanging with my crew—the same crew that had jumped me and him a few years prior. Then Russell and his mom moved after they had the second of two fires in their building. Although they stayed local by moving to Sixth Street, I didn't get to see him quite as often. Despite that, we somehow remained tight. I still remember his childhood phone number, which is weird since I can barely remember my own current one.

The Ortiz brothers hung in almost as long as we did, but they finally moved to Fourth Street, where our mortal enemies, the Monkey Brothers, lived. Once there, they promptly joined up with our former archrivals and became some of the worst kids in the hood. William and Booshawn were long gone. Harry Blackwell and his people had moved to the promised land of Connecticut. Last I heard, Lefty wound up in Spofford Juvenile Center in the Bronx after he got caught geesing a house or some dumb shit. And believe it or not, I even became cool with that dog. His name was King, a.k.a. Rey, and he was the first bilingual perro I'd ever known. I ended up missing that motherfucker, too.

Our apartment on Second Street, between Avenue A and B, had gotten broken into and we got gutted. Only a few months before, my mom and I witnessed our upstairs neighbor, Willie, run past us on the staircase and then shoot a man in our hallway during a drug deal gone bad. We were scared shitless. I remember the cops coming to the pad and asking my mom what had happened. She told them nada. It recalled her previous FBI-inspired diatribe in regard to snitching.

After the cops left, she explained that our neighbor, Willie, had a family and was our friend. After our pad got robbed, he came and gave us a new TV, a stereo, and even handed my mom a knot of cash. Willie was a stone-cold dope dealer, a dope fiend, and possibly a murderer, but he was good to us, and that's what counted to her. This is an ethos I have taken with me throughout my journeys.

Life is full of contradictions.

In the late 1970s, unbeknownst to me at the time, my dad had reached out to my mom. She was reluctant to have him reenter my life for various reasons that she didn't share with me. I now understand her fear of exposing me to someone who was probably on drugs and seeing me get hurt. She also was resentful toward my father for a multitude of things, including his infidelity and lack of child support. She had struggled and suffered for a long time, and she wasn't ready to let him back into our lives just because he wanted in. She was cautious, and I don't blame her for that.

Much to her credit, she eventually showed me my dad's letters and let me decide if I wanted him back in my life. Of course, she knew I wanted to see him, but she also knew his deserting us contributed to my being a wild little dude. My mom was looking out for me as best she could because she didn't know if I could handle the emotional challenges it would put me through.

Being abandoned by my dad caused me, at various times, to resent him. I could have really used him during those important preteen years. My mom was drunk after eight on most nights, making my call to the streets mighty as a kid. I never got into major trouble, God bless, but the kids I grew up with sure did, which is a testament to my mom's love for her children—and also my complexion. White privilege is a real thing and any white person who denies its existence is full of it. In my late teens, I once remarked that I didn't see color, and my friend Paul shut me down with a quick, "That's because you're white."

Thanks for that gem, Paul. My liberal bullshit needed to get checked that day.

In those years of my dad's absence, I became a basketball player of some note. Granted my game peaked when I was about twelve, I was one of the best kids in the schoolyard and definitely the best kid on my block for a brief, awesome moment. That was until I played on the courts in Brooklyn. Then I realized I was good—for my block.

Funny how that works, you know?

2

BROOKLYN'S THE BOROUGH

In 1977, the year *Saturday Night Fever* arrived in movie theaters, I was twelve and my mom decided to move us to Brooklyn. Sheepshead Bay wasn't Bay Ridge, but it had plenty of guidos, and I wasn't feeling them and they certainly weren't feeling me. To the guidos on the block, I dressed differently, talked differently, and moved differently. Shit, I was different. They thought I was a weirdo because I skateboarded. Even though I'm half Italian and share my name with the most famous Italian writer of all time, they did not accept me. In fact, they started calling me "City Kid." They alternated this with "Half Heb" for good measure. One group of Irish brothers just referred to me as "Jew Burger," which was somehow funny to them. Obviously, they lacked the gift of Jewish sarcasm.

They didn't intimidate me, though. Even though Brooklyn had the rep of being the baddest borough out of the five (or the Bronx, depending on who you asked), this wasn't Brownsville or Bed-Stuy. Sheepshead Bay wasn't nearly as tough as the LES in those days, and I wasn't going to be intimidated by a bunch of Tony Manero wannabes after all the shit I went through.

We had a beautiful three-bedroom, two-bathroom apartment on Avenue U. My mom was working and my sister was bartending, making a grip. Things were as stable as they had ever been for us. I was taking guitar lessons and really getting into music. For once in my life, I didn't have to worry about getting mugged and gangs jumping me; my mom didn't have to worry about the pad getting broken into or me ending up on heroin.

My time on Avenue U in Brooklyn was perhaps the happiest time of my childhood. We had trees in the backyard and Manhattan Beach was a short bike ride away. There was a decent basketball court right around the corner. Russell was the only one of my East Second Street friends who came to check out the new digs. Years later he told me how much he enjoyed the escape from his mom and our exploration of the Brooklyn suburbs.

The only thing that sucked was the blatant and nonstop bigotry courtesy of the guidos. They tolerated me, but I wouldn't say that I made many real friends in Brooklyn for about a year. Then I met Nicky Lanza, who became my main dude. He was two years older than me and always seemed to have a goofy grin on his face. We bonded over music, weed, and wrestling. Nicky's claim to fame was that Bruno Sammartino, the legendary WWE champion, was his uncle. Was it true? In Brooklyn, you never knew.

Nicky, a heavyset kid, was self-conscious of his size. Husky or not, the kid was a good athlete and a great pot smoker. We became teenage potheads together, and we used to go to the city and "bug out." He wasn't a bigot like most of the kids in my section of Brooklyn. He gave two shits about color; he just wanted to get high and rock out.

He liked good music, especially KISS. We used to hang out in Greenwich Village or roll up the Deuce (Forty-Second Street) to smoke weed and watch B-movie triple features. We used to burn it down and listen to Led Zeppelin, Boston, Jethro Tull, and even P-Funk. Sabbath was his favorite. He loved Meatloaf, too, but hated disco. This mattered because in the late-seventies, one of the most intense culture wars was disco versus rock.

I'll admit now that I secretly liked a lot of disco. I mean, I am from the Lower East Side. Back then I didn't want to risk getting clowned, so I kept it under wraps from Nicky. *Saturday Night Fever* came out around this time and, in my eyes, it was a low moment in the culture of Brooklyn and for Italian-Americans. Every two-bit guido jerkoff thought he was John Travolta and ran around eating two slices of pizza at once. To me, the whole scene was embarrassing and soured me on disco and its culture for the time being. I came to realize the brilliance of the Bee Gees, but it took me a solid fifteen years to get there. Years later, I would realize there was commercial disco and "Street Disco." Street Disco is amazing music made by people of color that rarely hit the airwaves outside of New York City. It was made for the clubs I was too young to go to. I love "Street Disco" to this day. It would become a strong component of and influence on hip-hop.

The main reason why I hated guidos was because they loved to snap on me and call me a hippie or a half a spic. I was far from a hippie. I was just a kid with long hair trying to figure it all out. One thing I knew was I didn't want to be like them. I just wanted to skateboard, smoke a doobie, shoot some hoops, and listen to music.

It's kind of ironic that I lived in the middle of *Saturday Night Fever*–era Brooklyn when I got into classic rock—Zeppelin, Hendrix, Cream, Lynyrd Skynyrd, Steve Miller Band, and Ted Nugent, much to my mom's chagrin. I still got down with the funk: for me, that's innate. I dug Slave, Ohio Players, P-Funk, and Earth, Wind & Fire. I still love all that stuff—Ted Nugent not so much.

Either way, it was quickly becoming apparent that music was a form of escape for me.

During our second year in Brooklyn, my father officially reentered our lives. My mother agreed that I should get to know my father, and she allowed him to visit us in New York. It was, in retrospect, a courageous and thoughtful choice—allowing a man who had abandoned her and his children to get back in. She had no promises he wouldn't do it again. My mom allowed me to make this choice, which I'm sure was difficult for her. I decided I wanted to get to know him, as uncomfortable as this was for my mother. And I'm sure it must have been even more uncomfortable for my dad, considering he was the person who did the deserting.

My dad was living in Humboldt County, California. He had somewhat gotten his life back together. He was writing and moving weed, something he did intermittently to supplement his writing income. He had stopped doing hard drugs and was as stable as he had been in a long time.

The night he came to see me, we went for a walk around the neighborhood. He expressed real regret for abandoning me six years prior. I didn't hold it against him. We quickly made up for lost time by bonding over music and watching a lot of basketball.

My dad split his time staying with us and his friend, Owen Dodson, a poet, playwright, and overall heavy cat who had collaborated with James Baldwin in the fifties. Owen lived with his sister in Midtown on Fifty-First and Ninth Avenue. (I recently worked a block away and would occasionally walk by his apartment building and smile.) Owen was an eccentric gay Black man, a heralded writer who was suffering from bad health. He was a warm person, as was his sister who took care of him. They had been friends with my grandmother and her second husband, Harlan, who was Black. Owen turned me on to *The Boys of Summer* by Roger Kahn and was the first person to give me ginger beer. To this day, every time I drink it, I think of Owen.

My dad was really making an effort, and we were all getting along pretty well—that was until my sister, Dylan, screwed things up for us.

She had confided in me that she was going to join the Navy. My mom was already in on the info. I knew she was going to break the news to my dad, and I also knew it would drive him up the wall. A few days before Christmas, while my dad was visiting, my sister arranged a dinner at a Chinese restaurant in Midtown, near the place she tended bar.

When I walked in, my dad was sitting at the big round table, doodling in his sketchbook. As soon as I sat down, he started interrogating me.

"What's going on?" he asked.

"What?"

"What's with this dinner your sister arranged?"

"You ain't gonna like it, Pops."

"Lay it on me, my man."

"Dylan joined the Navy. Can you believe that shit?" And just like that, for the first time in my life, I ratted—and it was on my own sister. I knew it was a lame thing to do, but I was deeply conflicted about her decision and I spilled the beans. The truth was that I was scared. My sister paid half the rent, and I didn't know how we were going survive without her. I'm pretty sure I was also trying to ingratiate myself to my father.

His face said it all. My sister had become part of the machine he detested.

A few minutes later, my mom and sister showed up. We ordered a pu pu platter and some other shit, and then my sister dropped the bomb.

"I gotta tell you something, Dad," she said. "I'm going to join the Navy."

My dad, who looked gutted, said, "Yeah, Dante just told me."

How do you like that? My dad ratted out the rat.

My sister gave me a look that could kill. It was a double-snitching event for the Ross clan—go figure.

She asked him, "How do you feel about it?"

My dad took a big gulp of his drink and said, "I think it sucks, but it's your decision." This was my dad trying his best to be diplomatic.

"It's my life, and this is what I want to do," my sister said.

"Okay," my dad said. "If you want to fuck up your life to piss me and your mom off, that's your choice."

I don't think I had ever seen my dad so flustered in our brief relationship.

The food finally came and instead of fighting he just dug into his fried rice. We ate the rest of the meal in near silence.

Things were about to get hectic. My sister was getting ready to leave for the Navy, which meant she wouldn't be kicking in for the rent. My mom was now an officially licensed Montessori teacher and could hopefully make a decent living, and she intended to do just that. Unbeknownst to me, she applied to a bunch of schools around the country and was ready to move and exercise her degree. That May, she received a letter from a school in Albuquerque, New Mexico. She read it to me with great pride and announced we were moving there in the fall. I was happy for her, but I really didn't want to leave Avenue U. And what the fuck was an Albuquerque?

I was seriously bummed out and so was Russell, who had remained my best friend. One day we were bouncing around the Village when we stopped on Eighth Street at our favorite store: the aptly named Poster Mat, a combo head shop and poster store. They had a massive map of the United States thumb tacked up on the wall. Of course, we were so stoned that we stared at the map for what seemed like an eternity. I couldn't believe how close Brooklyn and Manhattan were to one another. To me, the Hudson River was the widest river in the world.

At one point, Russell pointed to New Mexico and said, "Dude, look at that. You're gonna move all the way there."

"Yeah," I said.

"That's lame."

"No shit, Sherlock."

"At least we got the summer," he said.

"Yeah."

We were wrong.

Soon after my sister made her announcement, my dad made his way back to Cali. During that time, he bounced between San Francisco and Humboldt County. I don't know why, but just as school ended, he sent me a ticket to spend the summer with him.

The summer of 1978 was the first time I spent significant time with him in a parental setting. We lived in a small spot in Arcata, a city of about ten thousand and home to Humboldt State University. We lived with my dad's two roommates, Phil and Buck, on the second floor of a beautiful wood-framed house with high ceilings looking up at a hill near the center of town. I had a homespun basketball court within eye shot, which was a big plus for me. My dad and I shared a decent-sized bedroom. I slept in the loft bed, my dad on a mattress on the floor. We had a big kitchen with a sit-down table, two couches, and a large color TV. Phil had a groovy Irish Setter. All in all, everyone got along pretty well, and it was a nice break from being in New York with my mom.

Humboldt was a total trip. I discovered skunk weed (later known as "chronic"), BMXing, and a redhead hottie named Rickie. I missed Russell, but I have to say, I had an amazing eight weeks up there. I skated a bunch, got to ride an actual-half pipe almost every day, and made a gang of friends. I was pretty good at being a loudmouth New Yorker, and it helped me meet people. I was a novelty act of sorts to the kids up there. They had never encountered a city slicker like me before—a real live New Yorker, attitude and all.

In the middle of August, we stayed a few days in San Francisco. It was the first time I had stayed there since I was a toddler. We waited for my mom to meet us for our questionable move to New Mexico. I was seriously thinking about asking her if I could hang with my dad for the winter and stick it out in Arcata, but I decided not to. After all, my mom had raised me and my loyalty was to her. I didn't want to be a flat leaver, which was the only thing lower than a snitch in my book at the time.

What happened next was a shitstorm of booze and old emotions between my mom and pops. This came out of nowhere and evolved into the worst week of my life emotionally up to that point. My pops went completely off the deep end, as he took to boozing, drugging, and acting like a fool. He even got the cops called on him when he conducted a drunken rant outside the house we were staying at. During the ordeal, he got so obnoxious that I decided to fight him.

The next afternoon I went to see him at his friend QR's house, where he was staying, and he got belligerent and started bad-mouthing my mom during a midday drunken stupor. I couldn't take it anymore, I wanted to choke him. I thought to myself that this motherfucker was MIA for the last six years of my life and here he was talking shit about the woman who raised me when he was too lost in his own web of bullshit and too weak to do what a man is supposed to do.

I'd had enough. I got lippy and told him off. "She's more of a man then you are," I said.

I was ready to sock him, and he knew it.

He got in my face. I could smell the Christian Brothers on his breath. I shoved him and put my hands up, and he promptly whipped my courageous and misguided thirteen-year-old ass. If not for his friend QR, it might have gotten really ugly. I pulled myself together and stormed back to my mother. I had gotten real beatings before. This was lightweight, but it hurt far more than any other.

My mom quietly slipped deeper into her own brand of alcoholism and depression, and by the end of her San Francisco visit, she was emotionally battered and on an alcoholic run herself, and we limped out of San Francisco and into Albuquerque via the Greyhound bus.

Albuquerque was a weird place, almost the exact opposite of New York. It was flat and spread out, and my mom didn't drive, so we had to take the bus everywhere. We lived in a small two-bedroom apartment in a prefab complex in a random shitty section of town. It was nothing fancy and the nearest store was five blocks away. It was a depressing little scene. We had no car, and I had no friends. I retreated into my world of music and skateboarding, taking the bus to various places in the city, cutting school, and looking for spots to skate. To say I wasn't into Albuquerque would be a huge understatement. I knew from the jump that it just wasn't going to work out. We were too New York for the Southwest. My mom was too strong-willed and confrontational for these people. She didn't fit in, and neither did I. She was also boozing it up. My mom got let go from the school after three months. We were broke, confused, and she was on a drunken binge. She didn't want to stay in New Mexico. I was just turning fourteen and I was scared.

I didn't know what was going to happen next. We packed up our shit and headed back to NYC the way we came via Greyhound. The ride took three straight days and was totally lame. I remember realizing for the first time that I could have body odor after several days on the bus with no shower. I stank like a midget wino. Armed with my Emerson boombox and a mono earphone, I somehow made it through that ride. I recall listening to Cream's greatest hits and AC/DC's "Highway to Hell" repeatedly the whole trip.

Becoming a soul music aficionado and hip-hop record producer wasn't an obvious musical choice for me. It's cool how your ears and musical tastes evolve with time. The one thing I've noticed is that all great music remains great while the marginal stuff you liked in the moment is forgotten. I don't think I have listened to an ELP, Foghat, or a Jethro Tull record in twenty-five years.

And there is a reason: that shit just don't swing.

Teenage Dirtbag Playlist

AC/DC—"Highway to Hell"

Cream—"Crossroads"

Led Zeppelin—"Dazed and Confused"

ZZ Top—"Francine"

Ted Nugent—"Free-for-All"

Black Sabbath—"War Pigs"

The Who—"Baba O'Riley"

Jimi Hendrix—"Who Knows"

Aerosmith—"Toys in the Attic"

The Kinks—"All Day and All of the Night"

Led Zeppelin—"When the Levee Breaks"

Queen—"We Will Rock You"

DON'T KNOW WHAT I WANT
BUT I KNOW HOW TO GET IT

I had cut school and was hanging out at my friend Garvey's crib smoking dirt weed. We were listening to WNEW 102.7 FM, which for years had been the most influential radio station in New York. Their battle cry was "Where Rock Lives," only because they couldn't say "Disco Sucks." The DJ introduced a song called "Police and Thieves." I was vaguely familiar with Junior Murvin's reggae song from the seventies by that name, but what the fuck was this? "Police and thieves in the street, oh yeah / Scaring the nation with their guns and ammunition."

I had never heard anything like it. Of course, it turned out to be the Clash. I wasn't sure what to make of it, but I thought it was cool, different, and new. It wasn't reggae, and it wasn't traditional rock music. It was, however, cool. It had me wanting more. I was full of anger, and the notion of punk rock seemed cooler and cooler by the day. It fit in with my passion for skateboarding, and I hoped it would piss my parent / parents off. I was still a stoner dude on the outside, but my affinity for this new sound was growing. The seed had been planted a year earlier when I had seen Devo play on *Saturday Night Live*. They had piqued my interest in punk and new wave a bit. I remember none of my friends liked them, but I thought they were great. The Clash, though, were a whole different trip—one that was more up my alley. They had that thing I later would understand as swing. They were aggressive but had a groove like a motherfucker.

By the last month of the 1970s, my mom and I had returned to New York and proceeded to crash on people's floors. For a few months, we hit our all-time low—we were semi-homeless, relying on the compassion of others. My mom was forty-seven and I was fourteen. Of course, at the time, I wasn't thinking about how hard it must have been for an educated middle-aged woman to be in that predicament—I was caught up in teenaged angst, being more rebellious than ever and venturing deeper into drugs. I played hooky a lot, I dropped acid, and I shoplifted like a mad man. I also got into graffiti, and of course there were girls.

As we went from house to house, wearing out our welcome, my mom had a minor nervous breakdown of sorts. It was hard to witness. She was having a rough time holding it together and wasn't used to being helpless like this. Once again, my dad was nowhere to be found after having inflicted a load of bullshit on us both in San Francisco that summer.

Things went from bad to worse when my mom's friend (I think it was the third spot we had crashed at) chucked us out. We left our stuff there and slept on the subway that night and then in a shelter for a few days. Yup, we had gone from being semi-homeless to homeless in a matter of months. This was right before Christmas time, and New York was cold and dangerous. I didn't really understand exactly what was happening, but I didn't like it. In the midst of all this, my mom had just started a new job, which she actually went to while we slept on the train and in the shelter. Shortly thereafter, my mom sent me to Queens to see my sister's boyfriend and future baby daddy, who my sis had finessed into helping us out.

Tommy Ford was an Irish rocker burnout from Queens who I had always liked. A few years earlier, after I had broken my nose playing street football, he got me drunk as a skunk on cheap champagne over Easter holiday and we proceeded to ride my bike round the house trying to pop wheelies the whole time. He worked as a grip at Silvercup Studios in Long Island City, a stone's throw from the Queens-Midtown Tunnel, where I met up with him.

When Tommy picked me up, he asked me how I was doing and how my mom was. I tried to front, but he already knew what was up from my sister.

In his car that day we smoked a skinny seventies-style joint, and he turned me onto the Dire Straits, who I thought were pretty good. We scooped up my mom, and he checked us into the Paramount Hotel and handed my mom $3,000 so that we could find an apartment. I think he really was in love with my sister and wanted to help as best he could. He did, and then some. God bless that man.

We found a place on Avenue B between Thirteenth and Fourteenth Streets on the fifth floor of a shitty tenement. I was always embarrassed about where I lived and how I lived most of my life. I almost never brought anyone home from school. As a teen, when I lived on Avenue B, I lied to kids and told them I lived in StuyTown, the mammoth apartment complex that was subsidized for the middle class. Obviously, we were a long way from middle class. As a way to save face, when I got off the bus, I would walk into StuyTown, which was directly across the street from my actual house, then circle back when the bus was gone and head to my tenement building.

By now punk rock was starting to become an obsession with me. I shoplifted *Talking Heads: 77* and *Never Mind the Bollocks* around this time. I also starting trading tapes with friends and got hipped to Buzzcocks and the Damned. I still was a closet punk rocker—I wouldn't dare admit it to Russell or my Boricua friends from the LES—but I knew sooner or later I would jump into that world. I eased into it, rocking vaguely new wave clothes, my transformation looming.

I started to kick it in the West Village—Washington Square Park, to be specific. This was where you wanted to hang out if you were a teenage dirtbag downtown in the late seventies or early eighties. I ran with a bunch of weirdo skateboarder potheads, many of whom wrote graffiti as well. I was dropping a lot of acid at the time. I still rolled with Russell Lauricella. My mom loved him. Russell had stayed with us through his mother's various bouts of insanity and would occasionally live at our house. He had often trooped out to Avenue U when I was living there. We were pretty much raised as brothers and moving back to the hood meant we could hang more.

He later told me how much he loved hanging with the guidos and being away from all the madness that was the Lower East Side. He had transformed into a rocker himself and I got him into graffiti. I wrote "System," he wrote, "Reveal." Writing graffiti and skateboarding were a rite of passage for white kids in the late seventies and early eighties in NYC. We were no exception.

I was rolling around the Lower East Side as much as I could back then. Shit was treacherous, for sure, but having a skateboard made me mobile, and I dipped and dived all over the hood. A few of my boys got into hustling, something I didn't have the heart for. I wouldn't say I was a tough kid, but I was fearless and scrappy enough if the shit came down, mostly out of necessity. It was a survival instinct and luckily enough for me, I had long arms and wasn't scared to defend myself. Plus, I could run fast as hell.

I stayed out on the streets because my home life was depressing. We were dead broke, and my mom was drunk most evenings while struggling to maintain a new gig. I saw a cycle coming and in the back of my mind I knew that life for me, until I was a full-fledged adult, was going to be full of dysfunction. I feared I would be further subjected to homelessness, poverty, and alcoholism.

I don't blame my mom. She did the best she could with the cards she was dealt. But it does make having an evolved and mature outlook on life harder down the road. Kids are pure and innocent, and none of us are born bad. It's what happens to us as children, often things we have no control over, that determine our futures. One thing I can say that my mom did well was open my mind up to culture. I was exposed to art and music even at a young age. I went to museums, art openings, and a slew of concerts. My mom somehow knew that if she planted the seed of creativity, my curiosity would be piqued. I thank her for this every day.

In my journeys throughout the city, I met a bunch of skater kids like Harry Jumonji; the Godfather of New York City skateboarding, Andy Kessler (RIP); Bruno Musso; and Ian Frahm, among others. There weren't that many skaters around at the time, so when you saw a fellow skater, you usually became fast friends. It's how I met many of my fellow brethren, including my OGs Jeremy Henderson and Jules Gayton. I actually met Jeremy and Jules by asking them what the fuck they were looking at while they watched me skate around on St. Marks. Place. Next thing I knew, Jeremy was asking to see my board and doing a gang of one-foot 360s and a big ollie. From there I went with them to their house to get their boards and we skated all night long. That's just how it was back then. Skating is something I always have love for, the culture of it helped me create lifelong bonds that exist to this day. We had a lot of fun terrorizing the city back then. Those two cats were five years older than me. They took on a big brother sort of role to me, schooling me on a lot of shit, and subsequently helped change my life.

Another skater/wise-ass friend of mine, John Porides, a.k.a. Potatoes, had already gone punk rock. In late August of 1981, he convinced me to come see this band that he claimed was the best thing since tits. I was already into the Clash, having seen them a month or so earlier at Bonds. The Treacherous Three opened and it was the first time I ever saw live rap, but I was bored and barely paid attention. I doubted these guys could compete. I had shoplifted some new wave/skate-inspired clothes, including a corny black-and-white bowling shirt that I thought was fresh and wore constantly. (I was wrong, and thirty years later friends from those days still torture me over it.)

Anyway, Potatoes got me to go see this punk band, which to my surprise consisted of four Black dudes. The "venue," if you could call it that, was this funky little spot called 171 on Avenue A and Eleventh Street. Potatoes was right. They were the greatest thing since sliced bread. I had never seen anything that powerful in my life. Up until that point, I had been to handful of concerts like Parliament; the Police; Earth, Wind & Fire; Kiss; and the before-mentioned Clash, but nothing I had ever seen before or since compared to what I saw that evening.

Bad Brains's energy, music, and vibe made me jump into the river that I had been dipping my toe into for the past year or so. It was time to cut the hair, ditch the gear, pull out some scissors, and cut my shirts up. I was about to go full-on punk, and it's a decision I never regretted. I met more skaters, I hooked up with a few cute punk girls, and eventually became friends with my heroes, Bad Brains. Beyond that, I also linked up with a bunch of future creatives who became lifelong friends and allies. The whole scene was inspirational. You could say I was the in right place at the right time.

Let me try to explain the energy that was Bad Brains in 1981. They were four Black men originally from Washington, DC, playing the heaviest, fastest music ever unleashed. They were the changing of the guard, the flipping of the switch. They were inventing new shit daily. They reached a level of energy during their live shows that I have only seen hinted at by a few groups ever, and they were firing on all cylinders for a solid two years until their incarnation as a misguided reggae group called Zion Train derailed their run. Only a few bands I have seen have been in the same realm as Bad Brains in their prime, and none of them—including the fantastic Rage Against the Machine and the outstanding Fugazi—have surpassed them.

The ROIR cassette they made at that time (right at 171, where I first saw them) still stands up to this day as the ultimate hardcore punk rock record. I never get tired of listening to it. Great music does this for you, no matter the genre. We used to listen to the demos that became that record on shitty cassette tapes we traded back and forth. Whether it was live tapes, the so-called Black Dot recordings, or early versions of the ROIR cassette, it didn't matter—we were hooked.

During this time, I started running with the Westbeth Crew, a bunch of crazy kids from the West Side who were Bad Brains–obsessed as well. The Westbeth Crew originated out of the Westbeth Artist Community Building, a nonprofit commercial and housing space for artists in the West Village. A who's who of artists lived there over the years. The building gained some notoriety when Diane Arbus committed suicide there.

Westbeth had opened about a decade before I started running with those guys. They were different than the street kids I grew up with. Their parents were artists, so they were exposed to a wide range of art and culture, but by the time I got down with them, all they cared about was punk and causing mayhem. They fought everywhere they went and drank like grown men. We had our own thing. Hardcore punk rock was our own scene and it felt empowering. Bad Brains was our band, and we lived for shows at CBGB and A7.

The crew had a band called Frontline. They were great, but they fixated on rehearsing instead of gigging, and as a result they never really took off like they could have. Their revolving door of front men didn't help matters. People in the know certainly knew who they were. The Beastie Boys covered their tune "Time for Livin'" albeit with Sly Stone's lyrics on top of their backing track on *Ill Communication* years later.

They rehearsed in a studio located in the basement of Westbeth. Years later, the studio would transform into the SD50 Studio, where I recorded the foundation of Everlast's hit single "What it's Like," along with a slew of recordings with Leaders of the New School, Ol' Dirty Bastard, Brand Nubian, and KMD. If you had told me this back then, I would have asked you if you were smoking angel dust. It was in that studio after a Frontline gig where I would meet one of the biggest influences on me during my teenage years.

I initially hated John Berry from afar and was pissed that he was hanging with the crew, which he'd started doing when I was in Cali visiting my dad. Actually, I didn't hate him—I was envious of him. I had watched him sleep with every cute punk rock girl downtown, and one night after one of Frontline's rare gigs, we all got blind drunk and headed to the rehearsal studio for our version of an after-party. One thing led to another and soon John and I were moshing and wrestling like twelve-year-olds. After several hours of this stupidity, Berry and I stumbled out into daylight. He asked me if I wanted to grab breakfast; I said yes, but I was broke. He sprung for some scrambled eggs and invited me to crash uptown on 100th Street and Broadway in the infamous wooden-framed house he called home—a place where I'd live on and off for the next few years. You could say this was the day Berry adopted me.

Two of the other kids in the crew hanging that fateful evening, Geeby Dajani (a half-Irish, half-Palestinian madman and the singer for Frontline) and John Gamble (his socially awkward friend), would become an important part of my life later, but for now, I wasn't really thinking about the future.

4

GOING BACK TO CALI

Toward the end of my sophomore year, my mom had fallen behind on rent for the spot on Avenue B. She'd slipped deeper into her alcoholism and my dad had been trying to step up. My mom decided we were going to move in with her "friend" in Hoboken. Funny thing is he didn't want me to come along, and when she brought me with her two weeks later, we got the boot quickly and were virtually homeless again. I was fifteen and, not knowing which way was up, I decided I didn't give a fuck about school anymore.

I was dealing with a gang of shit. My mom later decided to stay with my sister in Rhode Island, where she was stationed in the navy. I ended up staying with a friend named Kerlin "Create" Smith, a high school graffiti buddy whose mom was cool as could be. His family did me a great service, and one day I hope to let his mother know how much she helped me during this period in my life. She encouraged me to stay in school, to get a job, and treated me like her own. I stayed with them until the end of the school year. As a kid in high school, I had a lot on my mind. I didn't know where I would live next fall, how I would graduate, or what the future held for me. Unfortunately, Kerlin passed in his early forties. I had not seen him for at least two decades.

Through this period, I had been in close contact with my pops. He was concerned for my well-being and held me down as best as he could. In early June, he sent for me to join him in Humboldt County, California. My dad picked me up at the airport and quickly noted the punk rocker kit I was now sporting on the regular. He chuckled and said I would dig the Mission District in San Francisco, where we were going to stay for a week or so before heading up north.

I remember being jazzed on SF. It was full of energy: skate, punk rock, and low-rider culture. My dad and I stayed with his friend QR in the Mission, and as predicted I felt right at home. I skated around the hood right away to check out the terrain. I discovered the "Punk Rock Mall" on Fifteenth Street and hung out there for a few days, making friends with a cute new wave chick from Berkeley whom I would never see again.

Much to my chagrin, my dad forced us to move on to Humboldt, making the six-hour car ride with my surrogate Uncle Sid and my erstwhile little bro, Zach, who was tripping on my punky look. I figured going up north, cats might be a bit behind on the punk thing. I was right, but as long as I wanted to play sports or smoke weed, nobody tripped too hard. As we drove up north that first time, Sid pulled into the Redwood Forest in Crescent City. I had been yapping about New York this and New York that, and Sid asked me if I had ever seen a redwood tree. I brushed it off with a "whatever" as we entered the Redwood National Park. As we exited the car, my pops urged me to look up, and as I sucked in the purest air I had up to this point ever breathed in my life, my crazy surrogate Uncle Sid looked at me, smirked, and said, "They ain't got trees like this in Central Park, kiddo." Sid was spot on, and for one of the first times in my life, I was stunned into silence by nature.

That summer, my dad wasn't around a whole bunch, often shuttling back and forth from SF to Humboldt and hanging with a lady friend half the time. It was tight quarters, but it was also a chance to relax for a minute, get my head together, and try to figure out my next move. I was going be sixteen in the fall, and I was feeling old. Many of the kids I grew up with on the LES were already dead or in jail. Others I knew from the Village were on their way to becoming famous. It was a transitional period, and one where my pops gave me a lot of freedom to figure things out for myself. In retrospect, he was figuring out things for himself, too.

I ended up spending a lot of time farther north up the coast in a little town called Trinidad, where Zach and Sid lived. It was pretty dope.

We would smoke buds and skate. I even learned to surf a little. I got tight with two kids, Chris Stanton and Russell Willet. They got me into soccer and BMX, and I got them into Bad Brains and Motörhead. They hipped me to Judas Priest and Van Halen, whom I wasn't supposed to dig but did regardless. Later, when I confessed this to Darryl Jenifer, the bassist from Bad Brains, he was like "Yo, D, stop playing—Priest are bad as hell," and it blew my mind that he was a metalhead on the low. I also showed my Humboldt boys graffiti and how to ollie. It was a fair trade-off.

I was often embarrassed by my family's dysfunction. I didn't like telling the truth about it, and I didn't dig being vulnerable, so I often made shit up. I hated the fact that my sister was in the military, so she became a "registered nurse" if anyone asked. I hated the fact that my mom was an alcoholic who couldn't provide for us, so instead of admitting our poverty, I told people she had "suffered a heart attack." I just wanted to get out of high school, to get laid before I died, and most importantly, I wanted to gain a sense of stability for a change.

In Trinidad, I put down my lies and told the truth to my new friends. I talked about my life and all the shit that had gone down. You know what? I wasn't ostracized. My friends didn't hold it against me, and best of all, I ended up with a girlfriend named Teal who was so moved by my tale that she got teary-eyed when I shared it with her one drunken evening.

Teal started writing me love letters, and I converted her to punk rock a bit later. All was happy in Humboldt, and I felt safe and dug my new friends. I loved learning to surf, even though I never got very good. I also dug being around my dad and his friends. It provided me with some male bonding I desperately needed.

I'd had a great summer, but it was coming to an end. I had spent a lot of time with Uncle Sid in a crazy crib called the Stink House. He lived with another single male father, Pete Stanton, and his three sons, plus various other bohemian types.

One of the best things about staying at Sid's house was having freedom and watching Pete and the Stink band play their crazy, drunken country blues every weekend. Pete wasn't only a musician, he was also a lover of music who had an amazing record collection. He and his housemates—which included Teal's uncle Keith Buehler, a six foot four drunkard Viking idol of mine—had an equally sick record collection.

That summer, I listened to every record in the house and learned how to really drink beer. I would ask Pete or Keith about a record, and they would say, "Don't ask me, go listen to it." That's how I discovered Coltrane's *Giant Steps,* the prose of Bukowski, and the beauty of Nina Simone. I also got much deeper into the blues and the Rolling Stones. Only thing missing was some good punk rock, but since I had brought along a gang of tapes, I was cool.

These were some of the best times of my childhood, and I didn't want to go back to New York. The truth is that I was scared. The unpredictability of my life with my mom over the last few years had been a lot to take in. I knew my mom wanted me back, but I knew it wouldn't be a healthy situation. I had already started thinking about how to make some bread to get out on my own. I was almost sixteen and I didn't want to burden her anymore.

On a more selfish level, I didn't want to be subjected to her depression and alcoholism. Growing up in that environment led me to struggle with depression for much of my adult life, something I am still troubled by today. I have never felt comfortable with my biggest successes. Somehow, I've always felt like I didn't earn them, and instead of enjoying them, I tend to feel hollow inside. I work on it, and I have been to therapy, but I suspect depression is something I'll have to deal with my entire life.

Music has been my Prozac at times. Shit, I tried that garbage, but it didn't work for me. Music, on the other hand, has helped me express myself, feel closer to a higher power, and reaffirmed my belief in people. Music is, for me and many others, the cheapest and most positive form of escapism known. It offers people a chance to detach from their hassles and enjoy the moment, if only for a brief few minutes. It has been a salvation for me many times. I see a lot of what some would call God in the power of music.

5

THINGS DONE CHANGED

It took a while, close to a decade, for hip-hop to move from the Bronx all the way downtown. Once we got our hands on it, though, we didn't let go. By the early 1980s, rap music and hip-hop (the culture rap had spawned) were in full swing. Soon we began incorporating it into our everyday style, mixing it with elements of punk rock, the culture of skateboarding, and our downtown vibe. Manhattan was one of the most electrifying and artistically stimulating places in the world during that time. Unfortunately, I was back living in Sheepshead Bay, an hour-long train ride from Manhattan.

When I returned from another summer of fun with my dad out in Cali, I was in for a rude awaking. My mom had gotten a job teaching in Manhattan, yet somehow we ended up in an apartment across the street from where we use to live on Avenue U in Brooklyn. It never made much sense why she chose to move us there. We shared a tiny one-bedroom apartment that made our old place look like a palatial penthouse compared to this piece of shit.

I was ashamed of how we lived. My mom slept in the living room on a fold-out couch, and I wouldn't dare bring anyone home. I would shoplift food on the regular, unbeknownst to my mom, and lace us with steaks and cold cuts to supplement our budgetary concerns. A part of me thinks my mother knew I was boosting stuff to put in the fridge and just looked the other way. My mother was not naive. She was drinking heavily again, though.

By now, I had pretty much worn out my welcome at Brooklyn Tech, so I enrolled in an "alternative" school called City-As-School, which happened to be in the same neighborhood as P.S. 3. Maybe I thought that I could get serious about school like I had back in my glory days of academia. I was wrong. I ended up attending City-As-School less than I did Brooklyn Tech.

All I thought about was getting out of my house. My mom was trying her best, but I knew the clock was ticking. My sister was stationed in Newport, Rhode Island. My mom kept hinting that she could go live with her after having stayed there the previous summer. I was getting the creeps. It felt like my days in New York were fading fast, and I wasn't having it.

I ended up moving in with a pretty catalog model named Elizabeth who was one year my senior. She was from Westchester and loved me to death. Elizabeth was a tall girl with piercing blue eyes and beautiful blonde ringlets that fell into her face. She fed me well and tolerated my baloney. Right from the jump, I didn't think it would work—she was too straight, too suburban, and too wholesome for me in those days. My mother met her once and later asked me, "Why would that nice girl be shacking up with you?"

I dumped her for an Asian model/actress Ariane Koizumi, who was more my style. She made her film debut in *The Year of the Dragon* with Mickey Rourke. I'm pretty certain Mickey was giving her the high hard one. She dumped my ass right around the time the film was released—very unceremoniously, I may add.

Karma, right?

Rap had started to become part of the musical equation for us post-punk rockers. A song had come out when I was in Cali during the summer of '82 called "Looking for the Perfect Beat" by Soulsonic Force. It was their follow-up single to "Planet Rock" and, to me, it sounded almost like new wave, which I thought was pretty cool. You could hear rap's influences on bands like the Clash, particularly in a song called "The Magnificent Seven." It was kind of disco sounding, which I dug. They also had a tune called "This is Radio Clash," where Joe Strummer basically raps, which I thought was even cooler. Bands like Blondie and the Talking Heads were looking to Black music for influences. The musical cultural exchange was happening. Rap was becoming our post-punk soundtrack's not-so-distant cousin, much like dub had been to first wave punk bands in England.

I started opening my ears and listening to 107.5 WBLS, the station whose moniker was the "World's Best-Looking Sound and WKTU." In addition to the punk rock stuff, my friends and I also listened to a lot of reggae. It was an exciting time in culture and in life. Even though I often had an hour-long train ride back to Sheepshead Bay filled with potential treachery when I wasn't couch surfing, I still made the journey six out of seven nights a week to see bands like Bad Brains, Minor Threat, the Fall, Grandmaster Flash and the Furious Five, Bauhaus, Hüsker Dü, Jimmy Spicer, Soulsonic Force, the Clash, Treacherous Three, and the Birthday Party. Funny how, later on in life, the love of seeing live music became a strong component in my career. Even as a teenager, I was an A&R man of sorts.

In March of 1983, one record forever changed my world both musically and culturally. Run-DMC's first salvo "It's Like That" and its B-side "Sucker MCs," transformed what I thought music was and could be. Run-DMC altered my perception of music much like Bad Brains had a few years prior.

Run-DMC's first show in Manhattan was at Danceteria, a three-floor nightclub on West Twenty-First Street frequented by a slew of future icons such as Madonna, Basquiat, and Stephen Sprouse. Danceteria would forever go down in hip-hop history not only because Run-DMC's first show was there, but because it's also where Jazzy Jay introduced Russell Simmons to an overweight white kid from Long Island named Rick Rubin. It's where Kool Lady Blue initially held her party, after moving it from Negril, before taking it to the famed Roxy. Negril was the first downtown hip-hop party, and my friends and I followed it everywhere it went.

Run-DMC, however, were a different sound and vibe than Afrika Bambaataa's Wheels of Steel Roxy parties. You could say they were the beginning of the end for the Bronx-driven, Zulu Nation–propelled branch of electro hip-hop.

At that Run-DMC show, I muscled my way right up front. The show was a virtual who's who of New York City scenesters. It was one of the first times I can remember feeling electricity in the air. I can honestly say that show changed my life. It furthered my belief in rap music. I don't know how many in the crowd of several hundred people realized that they were witnessing history. I'd like to think I did.

To me, their sound and performance were the epitome of cool. For one thing, I had never seen rappers perform who actually looked like their audience. During this time, rappers resembled broken-down versions of Rick James. These dudes were different. With black Stetson fedoras, leather pants and jackets, and fresh kicks with fat laces in them, Run-DMC looked like the illest Times Square hustler/stick-up kids around. It was a blurring of the lines, and it sent a strong message to an impressionable young man. Their music was raw—like Black punk rock—minimal, menacing, loud, and amazing. It scared the shit out of square white people (and square Black people, too) much like punk rock had. It was beautiful.

Prior to seeing them live, I remember first hearing "Sucker MC's" on the Zulu Hour mix show on KISS-FM when I was pregaming at John Berry's house on a Friday night. It blew me away. I had never heard anything like it before. It held the same primal energy as Bad Brains and the Clash. It had a controlled chaos to it that screamed cathartic energy to me. It was DIY music. A new ethos of sound had opened up to me. I had already dug hip-hop, but this was beyond just hip-hop, this was a sound that confirmed the power of the genre to me. It was akin to discovering The Clash while being a teenage pothead who had been listening to Led Zeppelin. It made the competition for the most part seem dated. It was cool, dangerous, and menacing. It was minimal and primal—there were no pretty keyboards or electro sounds. It was anti-music, if that makes sense. It was unique and original. It made me want to be a part of the movement like nothing else I had ever heard before. It spoke to me deeply, and from that day on, I considered myself a proud member of the B-boy Nation.

Somehow, my growing clique of friends and I had inadvertently been granted the keys to the city. We were a bunch of stylish, scrappy, hip kids who gravitated to great music and fun scenes organically. We gained entry almost everywhere just for being ourselves. It was as if us being at a party or art opening almost confirmed that a scene was cool. This all happened without the internet, with almost no self-promotion, and in the spirt of seeking a good time. Back then, all our information came from word of mouth—people hipping us to things, like Rammellzee telling me to go to Negril or Keith Haring inviting me and my friend, Dominic, to his opening at the Fun Gallery after bumping into him on St. Mark's Place one afternoon. The hip crowd wanted my friends and me at their events and happenings. An older group of somebodies had recognized us as future potential somebodies and embraced us. This acceptance and my curiosity made me a natural A&R person and my peers into soon-to-be-famous artists of various sorts.

The world of New York City nightclubs was the nexus point of this access. I saw damn near every band in the world play at Danceteria. I met a ton of ladies—mostly cute, trendy new wave chicks, as well as a few older women, who were looking for a wayward young kid who was up to no good. I still rank Danceteria as the greatest club I ever went to. It was more like our high school stomping grounds than a club. I probably went there more than I went to my last two years of high school.

It was at Danceteria that I made lifelong friends. I hung out with signifi-cant members of the culture who were in the process of defining themselves or raking in the dough. People like the fabulously witty Haoui Montaug, the world's greatest doorman and possibly the first person who recognized my young posse and me as future somebodies; Stephen Sprouse, who had me and John Berry walk in one of his neophyte fashion shows; DJ Mark Kamins, the man who discovered Madonna; my peer, the photographer and art director Josh Cheuse; and, of course, Russell Simmons, who would be-come one of the most influential people in my life. At the time, none of that mattered. What did matter was the genuine sense of camaraderie.

I worked my connections for all they were worth. My school was the school of life, and my classrooms were CBGB, The Roxy, The Mudd Club, Fun Gallery, Danceteria, The Park Inn Tavern, the Holiday Cocktail

Lounge, Madame Rosa's, Irving Plaza, Club 57, Tier 3, Area, and a bunch of crazy afterhours spots with exotic names like Am/Pm, Save the Robots, Continental, and Berlin. I learned more in nightclubs as a teenager than I ever did in all of high school—life lessons both good and bad that I would carry with me for years to come. Things like how to scam on hot chicks from out of town, how to finagle copious amounts of free drinks, and how *not* to get caught up in garbage like cocaine. I also figured out early on in my nightlife career that it was important to know the door people, a tip that has helped me endlessly in my career.

John Berry, the dude I wrestled with at Westbeth, became like a big brother to me. As a founding member and the guitarist of the Beastie Boys in their punk rock incarnation, he had a big rep to keep up, one he earned and then some. He was a hard-drinking punk rock lothario, which is a big myth to perpetuate when you're just out of high school. John was a lanky, good-looking kid with deep blue eyes and a reckless swagger. He bore a resemblance to John Lydon. He was a good painter, a great drinker, a half-assed troublemaker with a lot of heart, and a good skater. In fact, there was very little John couldn't do well. He was inspiring, and after a while he instilled confidence in me just by letting me hang with him. You could say some of his mojo started to rub off on me. He oozed something I lacked: confidence. He was great, a real superstar at eighteen. If I had to bet on who was going to become famous when we were teenagers, I would have thought it would be John.

He hosted lots of wild parties for our ever-growing clique of mad men and women. When John was in the Young Aborigines with future Beastie Boys Mike D and Adam Yauch, they would often practice and even perform small shows there.

Cool, right?

Not really.

When I think about it, the house was more like a squat with several broken windows, no heat, yellow water that trickled out of the faucets, and let's just say we didn't keep the spot very tidy.

When I lived with John, my rent was all of 125 bucks a month, but even that was a stretch. I finally bowed out and crawled home, having been defeated by a winter without heat or hot water. John and I would remain friends, though I saw him less and less after my early twenties. He was a special person—brilliant, insanely talented, charming, and reckless. A lot of people act like they don't give a fuck; John really didn't give a fuck. He walked away from millions when he quit the Beasties and, to his credit, he held no animosity, remaining great friends with Yauch and Mike D. Though he appreciated rap music, it wasn't what he wanted to do. It wasn't his shtick, so he just stopped going to rehearsals. Coincidentally, he was also doing a bunch of speed and drinking heavily around this time, further alienating himself from the Beasties, who later unearthed a nice sum of money from their early recordings and bestowed John with a lump sum that he squandered in his own wonderful, drunken, John Berry style!

Tragically, John had a neurological disorder that gave him early dementia and eventually left him unable to take care of himself in his late forties. He died at a nursing home in New Hampshire at the age of fifty-two. I had not spoken to him other than briefly in at least three years before he passed, which is something I deeply regret. As a matter of fact, I had not seen much of John for the last ten years of his life even though we were only a train ride away. I completely fucked up with that.

At a formative time in my life, John was a huge influence on me, someone who believed in me more than I believed in myself. Our friendship was legendary. The time I spent living and running the streets with him was the wildest and most reckless of my entire life, and I loved every minute of it, just like I loved John himself. I'm proud to say, I was the best man at his first wedding. As much as it pains me to think of his passing, I was incredibly honored to be able to help eulogize him at his memorial a few years ago. I will forever have a piece of John Berry's irreverent spirit with me everywhere I go. The guy was a gem.

John Berry's Playlist

Delta 5—"Mind Your Own Business"
Bad Brains—"Pay to Cum"
Angelic Upstarts—"I'm an Upstart"
The Fall—"Totally Wired"

Gang of Four—"Damaged Goods"
Johnny Cash—"Ring of Fire"
Pere Ubu—"The Modern Dance"
Funky 4 + 1—"That's the Joint"
Magazine—"Shot by Both Sides"
Augustus Pablo and King Tubby—"King Tubby Meets Rockers Uptown"
The Slits—"Typical Girls"
Public Image Ltd—"The Flowers of Romance"
Tom Tom Club—"Genius of Love"

When John left the Beastie Boys' original lineup, it allowed the Beasties to become a full-fledged rap group. The Beasties' first lineup after their transformation included a rapping Kate Schellenbach, the former drummer from the Beasties' punk rock days and a close friend of the fellas, who was featured on "Cookie Puss," the song that caught Rick's attention. Ad-Rock, who replaced John Berry, had been in the Young and the Useless, who were the Beasties' little bro band. It's often been said he came up from the minors when he joined the Beasties, which was true to some degree. It helped that he also knew the tunes, was a talented musician, and was a charismatic cat whether rapping or playing guitar. Ad-Rock had a lot of swag. "Cookie Puss" would not have happened if Adam—or Vitz, as he is often called—hadn't joined the band. That song was as much about Ad-Rock being in the band as it was about the forthcoming stylistic change they would undergo. The Kid Ad-Rock had arrived and with him came a new vibe.

When Rick Rubin "discovered" the Beasties, he quickly decided he wanted Kate out. He put the band to the test, and the boys acquiesced, I believe, not only to Rick's influence but also to Russell's additional pressure to show Kate the door. This decision changed things for the band and was an official goodbye of sorts to some of the band's punk roots, which they would later revisit starting with *Check Your Head*.

With Kate out, Rick had officially altered their course. We grew up loving punk, which was their core inspiration attitude-wise until then.

Rick threw in cock-rock influences, including Led Zeppelin, and images of rock and roll indulgence that a few years earlier would have seemed corny. I watched this from the sidelines and thought this Rick guy really had something slick going on.

That was the time when Rick's dorm was its own scene as well. I remember, albeit blurrily, hanging with the Boys at an NYU party that Rick was DJing. When we met Rick at the dorm, Jazzy Jay showed up with T La Rock, who was to be Rick's first rapper. He went on to make the first unofficial Rick Rubin Def Jam anthem "It's Yours," which was released on Party Time Records. Jazzy Jay was already a legend to us, and he lived up to his reputation, teaching us about the wonders of Brass Monkey, the cheap liquor the Beasties later rapped about.

My dad had promised that if I finished high school, he would finance my journey across Europe. I didn't exactly graduate; I got my GED, or as Chris Rock calls it, my "Good Enough Diploma." I spent four months kicking it across Europe, visiting my dad's mom in Spain as well as friends in London and Paris. I met some beautiful girls, smoked hash with Muslims in North Africa, and went to amazing museums learning about art, culture, and life itself. Probably the high point of the trip was going to Morocco for two weeks. I got my mind fully blown after hearing a whole city shut down and pray. For the first time in my life, I realized there was a big world beyond America.

My dad had hoped that taking me abroad would keep me out of trouble and show me something bigger than my own existence. It worked, because up until this point, I had never really been in trouble with the law. I mean, I smoked pot and wrote graffiti, but I didn't get caught doing these things. My dad, though, didn't raise me, so he really had no idea the path I was going down. Then I fucked up.

On my return to New York, I had inherited my former roommate Cliff's little side hustle selling crystal meth to NYU kids. This was before Adderall and Red Bull, and the kids needed to stay up to study. I thought

I was doing them a "service." I would hit the NYU dorm on a Friday night and move a quarter ounce of product and make a few hundred bucks. It was a very low-level hustle.

One brilliant day after throwing craze at the wood frame house on 100th Street, Mike D and I decided to cruise by his house for a sec and then head downtown. I had, at the time, a TA 800 key, which was a cloned master key that opened almost every lock in the New York City subway system. My friends couldn't get enough of it, and Mike D was no exception. After we left Mike's mom's palatial digs on Ninety-First and CPW, I had the bright idea to use the TA key to get us free rides on the train. Mike didn't object; the thought of "getting over" excited us. I had at least a hundred bucks in my pocket, and I'm sure Mike had at least that much cash, not to mention a credit card or three. I also had a quarter ounce of speed, which I had planned to sell to the nerds at NYU a little later. The fact that I risked using the key to save us ninety cents each, knowing I had the product in my pocket, shows just how reckless my behavior was.

And stupid, I may add.

We walked in the back end of the train station at West Eighty-Seventh and Central Park West, and I quickly opened the lock. Of course, there was a cop on the other side. Mike and I ran down CPW only to get intercepted by two other cops from the other end of the train station. When I look back at it, I cannot believe how lame we were. We had Central Park across the street and access to side streets as well. I could have easily ditched the drugs and just as easily ditched the cops. I guess I was a bad criminal, which was probably a blessing in disguise.

We got nabbed on Eighty-Sixth and CPW. They searched me, looking for the TA key but found the speed instead. I told them it was all my fault, that Mike had nothing to do with it, which was the truth. They let Mike skate. I remember him backpedaling up CPW, looking baffled and confused. He ended up getting a friend of mine to come to the court to bail me out. I got released on my own recognizance, so the bail wasn't even needed. I eventually ended up pleading guilty and was given probation for two years. Needless to say, that was the end of my career as a speed dealer.

I went back to doing what I did best: shoplifting. I had figured out a way to boost all day and sell my swag to a series of Lower East Side bodegas. It was another low-level hustle and one I can thank my boy Mackie Jayson, drummer for Cro-Mags and Madball, for putting me up on it. I more or less supported myself like this for a few months, sometimes boosting upward of a hundred bucks worth of shit a day. One thing I knew for certain, this was not the way to create a better life for myself.

I juggled my boosting career while making weekly visits to my probation officer on Adams Street in Downtown Brooklyn. She was a nice lady who actually cut my probation short. I can't remember her name for the life of me, but she made my probation pretty transparent, which I am grateful for.

I wasn't destined to be a career criminal; however, I had no idea what I wanted to pursue. I did know this: I had a deep passion for music, in particular hip-hop, which was vibrant and compelling as a lifestyle beyond just the music. I wrote graffiti. I was all right, nothing great. I attempted to break dance, but let's just say it wasn't my strong suit. I tried half-heartedly to rap, but I never made it out of the bathroom.

So instead, I smoked angel dust and hung uptown with the painter Doze Green and his cohorts. Smoking dust was one of the dumbest drugs I fucked with, but I cannot lie—it was a trip. You never could tell what was going to happen on that shit. Thank God I wasn't caught in its grips like a bunch of graf writers I knew. Smoke the wrong batch of that stuff and you may never come back to Earth.

One time, a couple of my boys and I went up to Harlem to cop some dust. We smoked it on some random stoop and then took the train back downtown. One of the guys, my friend Armand, had a bad trip, which turned him into a "dust muffin." He started muttering to himself that the train wasn't right and that we were going to hell. He started sweating bullets and then promptly threw up all over himself.

Did we help him? Hell no. We laughed our asses off, and when he wouldn't get off the train at our stop, we just left him there. God knows how he got home. That just shows you how warped that drug can make you. I am proud to report that I haven't touched that shit in over thirty years. Just the thought of it makes my head hurt.

Hanging with Doze and his partners wasn't that different from growing up on East Second Street. I felt right at home in any hood-friendly situation. By this point, I was past my punk skater phase and rocking running suits, BVDs, and Lee jeans—the whole B-boy persona. Skating was in a weird phase at that time, and I just couldn't fuck with it. Cats were wearing Vision Street Wear, a lot of pink and teal, and doing stupid tricks like hohos, a.k.a. street plants. It was looking goofy, and I couldn't relate to much of what was going down at that time. I had grown apart from my skater pals and lightweight removed myself from that world in order to put all my energy into becoming a bona fide B-boy.

As much as my childhood was a curse, I have to admit, I was blessed as I got older. Take my first carpenter job. I knew this guy, Ethan Miller, and like Ricardo Ortiz, John Berry, and many others, we started off with bad vibes, exchanging unpleasantries and almost coming to blows. Ethan was a lanky kid, heavily tatted, and handsome in a rugged sort of way. Ethan was a former hardcore kid, a skinhead, and had a crucified skin tat on the back of his head to prove it, which was no longer visible. He was not a soft kid.

Ethan and I started hanging tough, but how this happened is blurry to me. We spent time skating, chasing tail, and drinking together. He taught me some basic carpentry skills and plugged me in with some work hanging sheet rock. Somehow, he got us a job helping build a nightclub on East Second Street, which was one block east of where I grew up. That nightclub just happened to be The World, which in its heyday was one of the most groundbreaking clubs in New York and the only real club on the LES.

From the mid-1980s until 1991, when the owner was found dead on the balcony with three bullets in his chest, The World, which was housed in a former catering hall and theater, attracted an unbelievably diverse crowd.

Keith Haring hung there. So did Russell Simmons, RuPaul, and the Beastie Boys. House music pioneers Frankie Knuckles and Larry Levan both DJ'd there, as did Red Alert. It was one of the jumping-off points for the whole club-kid scene and a precursor to the infamous Limelight. The World was instrumental in launching the careers of several prominent nightlife figures including Michael Alig, Susanne Bartsch, Lady Bunny, and Dean Johnson, whose Tuesday night "Rock and Roll Fag Bar" party hipped New York to the gay rock and roll scene. It seemed like every cool music act made an appearance there, including David Bowie, Public Enemy, Dead Kennedys, The Ramones, and Salt-N-Pepa. The building, which was located at 254 East Second Street, like most of Manhattan, was subsequently demolished and replaced with a luxury apartment building.

Ethan had been living in a squat on the LES, so he moved into the club while we worked there. He put me on and I tagged along over the course of a few months, alternating between my then-girlfriend's pad and the nightclub. We had built a quarter-pipe that we would skate nightly, which the owners let us keep up for the duration of the gig. We actually had an apartment in the space, which later became the VIP section of the club.

Imagine giving two teenagers a 20,000 square-foot nightclub to use as a living room. We would invite all our friends over before the club was even opened, with the owners none the wiser. The only downer was that we had about fifteen cents between us and had to shower in the sink. Despite my slim pockets, I was a dog with the ladies. I am still embarrassed by my behavior at this point in my life.

While working/living at the future club, my dad came to visit. He actually stayed with us for a couple of nights and was totally jazzed by the set up. One evening, we decided to go see one of my favorites, the great rock and roll pioneer Screamin' Jay Hawkins, play at Danceteria. Screamin' Jay was a great singer whose main shtick was to come out of a coffin on stage. He had a famous song "I Put a Spell on You" that later become the sample source for Notorious B.I.G.'s "Kick in the Door." My dad had dug Screamin' Jay since the late fifties, so he jumped at the chance to check out the gig. We had gone to see a lot of music over the years, including Ornette

Coleman at the Village Vanguard and James Brown one winter night at the Lone Star Café. My dad had magnificent musical taste, to say the least.

The three of us hopped over to Danceteria where we had free entry and a few drink tickets bestowed upon us. I could tell my father was impressed with my hustle, the same hustle that would eventually make me a natural as an A&R person. We caught the gig and somehow my dad talked us backstage where we ended up hanging with Screamin' Jay. I always considered Screamin' Jay the predecessor of the Cramps and the Misfits, what with his creepy, yet comical imagery and tunes. Those acts both mined his genius, as did people like the great Andre Williams and even Dr. John.

My dad started rapping with Screamin' Jay, who offered us drinks and partook in a joint burning session with us. I remember Jay and my dad vibing. My pops told him he had seen him come out of his casket in the fifties at the Brooklyn theatre, which Jay appreciated. I thought, "My dad's pretty fucking cool, kind of like me."

I tell this story because to this day, it makes me realize how similar we both are. We both possess the gift of gab and have the ability to talk to artists on their level. We were not ashamed to be a fan, but we were also aware of how not to overstep the boundaries. I have always believed telling someone how you respect their art is almost a duty as a lover of music.

At that time, I was half a grifter, so the fact that my father talked us backstage and also scored us a couple of additional free drinks was a bonus. I really appreciated my dad. He took care of me when my mom blew it during high school, and he always threw me a few bucks when he could. We had a very nontraditional relationship, but from his actions I knew that he loved me.

Plus, he was a trip to hang out with.

My mom could never hang with us at Danceteria.

Even though I boosted almost anything I needed, I came to realize that I wasn't going to become a carpenter any more than I was going to be a drug dealer. I got a job at a trendy yuppie restaurant in the West Village called Tortilla Flats. My friends would come in, including the Beasties, who never failed to bust my balls. I'm not going to pretend being a waiter doesn't suck, but for a nineteen-year-old who was trying to figure shit out, there wasn't a better job. I'd come to work hungry and broke, and I'd leave with a full stomach and some cash in my pockets.

That isn't to say I took the job all that seriously. In fact, I might have been the worst waiter in the history of New York. How bad was I? Say a table of four ordered a bunch of shit and I was on the way back to the kitchen to put in the order and I happened to see a hot lady, I would think nothing of kicking game for a few. When I finally got back to put my ticket in, the four-top would be incensed. Then I'd have to get my boy who was tending bar to give me four free margaritas to calm them down, which wouldn't be that hard since he was always looking to buy some weed from me. Like I said, I was a half a grifter back then. I was also the restaurant's resident pot dealer.

During this time, I had moved out of The World and jerked my ex-girlfriend Elizabeth for a few bucks. I had also hit up my pops for some dough, and he flowed me enough bread to get my teeth fixed and pay a month's rent on a bedroom in a decent little spot in Windsor Terrace, Brooklyn, that I had found in a classified in the *Village Voice*.

I got myself a futon and quickly moved in with some hippie vegetarian types who liked to smoke a lot of dope, which was cool with me. I was waiting tables five nights a week at Tortilla Flats. Since I had a few bucks in my pocket for a change, I was collecting records at an amazing pace. Ethan had limped back to Santa Fe with a small dope habit and became, of all things, a ski instructor. I was without a hardcore running partner, which was a bummer, but other than that everything was looking up for me.

My mom was getting ready to move to Rhode Island to live with my sister. I was concerned for both of them but relieved at the same time. I hoped things worked out for my mom—she deserved a better life than the one she had been dealt.

My probation had ended as well, which was a weight off my shoulders. I was kind of proud of myself for that and for paying rent for the first time in my life.

6

RHYMING AND STEALING

The Beastie Boys were downtown kids, first and foremost. Ad-Rock was the only one of them who was actually from downtown, but that didn't matter. You didn't have to live downtown to be downtown, you just had to hang out there. And they had done a ton of that—from The Rat Cage, to CB's, to Danceteria— the Boys had soaked it all in. To their credit, they never appropriated the hip-hop styles du jour. They made up their own fashion rules, from MCA's skater punk look to Mike D's exaggerated B-Boy persona, VW chain and all. Each of them had their own skewed lo-fi fashion sense, and one that set them apart from the rest of hip-hop. The Boys and the crew attacked hip-hop style like only former-punk rock kids would. As long as it was funky, it was cool. Our small posse tried to look like we didn't give a fuck, but obviously we did.

Though I had distinct relationships with all three of the Beastie Boys, I was closest with Mike D. We were an odd duo. Pre-Beastie fame, we were always trying to invent a scheme together, most of them dubious. Mike and I got into a fair amount of trouble. His house on Central Park West was our hang pad, and it just happened to be the sickest house I had ever seen, complete with Brancusi's *Bird in Space* in the living room and a Picasso or two on the walls. It was beyond swanky.

We often got a bunch of us together, went uptown, and threw craze, drinking everything we could and raiding his restaurant-style kitchen. I think Mike looked at me as his streetwise charity case of sorts. He knew I didn't have much in the way of money or stability in my life, and he was always hooking me up.

Mike and I, like I said, had a bunch of dumb hustles. Even though Mike wasn't involved in my idiotic crystal meth venture, he had one that may have been just as moronic. He had a little cocaine skit he was running with his boy, Thom "Bellhead" Beller, up at Vassar, an elite and prestigious liberal arts college in Poughkeepsie, New York. Mike had dropped out of Vassar after one semester to "focus" on the band.

I was slightly involved, having helped set Mike up with the connect: the infamous Dave "Hondo" Hahn, former manager of Bad Brains and drummer in the Mad. We had a road trip in our sights, but first we had to acquire fake IDs on Eighth Street, in the Village. Then Mike scooped up a large amount of cocaine—large for us, anyway. I'm guessing it was an eight ball, but it may have been a quarter ounce. We were heading up to Vassar in Mike's mom's brand-new Cadillac Seville to flip it to his partner. Thom was a six-foot-five kid from Manhattan who one day wore a Kangol bell hat, hence the name Bellhead. Thom loved rap and was playing basketball at Vassar. He would wind up being a notable writer and the brain behind Mr. Beller's Neighborhood, a great literary blog site.

We met with him for a few minutes, did the deal, and headed off to the pub on the Vassar campus with a wad of cash. Of course, we got smashed, which was nothing unusual—it didn't take much. On the way out, Bellhead's jar of coke somehow flew out of the top pocket of his lumberjack coat and smashed onto the floor in front of the crowded campus pub. I'm going to blame his over-exaggerated hip-hop gait of a walk for this fiasco.

"I am so fucking out of here," I said to Mike.

"Go straight," he said, looking like he saw a ghost.

I followed his orders up the stairs, leaving Bellhead behind. Last I saw he was on his knees, trying to direct traffic and scoop his product off the floor.

"When we go outside, follow me," Mike said. "We're going right to the car and bouncing."

We hit the exit and sprinted to the car. My heart was racing—us and our fucking schemes. We made it to the Caddy with no cops anywhere in sight. Mike looked at me and then started the car.

"What do we do, Mike?"

"We're gonna go to town, get a beer, then call Beller," he said. "I know the spot in Poughkeepsie."

I have to admit, Mike was sharp for an Upper West Side blueblood. We went to the bar and quickly drained a couple of beers. Mike hit the pay phone and called Bellhead. For all we knew, he was now in cuffs, about to get arrested and kicked out of school. When Mike hung up, I asked him what was up.

"Esss alrgiiiight," Mike said.

"For real?" I asked.

"Yeah, Bellhead scooped it all up and is running it through a strainer," said Mike. "He's gonna come meet us in a few."

Sure enough, about a half hour later, Bellhead met us, and we drank too many beers and went back to his dorm where he showed us his strainer operation. We smoked a fatty, listened to a Pere Ubu record, recounted the madness that had occurred earlier in the night, and counted our blessings.

My friendship with Yauch was different, as there were no schemes to speak of. In our youth, Yauch was the fire starter, and he often didn't care what he burned down along the way. He was also a lot of fun, and his reckless behavior was a good match for mine.

I was about fifteen when I met Yauch at the Rat Cage, Dave Parsons's record store on East Ninth Street that is now Mudd Coffee. Parsons's Rat Cage Records produced the Beasties's first EP *Polly Wog Stew* and their single "Cookie Puss." Yauch and I hit it off immediately, and we ended up taking the train back to Brooklyn, talking punk rock and girls. As the band got more into rap and fame approached, we ended up hanging a bit with or without the rest of the crew. When we hung, shit was known to get loose. Yauch brought out the crazy in me and vice versa—not a good combo.

One evening during the holiday season, right before the Beasties blew up, we had gone out to The World early and got wasted with two girls we were seeing and one of us got the bright idea to crash an architects' Christmas party on the West Side. How we knew about the party is anyone's guess. Needless to say, we stuck out like sore thumbs. I was wearing standard issue downtown hip-hop gear, which included rolled-up, faded Levis, a ski hat, a lumber jack coat, and some Adidas high-top Patrick Ewings. Yauch was wearing his ever present black-and-red flannel shirt and black leather jacket combo, a baseball hat, a pair of old rolled-up Levis, and his funky Stan Smiths.

As we scoured the bar for liquor, an older guy in an ugly blazer came up to us. He asked, "Who are you guys here with?"

Yauch mumbled, "John."

"John, who?" the architect shot back.

Without skipping a beat Yauch said, "Horsencock."

"Excuse me?" the architect said.

"John Horsencock," Yauch said, pointing across the room. "He's right over there."

Our chicks were watching us. They knew some shit was in the air, and I could tell they were getting stressed as Yauch gestured across the room and the architect looked where Yauch was pointing. We took this as a cue and tried to dip. We slipped into the crowd. The architect, a half-jock douchebag, followed us. We weren't hard to find in the sea of schmucks.

Needless to say, the architect caught up to us and grabbed Yauch by his collar. At the time, Yauch weighed about a buck thirty-five and I rocked the scales at about a buck forty. The architect probably had us by forty pounds—but he was still a fucking architect.

"Look, asshole, there's no John whatever the fuck his name is here," he said. "Time for you to go, fucko."

He was shaking Yauch like a rag doll. I jumped between them and told the guy to fucking chill. He was no nicer to me and basically threw me halfway across the room after I pried him off Yauch. I thought, *Fuck, we're gonna get beat up by architects for Christmas. Could it get any worse?* Quickly, his friend, another jock jerkoff, joined in the fracas. It was apparent the architects were smelling blood.

Just as we were about to throw down, Yauch came out with one of his all-time great lines. He got between the guy, his friend, and me, and said: "Hey, guys, relax! We're all draughtsman here. From one draughtsman to another—can't we just chill?"

The architects didn't see the humor in it. The first guy shoved Yauch out of the way and went for me, and we started wrestling, going back and forth. The girls were screaming. The whole party was watching, and other architects were hovering.

Then, out of nowhere, just as I was going to get my bell rung, I heard a *boom*, and the architect dropped like the turd he was.

I poked my head up and saw Yauch with a standing ashtray in his hand, swinging it at anyone near him. He had leveled the guy with it. I grabbed a beer bottle and was ready for battle. The girls got between the ensuing crowd of assholes and told us to jet, throwing interference for the clearance as we tore ass for the stairs. We made it out and hid around the corner. The girls followed quickly, one of them saying, "We gotta go. They're calling the cops."

I spent less time with Ad-Rock, most of it at his apartment downtown. His mom, Doris, was the coolest lady ever. Like my mom, she was a bit of a hippie and a real free spirit. She encouraged us to embrace all the happenings around us. She let us hang at the crib and bug out. She was extremely nurturing, making sure there was some food for us to nosh on, and even letting a few of Adam's friends—including future Beasties' art director, Cey Adams—live there. She was the Beasties' biggest fan and one of the best mothers I ever met. She was up front at every one of their early gigs. Doris was so cool she even went to a Bad Brains show or two with us. Unfortunately, she passed before Adam got famous, something that always made me sad. She was his ace, and she, if anyone, deserved to see Adam conquer the world.

Russell Simmons somehow finessed the Boys a slot on Madonna's tour, and voila, they were barnstorming the country, opening for an unsuspecting and unappreciative audience of Madonna teenyboppers. I saw the Boys open for her twice at Radio City Music Hall. Let's just say the crowd wasn't ready for the Beastie swag, and the Boys didn't go over too well.

After one of the shows, we got drunk backstage and went to the after-party in the basement of Radio City. Ad-Rock had his ghetto blaster pumping the classic Busy B and Moe D battle as the Boys entered the room like total delinquents. Next thing I knew, we were hanging with Keith Haring, who had a very young Sean Lennon with him. It was a trip. Our posse was acting up, and Keith rolled with us.

The bravado the Beasties showed at the after-party was a sign of things to come. It was like they were saying, "Yeah, teenybopper Madonna fans don't get us, but guess what? We're the shit, and we know we're the shit."

And you know what? The Beasties were, and are, the shit. Fuck a teenybopper.

They had a rough time the rest of the Madonna tour. They also had a rough go of it opening for Run-DMC the first few times. Not to mention the fact that they were white—an aberration for rappers at the time. The Beasties rapped in a uniquely awesome, goofy style that cross-pollinated punk and Run-DMC. It wasn't an easy sell. But they had learned to overcome adversity. I actually think catching bricks that whole Madonna tour made them an unstoppable band. They opened for Whodini and Run-DMC in 1985, pre–*Licensed to Ill*, as they were figuring out how to rock a crowd—not an easy task. The fellas were in the process of finding their confidence and that run, I believe, was crucial to their growth. Still, their first Def Jam singles distributed by Columbia—"Rock Hard" and "She's on It"—had stiffed.

One gig that holds a special place in my heart is the time they opened for Kurtis Blow at Roseland. This was early on in the game for them, pre–"Hold it Now, Hit It." The crowd wasn't really feeling them, which was uncomfortable for me. Roseland was a pretty dangerous club in Midtown. (Years later, at a freestyle show, I would get sliced in my back with a razor there unknowingly.) It had been the center of ballroom dancing in the forties and fifties, but suffice it to say, that's not what this crowd was here for. The vibe was tense. Besides the Beasties, Dave Skilken (a.k.a. the real fourth Beastie), and myself, there were no other whiteys at the show. I could smell angel dust in the air and people were definitely vibing Skilken and me. Cey Adams, the Beasties' longtime graphic designer/friend, was rolling with us as well. If Cey, who is Black, hadn't been with us, I suspect we might have gotten a beating. It was kind of scary, to be honest. As the Boys did their best to rock the crowd on stage to little or no avail, a group of four or five thugs turned to Skilken, Cey, and me.

"That's your people up there?" they said.

I mumbled back some weak shit. They didn't hear me. I'm still glad to this day.

"Your boys suck, yo," one of their crew barked at us.

Cey quickly motioned us toward the side of the stage near security. Cey had street smarts, and I followed his lead on this one. It was the smart thing to do.

As the Beasties got offstage, the crowd continued. What happened next, instead of a bloodbath, was amazing. Kurtis Blow came on and started to perform his hit, "Basketball." He was also working an ugly-ass Jheri curl at this point in his career. During his performance, he pulled out several hand-sized promotional basketballs and threw them into the audience. Toward the end of his song, someone in the audience took one of the balls and threw a fastball to the side of Kurtis's head, splashing Jheri curl juice all over the place. We could literally see the activator fly. That shit was comedy. The audience started rolling, and Kurtis did his best to saunter off the stage, tight leather Eddie Murphy suit and all, but he was pissed. It was a classic moment in my hip-hop memory vaults. I mean, who was rocking a Jheri curl in New York besides Kurtis Blow?

On April 19, a warm Saturday afternoon, I rolled with the fellas to the show at the world-famous Apollo Theater on 125th Street in Harlem. Don't get this confused with how it is today. This was Harlem in the middle of the crack epidemic, when over two thousand people a year were getting merked. There weren't a lot of white folks milling around. But that didn't stop us. Shit, we were going to the Apollo.

The Beasties had rented a passenger bus and imported a bunch of the crew uptown that day. I rolled to the show with the fellas, and we were hanging with Jam Master Jay; Captain Pissy, their infamous road manager and confidant; Cey Adams; Dave Skilken; and a bunch of girls. We were all psyched to be hanging at the Apollo. This excitement led to the usual Beastie beer guzzling backstage, as the Boys and the crew quickly drank everything in sight. I ran out between sets with Jam Master Jay and his sidekick Runny Ray (RIP) to get Blimpies and a case of Heinekens, courtesy of JMJ. *What the fuck am I doing at Blimpies with JMJ on 125th Street drunk out of my mind?* I found myself thinking. He was the Beasties's biggest supporter that night. He also liked to see the crew get faded and have fun, so he supplied more brew to keep the good times percolating. (I got to know Jay that day and will always remember him as that cool dude who just wanted to hang out and have a blast.)

This was a two-show performance—one afternoon gig, another in the early evening—and then a third scheduled show at my old crib, a.k.a. The World. Russell had seats on the side balcony VIP area of the Apollo so we could all enjoy the show hassle-free. The Beasties opened with a shortened version of "She's on It," which got a half-hearted response. Ad-Rock then addressed the crowd with as much bravado as I'd ever seen him muster. Not sure if it was the beer, the Apollo, or the time he'd spent on the road, but he was tremendous. Homie had transformed himself into a punk rock version of Run somehow.

"First, I gotta say I'm honored to be here tonight…"

This didn't exactly thrill the crowd. You could feel a slightly uneasy tension, like the audience was thinking, "Who the fuck are these white boys?"

Unfazed, he went into a little more crowd hyping and demanded that the crowd acknowledge him and his crew onstage. "Let me ask you people, are you excited to see Run-DMC?"

This got the crowd involved a little something. And with that, he had gotten them to acknowledge him. They were responding to his command. They were now almost on the Beasties' side.

"I can't hear y'all. Are you excited to see our boys, Run-DMC?" he roared.

The crowd responded louder now.

MCA jumped into the fracas, raspy voice and all, and said, "Let's hear some uptown noise for Run-DMC."

The crowd turned it up. It was getting serious in the Apollo.

Mike D chimed in with his nasal yelping: "I can't hear you, Apollo. Do y'all wanna see our peoples, Run-DMC?"

The crowd got louder.

"I can't hear youuuuuu," Mike D barked again.

The crowd got dumb loud. The Beasties had won already, and they hadn't even done their "hit" song yet.

Ad-Rock chimed in with his classic snarl—half-Slick Rick, half-Pee Wee Herman. "I can't hear you, I SAID. One mooooooore time for our boooooooooys, Run-DMC," he screamed at the audience.

The crowd lost it.

Mike D charged into the intro of the then-unreleased "Slow and Low." By the time the beat dropped with its tremendous 808, the Apollo was rocking.

I watched as an initially skeptical Apollo Theatre lost its shit watching three crazed white boys run all over the stage, delivering lyrics in unison, on point, just tearing it up. Most of the crowd, I might add, probably had no idea who they were, and those who did know were not exactly fans. But now the crowd was with them one hundred percent.

Halfway through the song, people got out of their seats and started dancing, yelling, and generally bugging the fuck out like only a Black crowd will do. White motherfuckers just don't get involved like that. Fame looked like a layup at this point. They had just won over the hardest crowd in New York, maybe in the whole country. I was excited for them; all their hard work was going to pay off. And they still hadn't performed their "hit song" yet.

The Boys ended "Slow and Low" and readdressed the crowd.

"It's an honor to be here, uptown at the Apollo," Ad-Rock shouted, half drunk.

"I feel like James Brown," Mike D chimed in. He got nothing from the crowd, but I laughed out loud. Hard as it was to believe, the reference to the Godfather of Soul's iconic Apollo run had gone over the fans' heads.

It was time to drop the "hit." As the intro to the now-famous "Hold it Now" started up, and just as Ad-Rock uttered his infamous, "Ahhh yeah, yeah. Why don't you hook up that Def Jam right about now?" the entire Apollo audience knew THAT song and now knew who these kids were and what was up. I honestly believe most people who'd heard "Hold It Now, Hit It" up to this point thought the artist performing the song was Black. When Mike D hit the line "I can do the Jerry Lewis," and did the Jerry

Lewis, a popular dance at the time, the whole crowd went off. Up until this point I had never seen the Beasties rock it like this.

A chant began to build from amid the frenzied crowd: "Go white boys, go white boys, go white boys…"

I knew my friends had arrived, and then some. I also suspected white America might never be the same. The crowd had come to see Run-DMC but left remembering the Beastie Boys.

After the show, we all got hustled into a waiting shuttle bus to The World for the after-party and for the Boys's third show of the night. We were all drunk as skunks. Ad-Rock had his box blasting Funkmaster Wizard Wiz's "Crack it Up" (a long-forgotten ode to the wonders and joys of crack) as the Boys kept the ruckus moving.

The World show also rocked. With that, the Beasties had slayed the Apollo and the biggest downtown club of the moment, all in one eventful evening.

The fellas never really looked back after that. I mean, who could blame them?

A few months later came the Garden opening for Run-DMC, LL, and Whodini, and they killed shit. It was a sign of things to come. The Beasties opened the entire northeast on that tour and figured out how to rock an arena. They had put in the work, and now it was time to go become world famous. So they did.

The Beastie Boys had come a long way from "Egg Raid on Mojo," from their first EP, *Polly Wog Stew*. I saw them rock a lot in the next year, and their momentum continued to grow. One night that holds special significance was when they played the Ritz. *Licensed to Ill* had recently dropped and was looking like a big hit. We had all seen tons of shows there over the years. It was a thrill to know my friends were going to be headlining the biggest club in town. Next stop after the Ritz tended to be Madison Square Garden.

The Boys were in rare form. It was one of the first performances to feature their bovine, scantily clad dancer, Eloise, in a cage. I was bummed

I didn't get the gig tossing them beers on stage that night, but *c'est la vie*. They stomped, and the crew and I got wasted watching the fellas.

That evening was special for a couple of reasons. All of the young cool kids I knew from every scene in New York—whether punk, skaters, or hip-hop kids—were at the Ritz getting rowdy. Our old punk rock friends Murphy's Law opened for them. The after-party was its own special event because it was so steeped in humility. We literally walked a few blocks over to the newly opened, and soon to be closed, Fatburger, a mere four blocks away and drank brews and ate burgers. A photo I have from that night shows how small the entourage was. It included future-3rd Bass producer and old Beastie friend Sam Sever; my big-haired then-girlfriend, Jessica Ford; Lyor Cohen; Cey; Captain Pissy; the Boys; and a few Beastie girlfriends. We were young kids, just having a good time, celebrating our friends who had just tore the roof off the biggest club in town.

That same year, I tagged along as the fellas hit the *MTV Video Music Awards* for the first time. The Boys bum-rushed the stage during "Weird Al" Yankovic's performance. We were quickly deemed not fit to hang with the rest of the party dwellers and were sequestered in a private lounge upstairs. The Boys, who had already performed earlier in the night, didn't comply with the rules and we quickly made a mess of the lounge. Before it was all over, our friend Bosco had passed out and got the magic marker face treatment and we had a big beer fight. We were young, bad drinkers, and enjoying whatever was there for the taking. Just the thought of that night makes me relive my hangover the next day.

Nothing lasts forever, though, and it was about a year into the tour that the Boys and Def Jam started going in different directions. The tension started with a movie deal for a picture called *Scared Shitless,* which would never happen but nevertheless started the divide between the band, Rick, Russell, and Lyor Cohen. Rick had demanded he direct/produce it. For obvious reasons, the Boys were angling for Ivan Reitman, who had done *Stripes*—and, I mean, have you seen *Tougher Than Leather?*

Things escalated after Ad-Rock got arrested in England for allegedly hitting someone with a beer can. The Boys were already overworked and feeling exploited. Ad-Rock almost missed a trip to Japan on the last leg of the tour. He was basically over it, dating Molly Ringwald, spending time in LA, and starring in an upcoming movie.

Rick decided to put his foot down, though, and play his trump card: No royalties if the Boys didn't start a new record. This shit did not fly with the Beasties. They hired a top-tier lawyer, Ken Anderson, who knew where all the Def Jam bodies were buried, and waited Def Jam out, eventually getting out of their contract, which was possibly the biggest mistake Rick Rubin and Russell ever made. The Boys quickly inked a three-million-dollar deal at Capitol, refusing to be defined by Def Jam, Russell, Rick, or Lyor Cohen.

They moved to LA, leaving the bad mojo behind them, and linked up with Matt Dike and the Dust Brothers. They created a misunderstood masterpiece, *Paul's Boutique*, which initially tanked. The Boys gave two fucks. For me, it's still my favorite Beastie record, and it's now hailed as a piece of high art. Funny how that happens sometimes.

My friend Tim Carr (RIP), who swiped the band from Def Jam in the midst of a legal battle said that when the record tanked, he was promptly blamed for making Capitol the laughingstock of the business, having spent millions to sign the Boys, and he was shown the front door—escorted by security no less.

I liked the new, leaner version of the Beasties better than before. The Boys regrouped and built G-Son Studios where they created *Check Your Head*, my second favorite Beastie Boys album. That time period in LA, when they created those albums, is part of the foundation of the band's career. It made them stand on their own. Many thought *Licensed to Ill*, and the band themselves, were a creation of Rick Rubin and Russell Simmons. Yes, they were definitely influenced deeply by both of them, but they were the MCs on that record—something people somehow forgot. Rick and Russell weren't writing those songs—the band was. After more than a year of globetrotting, the Boys had had enough of being led around like they didn't have a clue.

They outran any questions about their artistic merits. They helped invent the LA slacker cool guy—retro sneakers and all. And they never forgot where they came from. They continued to look forward as they rewrote the rulebook. In doing all of this, they indirectly inspired me to make Everlast's *Whitey Ford Sings the Blues* many years later and inspired countless kids to do their own thing. They made DIY music and went platinum. They defied the way things work in the music biz and remained empowered and creative. Nobody remembers the doubts that arose when they left Def Jam or when *Paul's Boutique* flopped. All of this is a testament to their collective genius.

I continue to marvel at the Beastie Boys. Over the years, I've seen them reinvent themselves again and again: from punks, to MCs, and then, when the novelty of being the guys with the exploding penis on stage wasn't cool to them anymore, they came back and invented psychedelic hip-hop on their sampledelic masterpiece, *Paul's Boutique*.

From the beginning, they were fearless, albeit with a healthy sense of humor. I was lucky enough to be around when they walked through emerging cultural landscapes and reinvented the young, cool white boy experience. The Beasties were always on some other shit.

I had a long, weird relationship with the Boys. I love them, respect them, and though they are my peers, I always looked up to them. I think they make great music, but I could never hover around their world too much. Once I started making my own records, signing groups, and forging my own path, I remember them telling me how dope De La Soul was after De La's initial single "Plug Tunin' (Last Chance to Comprehend)," dropped. I was honored that a group I had the privilege to work with was being given props by the Boys, who often just liked to bust my balls. They also clowned me for staying at the Holiday Inn when I was traveling in LA with the De La's our first time out west—but, hey, that's what friends are for.

I shared a lot of teenage laughs with the Boys. I was sort of a myth to their LA friends, and whenever I would meet them, they would ask me about some crazy shit the Boys had told them I'd done. Whatever the story, it was usually true, though often greatly exaggerated. I was, and am, proud I held that place with the dudes. I also have no recollection of telling them they had like two records on *Paul's Boutique*, though, that's something they shared with the world in their great book. In fairness, it sounds like something I would say. What I probably meant was that they had two singles on the record, but I'm half embarrassed and half honored that this became the yardstick for how they measured people's records and an inside joke with the fellas, one I didn't know about till I read their book.

As for my friendship with them, these days we usually only connect when an old friend of ours passes, unfortunately. I think I may have been a bit too raw, outspoken, and politically incorrect to be in the Beasties' inner circle for the last twenty years. I am totally cool with that. I march to my own drum, for better or worse.

Looking back at the group, they have lived a charmed existence, no doubt—but there's also been some serious loss. Dave Skilken, the real fourth Beastie and Ad-Rock's best friend, died from a drug OD at twenty-six. We all loved Dave. Our dear friend and nihilistic ringleader of sorts, Sean "Captain Pissy" Carasov took his own life in 2010. From the outside looking in, it all seems so perfect. But up close, it's not all sweet, and this is another thing that I believe lends them so much depth.

Of course, the most devastating loss is the one that claimed their brother, Yauch. For Mike and Adam, it is something I can only imagine. Musically, the Beasties was always the sum of its parts, interchangeable rhyme patterns and all. Those guys were like brothers more than any group I have ever seen. I also believe that, collectively, they handled fame as well as any artists I've ever known.

I remember my friend and hardcore Beastie cohort Nadia telling me Yauch had name-dropped me in a tune called "Flute Loop." I had just shot some hoops with Yauch backstage at MSG on the *Ill Communication* Tour, and he hadn't mentioned it to me. (He never did, which is so cool.) I had my head up my ass and hadn't listened to the lyrics on the record too closely. When I finally peeped it, I was honored, to say the least.

About six months earlier, Yauch was running around New York living on Prince Street and had come by my cramped little studio SD50 (in the basement of Westbeth) one night and laid down a few bass lines for me. We just talked a gang of shit, joked around, and caught up. It was a very chill hang. We were speaking on our mutual friend Rob Perlman, who was always showing people cool records but wasn't making beats with them. Musically it was nothing epic, just two old friends shooting the shit, talking about music and whatnot. I never thought twice about it. Funny, though, I guess it's what inspired the lyric Yauch dropped:

Perlman's got beats and it ain't no secret
Dante found his shit but you know he freaked it
And so the story goes on and on
Down in SD50 'til early morning

I never got to tell Adam how psyched I was that he mentioned me on a song. It's for the best; he would have probably just cracked wise about it. He was good like that.

He was an amazing cat with a killer sense of humor and wonderful freewheeling spirit. He helped raise peoples' consciousness with his dedication to Milarepa and his overall want for peace and understanding, which he so courageously shared with the world. Through it all, he never lost his irreverence—I mean, how cool was his alter ego Nathaniel Hornblower's epic appearance at the 1994 *MTV Video Music Awards*? He was the main force behind the exploding dick on stage and most things epically juvenile circa *Licensed to Ill*. For all his recklessness as a kid, he became the most conscientious of all three Beasties, leading the way for him and the crew to show people that maturing can be pretty cool if you do it the right way. Besides all the highbrow stuff, I also remember the great joy he took in slapping stickers on peoples' backs unsuspectingly one night. Yeah, he was that guy, too—and that's why he was so great.

I will always be indebted to the Beasties for helping change my life in so many ways. For these blessings from the Boys, I will forever express an immense level of gratitude—even if they would probably clown me for it.

7

KICK IN THE DOOR

Through a close friend, Matt Robinson, I was introduced to the first love of my life, Jessica Ford. We quickly hooked up and within a matter of weeks, I decided to leave behind my hippie pad in Brooklyn. I moved in on Grand Street with Jessica, Matt, and another roommate who turned out to be a weirdo. Our time there didn't last long, due to the creepy roommate. We moved to a swanky little spot off Fifth Avenue in the heart of the Village, all on her dime.

Things were looking up. I was making decent money waiting tables at Tortilla Flats. I even broke my mom off a few bucks before she left for Rhode Island to live with my sister. Things were good. I mean, I was living off Fifth Avenue. Who could believe it?

Jessica and I ended up moving from Fifth Avenue to Canal Street, right by the Holland Tunnel, which was one the worst apartments I ever lived in, and I have lived in some dumps. It was so noisy at certain times of the day you'd think you were in an airport. The one redeeming thing was that I got to hang with Sam Citrin, a.k.a. Sam Sever, whom I met a year or so earlier through some graffiti friends. We came to realize we had known each other as grade schoolers via our parents' mutual friends. He was a blue-collar Manhattan kid just like me. We became fast friends and he inspired me on a lot of levels.

Sam was a burgeoning whiz-kid, beat maker, and record producer who was part of the Mantronix team. He had done the tune "Is It Live" for Run-DMC on the *Raising Hell* album when he was only seventeen. We had become tight, so when the downstairs apartment became available, Sam moved in. Taking note of my ever-expanding funk and soul record collection, Sam would end up borrowing a few joints from me that later ended up being used as samples for a few of the beats he made. In return, Sam hipped me to the original Paul Winley *Super Disco Brake's Beat* records, one of the building blocks for the sample era of hip-hop production.

I believed in Sam's talent, and I was one of his biggest cheerleaders. I had also become tight with a crazy Englishman by the name of Sean "Captain Pissy" Carasov. He would swing by my gig at the restaurant where we would get drunk then go out and raise hell together. Pissy was an early punk rocker who cut his teeth as a roadie for the Clash. He was a seasoned touring veteran who had become the Beastie Boys' road manager during the *Licensed to Ill* era. As an A&R man, he later signed A Tribe Called Quest to Jive Records. He was endlessly entertaining and possibly the first person with any clout to believe in me. Above all else, Sean was a real G.

The restaurant thing was decent money, but I wasn't trying to become an actor. I loved music and wanted a career. Captain Pissy told me about a possible job opening at the fledging Rush Productions, which was owned by the most important man in hip-hop, Russell Simmons, and his partner, Lyor Cohen, who would go on to become one of the most important people in all of music. At the time, they managed Def Jam's artists, including Run-DMC, Public Enemy, the Beastie Boys, and LL Cool J, among others.

There was apparently an opening for the recently vacated office messenger gig, which at the time belonged to my boy, the crazed photographer and New York fixture, Ricky Powell. This was decades before Ricky would cement his personal legacy and become a legendary New York character. With Ricky gone, I saw the opening and wanted in. And with the Captain in my corner, I decided to go for it. (We recently lost Ricky, another real New York City character gone way too soon.)

Rush Productions was a nascent management company started by Russell Simmons, a party promoter, who was using this moniker for his party promoting business. Russell started managing Kurtis Blow, and thus Rush transformed into a management company.

Back then, hip-hop management, much like hip-hop itself, was making up the rules as it went along. Russell was no different. As he progressed from working solely with Kurtis Blow to working with Whodini, Run-DMC, LL Cool J, Public Enemy, and the Beastie Boys, Russell soon became known as the best manager in hip-hop.

Rush was initially located in a loft on Nineteenth Street off Park Avenue that doubled as Russell's house. I only went there a few times to pick up tickets and to meet Mike D for God knows what. This is where I first encountered Lyor Cohen. He was an intimidating cat physically—a big motherfucker who was loud and obnoxious, with a weird bootleg Israeli hip-hop inflected accent. I couldn't figure the dude out, but I got the sense he was kind of important. If nothing else, he made sure you knew that much.

The Captain set up a brunch with Lyor Cohen on the Upper East Side at Barney Greengrass. I brought along Jessica, who Lyor seemed more interested in than in me. But once Lyor realized he wasn't going to get anywhere with Jessica, he took a shine to me. Maybe it was my preceding rep as a knucklehead and Beastie cohort. When he offered me $236 a week before taxes, I took the pay cut, quit my waiting job, and never looked back.

My first real gig in the music biz was at Rush Productions. Contrary to popular belief, I never worked at Def Jam, though I later had an unsuccessful production/label deal there. I worked for Rush Productions as the office messenger/resident troublemaker.

By the time I was hired, Rush Productions had moved to 298 Elizabeth Street, not far from where I grew up. Their office, combined with Def Jam upstairs, took up two entire floors. The idea that I was working at the nerve center of rap music was pretty invigorating for a skinny, broke white boy whose last job was waiting tables. But no one would have guessed it by looking at me. I was a rebel, an angry kid but with just enough smarts not to completely blow it. I was busy trying to play it cool.

I started working there in the early summer of 1986, right before the Beasties went on their first real tour. This was also smack dab in the middle of the crack epidemic, and there were real-life crackheads trolling this area, often smoking rocks right next store to our office. The Bowery was a block away, and Bowery Bums were still in effect. CBGB, which was only a block and a half away, was still attracting kids from all over the world who were trying to get a whiff of what had transpired earlier. The area was sketchy, and that's as real as a ten-dollar rock.

How sketchy? Once in broad daylight I saw a crackhead take a shit in a garbage can right on the corner. We chased crackies away from the entrance on the daily. There were stickups and muggings; hustling was at an all-time high. And in the middle of the madness, LL Cool J or Eric B or whoever would pull up in a Benz or Beamer wearing a year's salary around their neck.

The building itself was a red brick four-story walk-up. Def Jam was on the second floor, Rush on the first. It was a long, loft-like space—Lyor had set up his office in the back. The full-time employees, like me; the publicist, Bill Adler; and the tour manager, Tony Rome, each had a cubicle. Everyone else camped out wherever they could.

Rick Rubin lived on the third floor but was hardly ever there, instead opting to stay at his peculiar apartment on Broadway off Houston, which was known for its blacked-out windows. Whenever he was around, Rick was almost always flanked by his goofy sidekick, George Drakoulias, who would eventually morph into a major record producer a few years later. I wasn't close with Rick, but I had spent some time at his infamous NYU dorm room when he and the Beasties first started cooking up their magic together. He was slightly condescending to me, which changed later on when I did a few things with my career. Back then, I felt like he wasn't checking for me, which kind of bummed me out. I think he looked at me as a hanger-on of sorts. I can't blame him, because God knows there were a lot of them around the office. On the other hand, Russell embraced me from the jump. I think he appreciated my madness and sensed that I knew a little something about music as he was constantly picking my brain about records.

As stated, the only time I liked school was at P.S. 3; however, in 1986 I took some incredibly valuable classes in "Music Business & Management" and "Hip-Hop Theory" upstairs in the restaurant area at Nell's, a nightclub on West Fourteenth Street. Professor Simmons led the class, and Andre Harrell and Lyor Cohen were his teaching assistants. I was the lone freshman. Like any good teacher, Professor Simmons wouldn't spend the whole class lecturing. On the contrary, he even wanted to hear what I would say. In fact, he would ask me what records were popping at the infamous Latin Quarters night club, which I frequented, as well as what was in the streets—which is funny thinking back on it, as they were one and the same. The irony is that a former punk rock skateboarding kid from the LES was putting these guys up on what was hot in the streets. By the way, this is a practice I still carry on thirty years later. I make it a point to talk to assistants and interns because they're usually the ones who have their ear to the ground.

No matter how late I stayed out at the clubs, I made sure to get my ass to work the next morning or Lyor would rip me a new one. Besides, I loved going to the office.

That's where I got to chop it up with luminaries such as Chuck D, Rakim, DJ Red Alert, and many others. I used to play hoops with Jam Master Jay after work with my friends over at the Carmine Street Recreation Center in the West Village. It was at 298 Elizabeth Street where I also got to know Stetsasonic, a rap "band" from Brooklyn. They had a LQ classic called "Go Stetsa I," a veritable Brooklyn chain-snatching anthem at the time. Knowing Daddy-O and Prince Paul, who were both members of Stetsasonic, would later change my life.

Possibly the best part of the gig was having the honor of delivering test pressings to the biggest DJs in the game. Later on, this became a real entry point into the biz for me. I know it may not seem like a big deal, but I cannot tell you the rush I got handing Red Alert the test press of Public Enemy's "Bring the Noise" at the Latin Quarters and watching him play it later that night. The song baffled the crowd for a brief second when he first played it, but eight bars into it the dance floor went nuts. I had suspected this song was going to connect with the dance floor and watching it do so confirmed my thought. This was another small step toward me believing I had what it took to be an A&R person: good ears. Being out at nightclubs, watching crowds react, and meeting artists were some of the most enjoyable parts of my job. I still enjoy it to this day.

Of course, my job wasn't always fun. I was firmly entrenched as the lowest man on the totem pole. My day started with fetching Lyor his morning coffee and toasted butter roll. I delivered mysterious packages all around town on my skateboard, often to Sony, who distributed Def Jam at the time, and I occasionally cruised all the way uptown to the Jive offices, which were then located on the Upper East Side, to pick shit up on Whodini's behalf. The most stressful part of my job was getting lunch for Lyor. I often screwed up his order, which would result in me publicly being told I was "a fucking idiot" and that he wanted shrimp fried rice, not pork in front of the entire office. It didn't matter. I was paying my dues and counting my blessings.

This is where and when I became fascinated with the idea of becoming an A&R person. Rick was not only a producer, but an amazing A&R man and looking back, my desire to do the same probably came from watching Rick, and to a lesser degree, George Drakoulias. They would have in-depth conversations about record producers, studios, mixes, and sonics. Though I was a rookie and never dared to open my mouth, I wanted to participate in that dialogue. The fact Russell and Lyor were picking my brain about what was popping in the streets, coupled with Bill Stephany telling me I would be a great A&R person, started the ball rolling. Little did I know that it required a lot more than just knowing what records were hitting in the streets.

It requires a vast skill set. Yes, you have to be able to spot talent and records early, but that's just a small part of it. You also have to know how to set the record making process in motion once you sign an act, which requires an intimate knowledge of studios, producers, songwriters, and engineers. It also requires people skills and a lot of patience. To sign a band, you have to make them love and trust you. This is critical. In today's playing field, where everything is research driven, there are no secrets, meaning everyone knows everything most of the time. The idea of selling yourself to artists and managers has never been more important or more difficult than it is now. It's necessary not only to seal the deal but to hold some form of gentle (or not so gentle) influence over a group—to guide them in the record making process, if you will. You also need to have political skills within whatever company you are working at—something I have never been great at. It is vital to be able to walk a group and a record through the label's many departments in an effort to drum up support and enthusiasm. You are a cheerleader, of sorts, and you have to inspire your coworkers to believe in what you're putting in front of them. This is beyond important to any record's success.

In addition, you also have to be able to pick singles, which is not always easy. What an A&R person thinks is the single is not always what the artist thinks the single should be. This is always a tricky area. You want to make the decision you feel is most prudent, but you do not want to alienate the artists or manager. I have had some rough moments in this area; all A&R people have.

You also have to pick and choose your battles with management and with talent when it comes to making important decisions. It is a plus to maintain a good relationship with management and talent, but it's not always possible. When things go sour, repairing the relationship is never easy, and sometimes it's impossible. Couple all of this with the need to manage budgets, oversee sample clearance, and walk artists through the video making process, and it's a complicated job. Yes, it all starts with spotting talent, but it encompasses so much more. I see a lot of kids on social media these days proclaiming themselves A&R people. I'm sure some of these kids are actually A&R people. I am also sure a lot of them can spot talent and have no idea about the other components that are needed to actually be an A&R person. I learned a lot of what I know from my time just watching and listening at Def Jam. Later, I would learn the nuts-and-bolts side of things from Monica Lynch, too, but let's not jump ahead.

My first real assignment had nothing to do with my ability to sniff out a talented act. After a few weeks working in their office, at Yauch's urging, Lyor sent me on a trip out west in an effort to capitalize on their ever-growing legion of fans in the world of action sports and get them a skateboard deal. I had conspired with MCA to plant the idea for the deal, and he sold the dream to the rest of the clique.

I headed out to LA along with my OG, the infamous graffiti writer/ graphic designer Eric Haze. Together, we were planning to creep out to the ASR trade show in Long Beach to get the Beasties their deal.

Rush rented us a car—a piece of shit Suzuki Samurai. Of course, we wanted something flashier, but we held steady and waited two days for the Boys to finish shows in San Francisco before they made it to LA. We checked into our hotel, Le Parc, the site of much future Beastie craze, as well as the home to many a rock-and-roll band, and headed to meet my homie, Matt Dike, the owner of Delicious Vinyl; the actor, Max Perlich; and Matt Robinson, who was a DJ, club owner, and all-around scenester.

First up, we went to Matt Dike's studio and smoked some hash oil while listening to a few unreleased Young MC records and what would later become Tone Loc's mega hit, "Wild Thing." Matt Dike would soon make history himself by making Delicious Vinyl one of the first successful West Coast rap labels. Back then, the world was a smaller place and we were all somehow seemingly connected. A lot of cats who were into the punk and new wave scene had moved on and ended up in this emerging rap netherworld. It was like an underground vibe line that had stops in multiple cities along the way. Matt Dike's pad was another outpost of cool, much like Rick Rubin's dorm had been.

We hung with the two Matts and crazy Max Perlich and then headed back to the hotel. I had been to LA a few times, but this was the first time I felt like I was really doing LA. I thought I could probably live there one day— why not? I had always been fascinated with the West Coast and the legends of LA intrigued me—from the Lizard King all the way down to The Germs. I was never a New Yorker who hated California. Quite the opposite, I always dug it. From the women to the weather—what wasn't to like? I mean, I actually live in LA these days, something I'm still a bit confused by.

The next day, we headed to Long Beach, blasting the Public Enemy demo of *Yo! Bum Rush the Show* that I had scored from the Beasties. It was one of the first times I had an advance cassette of anyone's music. It made me feel special, and it didn't hurt that it was Public Enemy's debut. I later made it a practice to get the music of every group I loved before it was released. It was what A&R people did before the internet. We loved that shit and knew when it came out that everyone else would, too.

We hit Long Beach and quickly hooked up with Christian Hosoi, Skatemaster Tate, and Ivan Hosoi, who was Christian's very groovy dad. I had met Christian Hosoi a few months earlier when he was skating at the Brooklyn Bridge banks. He was a skateboarding superstar, one of the coolest dudes ever. In my eyes, he was at least as famous as the Beasties. We walked the floor of the trade show, giving out Beasties T-shirts emblazoned with the slogan "Get Off My Dick" on the back to all the people who ran the skate companies we thought would be a good fit for the Beasties board they were planning.

The infamous Tony Alva was cool, but it wasn't his thing. We hit him with a shirt and he gave us some Alva swag. We kept it moving. We linked with the Dog Town skate cats and they gave us the same answer: no dice. They weren't into spending bucks, but Jim Muir did give me a killer Dog Town sweatshirt I had for years. We bumped into Shawn Stussy, for whom I had shot an ad the year before. He was the homie. Shit, he helped invent "street wear," which Haze would later profit from with his own brand. Shawn gave us a gang of swag and we made time with his cute salesgirls. I had never been to a trade show before and I was juiced. The ad I'd done for Stussy was on display at the booth. My fame preceded me, or so I thought.

Eric and I walked the floor a bit more and linked with Scott Oster, Steve Olson, and several other skateboarding heroes of mine. We bonded while partying and chasing chicks. We invited them to the Beasties' show later that week at the Palladium in Hollywood and the rest, as they say, is history. Just like with Christian Hosoi, I've stayed friends with the cats I met on that trip for the next thirty-plus years.

The next day, Eric and I went to lunch with the legendary kook, Brad Dorfman, who had a mullet and looked like a chubby Sammy Hagar in dorkier clothes. Brad owned Vision Skateboards and is credited with inventing the term "street wear." Vision was one of the hottest brands out there, and Brad never failed to remind anyone he came in contact with of this. (The brand has had a revival of sorts the last few years, though I still think shit's goofy.)

I let Haze lead the way. He was my elder. He also had a lot of game.

Haze opened up big.

"So, Brad, we want to see how we can get this Beastie Boys deck rolling," he said. "We have a lot of interest, but we think Vision would be the best fit."

Dorkman cut him off *quick*. "Of course we're the best fit," he said. "We're the best."

"We know this, Brad. This is why we're here with you right now."

Haze was good, and I learned some shit that day.

"I love the Beasties," Brad said. "Everyone does. We can sell a ton of Beastie boards. What do we have to do to make this happen?"

I jumped in, rather weakly I might add, and said, "We have to talk to our team and connect you with them." Our team was Lyor. I was lame, but I was trying. Haze gave me a look and a half.

"When can we talk?" Dorkman said. "I want to make this happen."

Haze took over again saying, "After this lunch, I will call Mr. Cohen and set up a call for you two."

He gave Haze the number to his primitive cell phone.

We left Dorkman and ran back to our room to call Lyor and discuss the news. He immediately asked how much money we could get. We hadn't talked numbers. He was disgusted with me. I didn't know what to do. Two days later, Lyor called Dorkman and negotiated a $70K advance, which in retrospect is baby money compared to what the Beasties were making at the time. He did all of this from the payphone at Dukes with a calling card while we ate breakfast. I was psyched, I had nailed my first deal. Actually, Haze had, but what the fuck, I was part of it.

I was on my way...maybe.

The board was never produced beyond a few prototypes for reasons only Dorkman and Lyor really know. But I had met most of my skateboard heroes that weekend, and they were cool.

The next day, the Beasties arrived in LA with Russell, the road crew, security, and our boys from Murphy's Law, who were one of the openers on that tour. That night, I went cruising all along Mulholland, down to the beach, and back through Beverly Hills in a red Ferrari that Yauch had rented. That's when we spotted some cute LA girls in a white cabriolet.

Yauch was famous, and I was bold, so we pulled up alongside their car.

"Hey, girls," Yauch said. "How's it going?"

They looked the car up and down, and then us. *Two of them, two of us. We might just get lucky,* I thought. There was a blonde and a brunette. They looked a bit older than us, but whatever. We had a Ferrari, and Yauch had a hit record.

"Pretty good," the driver said. "Nice car."

"Yeah, you know. Where are you ladies from?"

"LA, where else?" the B-rate Farrah Fawcett in the passenger seat replied. The brunette asked us where we were from.

I couldn't wait to chime in. "New Yawk City," I said.

"Really?" the brunette responded.

"Really," Yauch, said in a Valley Girl accent.

This was not the move.

The blonde turned the tides on us. "Let me ask you something, New Yawk," she said. "When do you have to return the rental?"

Then they burst out laughing and drove off. We were done. All we could do was laugh. Strike one, red Ferrari and all.

That week, I also got pushed into a pool with all of my clothes on, and then returned the favor. Went to a crazy dinner with the people who ran Adidas (who were wooing the Beasties), figured out how to get sent free kicks for the first time, and generally had a blast being a member of the entourage.

We went to a bad movie screening, ate a lot of free food, and scammed chicks. Haze and I met a kid who worked at Sunset Car Rentals and convinced the youngster to rent us a Porsche 928 with Eric's bankcard as collateral, in addition to a few hundred in cash, plus two tickets to a Beasties' show. It was one of the most amazing hustles ever perpetrated; like I said, Haze had a lot of game. We now had a black Porsche 928 to cruise back to ASR in as we bumped PE loud as fuck. Talk about living large. I was twenty-one, a few weeks out of working at a Mexican restaurant, and here I was going "big."

Eric and I still laugh about that week in LA to this day. I basically had the time of my life. Shit, a few years down the line, Haze ended up moving there.

We went to *The Joan Rivers Show*, where the boys clowned writer Chuck Eddy, who was on assignment from *CREEM* magazine, eventually breaking into his hotel room and throwing water on him. I was the victim of one of their pranks as well when I stepped out of my hotel room and had an egg cracked over my head. They had taped it over the corner of the door, which was a favorite trick of the Beasties, and getting got made me feel like part of the gang.

The LA shows were amazing. They played the Palladium on Sunset and just tore shit up from the opening bar to the last 808. One of the highlights was when Jam Master Jay threw a massive stage dive and lost one of his Adidas. The other opener, Fishbone, killed as well. (Why they never connected and got big is a mystery to me; they were, without a doubt, one of the best live bands I've ever seen.)

That night we met the Suicidal Tendencies cats, which was cool. I got shit faced, hit up the after-party, and went home with some crazy chick. I got a taste of what tour life was like, and it seemed pretty cool. I wanted in, and I was off and running after this week in LA. I was amazed at how famous the Beasties had become, and it seemed like it had happened overnight. I was a little envious, to be honest, but also super proud. This was when I decided to really dig in and take the chance I'd been given to get knee-deep in the music game. I actually had a few valid ideas, like getting the Beastie board made, and I had figured out I might know how to put together a business deal. The opportunities seemed endless.

I knew one thing concretely: This was a way better hustle than being a waiter.

I really loved rap music, and I was passionate about being involved. I was also a reckless twenty-one-year-old kid. This worked for and against me at times. Certain groups like Eric B. & Rakim loved me for my punk rock recklessness and overall hustle, while bougie record business cats shit on me just for being me.

During my tenure at Rush, I went through a painful breakup with Jessica, which only exacerbated my wild behavior. I was hoodwinked by a big homie of mine, Fred Sutherland, a downtown mover and shaker while on a mini tour with one of the Rush artists. I came home to learn he was fucking my girl on the side. I was out of my mind, and this culminated in me destroying his new BMW motorcycle with a baseball bat one drunken evening. This had our gang of mutual friends in a bind, as I was letting my temper get the best of me. I was a long way from East Second Street, yet I still had a lot of that in me. I was a half-goon, half-downtown cool guy, and despite my running buddies like the Beastie Boys, my collar was distinctly blue. Breaking up with Jessica alienated me from some of the downtown cognoscenti, which was weird to me, but hey—love hurts, and losing it hurt even more. Fuck it. They ended up having kids and getting married and later divorced. All of this just shows what an idiot I was for tripping—God bless them both. I was a terrible boyfriend, to be honest, and if I hadn't gotten dumped, I'm not sure I would have pursued my career with so much determination.

Meanwhile, I sunk my hooks into rap music on a much deeper level while working at Rush. I had linked with a number of emerging rap promoters/managers and artists. One in particular, Paradise Gray, was a promoter at the infamous Latin Quarters or LQ, which at the time was located on West Forty-Seventh Street. Paradise and his man, future X-Clan manager Lumumba Carson (RIP), the son of infamous Black militant, Sonny Carson invited me to the LQ. I eagerly accepted, knowing it was a wild place where cats had gotten into shootouts and chains were known to get vicked. I figured I didn't have but twenty bucks to steal, I wasn't rocking any gold chains, and I wasn't rolling with any loudmouths or fine ladies, so I should be all right. I remember the first time I went there it was specifically to see the Ultramagnetic MCs, a group of brilliantly bugged out rappers that did my favorite song at the time, "Ego Tripping."

The Latin Quarter was a ballroom in the forties and fifties. By the time I got there, it was in a dilapidated state and the smell of angel dust and dirt weed permeated the room. The notion that violence was right around the corner was exciting and the crowd's reaction to the music was a real litmus test as to whether a song was official or not. I had been to a few bonafide hood clubs before, venturing to Union Square and the infamous Rooftop in Harlem a few times, but the LQ was a different trip all together. This was also the place where I mastered the art of going to a club alone. I realized early on that I could finesse my way into any nightclub alone with just the gift of gab and a business card. It also made it easier to move around in treacherous environments like the LQ. I still roll out to shows by myself all the time—it's just easier.

The Latin Quarter had a big dance floor and an unusually high stage. The dancing was unparalleled. This was the post–break dancing era when new dances, new styles of dress, and new rhyme styles were being invented daily. The LQ might have been the most exciting club I have ever logged time at. I could feel the history being written while I was hanging out. I can't say it was always comfortable, but it was always vital.

I walked around and saw MC Serch, a fellow Caucasian member of the hip-hop nation and a future cohort of mine. He knew his way around the spot, and he quickly took me upstairs to hang in the DJ booth. While I was there, I saw Red Alert, the house DJ. I had met Red a year or so earlier with the Beasties and had seen him at Rush a few times. He was the most important hip-hop DJ in the world at the time, and he showed me nothing but love. Up to this point in my career, the cosign from Red really made me feel like I was making something happen for myself—even though I still wasn't sure what that was.

Other cats I connected with around that time at the LQ were Positive K, who I ended up running the streets with a bit, and of all people, King Sun. He was a six-foot-four behemoth of a man, a Five Percenter who took a liking to me for some reason and made it implicit to the club security that I didn't have to check my coat, which is always a no-no in any thuggish environment. In the rush out the door during an outburst of violence, getting your jacket at coat check might get you shot or trampled. As a rule, I still never check my coat if I don't have to. This is one of the all-time hip-hop nightclub rules for me. And God bless King Sun for the hook-up— it saved my ass on more than one occasion.

I started going to the LQ every Friday when Red held court. I met the who's who of future rap stars. I hung with Biz Markie, who took a shine to me cause as he told me, "I use to see you on Fulton Street," which was true. I had a broad in Brooklyn Heights and probation on Adams Street, smack in the middle of downtown BK. Not to mention that I was technically enrolled at Brooklyn Tech in Fort Greene for a while. Fulton Street was one of my favorite spots to check out when I was cutting school.

Of the many lessons I learned at the LQ, the biggest was that the art of networking is key. This was years before the internet, going to a nightclub was how we made contacts and exchanged info. Besides the networking, I witnessed some epic performances by up-and-comers KRS-ONE and BDP, Kid 'n Play, Stetsasonic, Public Enemy, a very young Big Daddy Kane, Salt-N-Pepa, Rob Base, Just-Ice, Doug E. Fresh, Masters of Ceremony, Biz Markie (a real LQ Favorite), and MC Lyte—who was playing her first show ever. All of these acts would go on to have serious careers and help shape the so-called "Golden Age of Hip Hop."

I ended up rolling with MC Serch a lot. I hooked him up with his future producer, Sam Sever, and then along with Sam helped get him and Pete Nice to join forces and become 3rd Bass. As a side note, I often get asked if I hate Serch for giving me the gas face at the end of the aforementioned tune. This was an inside joke between Serch and me that got outside our ecosystem. In all honesty, I hated that shit because it gave the general public a license to bust my balls. I had snapped on Serch plenty, so his dissing me on a record was karmic payback. Down the road, along with my production partners, I actually ended up producing 3rd Bass's biggest hit, "Pop Goes the Weasel."

But for now, I was just getting my feet wet and making as many connections as I could. Other notables I became cool with included the Boogie Down Productions crew, consisting of KRS-One, D-Nice, and Just-Ice. I once tried to get BDP to sign with Rush Productions. We had a crazy meeting at Norby Walters Agency that was brokered by Eric B. and me, of all people. I thought I was in over my head, but I was going for it regardless. I distinctly remember Scott La Rock, whom I didn't know very well, listening to Lyor Cohen and Russell Simmons's pitch, not to mention Eric B.'s hard sell.

Scott La Rock was poised. I mean, after all, BDP had an independent hit record, *Criminal Minded*, which became a highly influential hip-hop album. The record was on the radio from New York to LA, and Scott La Rock, KRS, and Ultramagnetic's Ced-Gee (who helped produce it, though he is often overlooked) had done it themselves, aided by a powerful cosign by

DJ Red Alert. *Criminal Minded* was also one of the initial salvos in what would later become known as gangster rap, which is often forgotten due to KRS-One's later consciousness-raising music. At this point in time KRS, along with Rakim and Big Daddy Kane, sat on top of the MC throne. To a lot of people, they still do.

I really wanted Rush to manage BDP, but Scott La Rock and KRS didn't seem particularly interested. I remember KRS asking what was up with Def Jam and then sarcastically inquiring if Lyor had heard his song "Dope Beat," which used the same AC/DC "Back in Black" sample the Beasties used for their song "Rock Hard." Lyor admitted he had not, and KRS laughed mockingly at him. BDP wasn't going for it—they had their own point of view and Rush wasn't going to be a part of it. Even then, KRS was a contrarian. He was already going against the grain, and I felt that he took great pleasure in rejecting Rush Management's wants. Scott La Rock made a big impression as he, in contrast to KRS, politely brushed off Russell and Lyor. BDP had gotten a few dates on the upcoming *Dope Jam Tour*, which included Eric B. & Rakim, Kool Moe Dee, and Biz Markie. Since they had a few shows on the tour, Lyor and Russell were trying—to no avail—to leverage this opportunity.

When they left the conference room, Lyor turned to Russell and said in his Israeli inflected hip-hop speak, "They are *not* fucking with us."

Russell said, "Word. They weren't feeling our bullshit." He then turned to Eric B. and said, "I thought that was your mans?"

Eric B. said, "I thought so, too, but he just played us like a brick parachute."

We all laughed at this. A few weeks later, Scott La Rock was killed in the streets over a dumb beef revolving around D-Nice and a girl. He was one of the twenty or so hip-hop stories I know like this—young Black and Latin men getting taken out over some stupid shit. I hadn't seen this in the punk world; punks only died from dope. Two different worlds, two different ways to die. Both of them sucked, and this was a dynamic I fully understood.

I will never forget watching KRS-One performing at Madison Square Garden a month or so after Scott's passing, opening for LL Cool J on the aforementioned Dope Jam Tour. A big picture of Scott La Rock with flowers set up in memoriam at the turntables and no DJ behind the tables as KRS rocked off a quarter inch tape played on a reel to reel. He played to the crowd, showing very little sentiment while acknowledging his fallen brother Scott La Rock, which said a lot, as he was never overtly emotional. This performance remains etched in my mind like it was yesterday. It was poetic for me in a lot of ways.

LQ Playlist

Stetsasonic—"Go Stetsa I"

Just-Ice—"Lyric Licking"

Big Daddy Kane feat. Biz Markie—"Just Rhymin' with Biz"

Audio Two—"Top Billin'"

Boogie Down Productions—"South Bronx"

Ultramagnetic MCs—"Ego Tripping"

Public Enemy—"Rebel Without a Pause"

Boogie Down Productions—"The Bridge is Over"

Jungle Brothers—"Jimbrowski"

Jungle Brothers—"Because I Got it Like That"

Positive K—"Step Up Front"

Masters of Ceremony—"Cracked Out"

Latee—"This Cut's Got Flavor"

Salt-N-Pepa—"My Mic Sounds Nice"

Heavy D & the Boyz—"The Overweight Lovers in the House"

Eric B. & Rakim—"My Melody"

Eric B. & Rakim—"Eric B. is President"

Black, Rock and Ron—"That's How I'm Living"

Maze—"Before I Let Go"

Keni Burke—"Risin' to the Top"

By 1987, hip-hop had returned downtown after a short hiatus. Even predominately white clubs started booking rap acts and DJs. I was psyched on this since I could now see the groups I liked in my own childhood stomping grounds. I had the hooks at a lot of these spots and usually rolled with a bunch of scary looking goons. I was notorious for fucking up parties and causing trouble. I would get drunk and act up—something I wasn't even thinking about at the Latin Quarters. I might get killed for trying that bullshit there.

Me, I was a brawler—not a gangster.

Worst-case scenario, brawlers get beat up. Gangsters get killed.

One of those moments of madness occurred at the reopening of my former living room, The World. Russell and Lyor had me given the responsibility of navigating the performances of Public Enemy and Davy DMX, Def Jam's newest signing. There were a few problems, though: the club wasn't set up to do hip-hop shows, and the tech crew had little experience setting up turntables. After a haphazard soundcheck, during which the turntables that were set up onstage were skipping due to the PA system and the stage monitor system, Davy DMX screamed at everyone, including me as I set his turntables up in the balcony DJ booth, much to his disliking. I was prepared for the worst, and the way I decided to prepare was by drinking heavily.

The opening was delayed a good ninety minutes. Frank Roccio and Arthur Weinstein, the owners, weren't very helpful. They still thought of me as a half-ass carpenter who used to live in the club. When I complained that the records were skipping, Frank said, "Go hang up a piece of sheetrock, ya fucking hard on."

I wasn't particularly feeling Frank's bullshit. The guy was a cardboard wise guy at best. A few years earlier, Ethan and I literally had to go to his house after he had written us two separate checks that had bounced like spaldeens in order to get him pay us in cash, which he only did under threat of getting hit upside his head with a hammer. To be clear, we did not like each other, and this was his chance to pay me back—so he did.

Next, Public Enemy came on, and to my pleasant surprise, they rocked it. They were smart, they had the SW1s in tow, and had no problem with the DJ rocking in the balcony DJ booth. They had their shit together and then some. Chuck and Flavor owned the stage that night.

By the end of the show, I was smashed. So I decided to do what I usually did in those days: get more smashed. I have no idea how or why this happened, but I ended up backstage with DMC in the dressing room

(Ethan's and my old bedroom) drinking 40s of OE. In a drunken haze, DMC told me he was the Green Lantern. He showed me his Old English Bottle cap ring.

I laughed at his comic book hero fantasy.

"Fuck you, Dante," he said. "I'll prove it, motherfucker."

"Then prove it, my G," I said.

He barked back that he would.

There were two bay doors at the front of the dressing room, my former bedroom. There were 8' x 10' panes of glass across the bay doors. DMC proceeded to punch a pane of glass out with his OE/Green Lantern ring. I was jazzed.

DMC screamed, "You see that, white boy? I'm the Green Lantern."

I laughed and said, "I can do that shit man."

"Do it then, you drunk motherfucker," DMC said.

I took my fist, with just a pinky ring, and popped a pane. The shit cracked, and my hand was fine.

DMC loved it. He hugged me. "You a crazy motherfucker," he said. "Now we're gonna get illy."

DMC knocked another pane out and then screamed in my face. As if I weren't drunk enough, I grabbed my 40, took a big swig, and popped out another pane. Shit shattered and my hand was fine. DMC threw me in a half headlock, hugging me, and screamed, "Yeah, boyeeee!"

At this point it was me, DMC, Big D, Run-DMC's road manager, and various members of DMC's crew. I idolized these cats; getting wasted and causing trouble with them was like a dream come true.

DMC said, "You up, you skinny motherfucker."

He was right. I was skinny, and I felt like a motherfucker.

I stepped up to the pane and popped the glass out again. This time, though, I also cut my hand wide open. I was bleeding and had a big gash over the lower part of my middle finger. At this point, Davy DMX had entered the room. He looked at me and laughed and said, "You fucked up playing with the Green Lantern, kid."

We all busted out laughing. I made a fist and blood flowed down my hand.

I declared the game over. DMC, sealing the deal, knocked one more pane out and laughed. He said, "Don't ever test the Green Lantern, a.k.a. Captain Waxan****—ya heard!?"

This caused more laughter, some of it at my expense. I was bleeding like crazy. I poured some OE over my hand. Davy DMX found some napkins and told me to wrap up my hand. He also told me I probably needed stitches.

In front of the club, I bumped into Russell, bloody hand and all.

"You pissy as hell," he said, laughing. "You best go get that hand checked out."

I bummed twenty from Russell and stumbled into a cab and went to Beth Israel. I ended up getting six stitches and an ugly scar on the lower knuckle of my middle finger that I carry to this day.

It was all fun and games that night, sure, but the next time my antisocial behavior kicked in, it almost cost me my career.

I was hanging out at the rotating East Village club, Payday. I went out every weekend back then, and it usually ended in a fight. Win, lose, or draw—I didn't give a fuck. My office coworker, Hank Shocklee, who was a member of the production crew, The Bomb Squad, which had Public Enemy and Slick Rick credits under their belts, got into a little fracas publicly. This was around the time I had started to win more of my fights, and I was getting a rep as a real troublemaker.

The whole thing sparked off after Hank got annoyed at my drunken antics and we started throwing insults back and forth at each other. After I slapped him on the back of the neck playfully, he slapped me upside my head. Being the drunken fool I was, I slyrapped him. Hank didn't expect it. To make matters worse, Hank's brother, Keith, also a member of the Bomb Squad, who I dug, tried to break it up but got roughed up by another crazy friend of mine, a maniac of an Albanian I will leave nameless. As if this wasn't bad enough, after we got separated, my goons and I ran around the club looking for Hank and causing a scene.

After the smoke had cleared, I realized I had got into it with the man behind Public Enemy. Not smart, and, honestly, I blame it on alcohol. I was a terrible drunk back then. Needless to say, Russell Simmons wasn't pleased. When I arrived to work at Rush the following Monday morning, he called me into his seldom-used office.

"Are you out of your fucking mind?" he said.

"Russell, I was just defending myself," I said. "Hank was bugging."

"Look, motherfucker. Hank makes hit records. Big hit records," he said. "Make me a hit record—you can whip his ass all day long. Till then, chill the fuck out. You're gonna end up getting fired and getting your ass kicked bad someday, you dumb motherfucker." After he handed me my ass, I somehow still had a job. A lesser person would have fired my dumb ass on the spot.

That week, I had also received a call at the office from Professor Griff, the leader of Public Enemy's SW1s. The SW1s were known for their aggressively militant stage presence. They wore military uniforms and would carry plastic Uzi submachine guns while PE performed. Some of the SW1s were members of the Nation of Islam and studied martial arts. Griff was no different. He was always cool with me, but he was also kind of scary. He was an army veteran, knew Kung-Fu, and to my knowledge, had fifty SW1s waiting in the wings.

I was a little shook to be honest, but picked up the phone anyway. "What's up?" I said.

Griff said, "What happened with Hank, my man?"

"He put his hands on me, I was pissy, so I blacked out," I said.

Griff laughed, which I found kind of strange. Then he asked me, "Who was the Spanish kid who hit Keith?"

I let him know right then I wasn't a rat. "He's nobody, just some crazy kid I know."

It was true—except he wasn't a Latino, he was Albanian. In a way, I was doing Griff a solid, because my man would have shot those cats, no worries. Albanians weren't to be fucked with. Later in life, him and his boys did indeed get in a heap of shit and he ended up getting convicted of murder.

There was a pause on the line. Finally, he said, "You know cats wanna come see you, right?"

I weighed my options. I had mad beef with crazy Puerto Ricans half my life and a recent beef with some skinheads that left me with three stitches in the back of my head. I had learned through experience that if cats wanna see you, they're not going to tell you. They just see you— end of story.

"Hey, man, Hank and me can shoot a fair one, whatever," I said. "But I don't want problems."

"Yeah, I know you don't want problems," Griff said, laughing menacingly. "You got a pass this time. I'm gonna make sure nothing happens with that."

"I appreciate that," I said, mumbling. "Thanks."

He hung up the phone. I was slightly humiliated. I can't lie. I spoke to Ant Live, Eric B.'s brother, a few days later, and he laughed. He told me, "Don't worry about that." This meant a lot to me, because Eric B. and them were gangster-ass dudes. Me, not so much.

I had the "pleasure" of road managing Eric B. & Rakim a few times and helped babysit them for the "Move the Crowd" video. For some weird reason, they took a shine to me. I ended up escorting them to LA for Lyor and Russell while MCA Records and Warner Brothers slugged it out over who would sign them. I remember Rakim tripping out on my chocolate and cream brown high-top Nike Air Forces. He called them Terminators. He wanted to know where I copped them. I told him at the infamous Jew Man sneaker spot in the Bronx, and upon returning to New York, Rakim took his waiting ride right to Jew Man and copped the same pair—a story he told to a crowd full of people when he performed at my fifty-first birthday party a few years back.

While we got put up in slick hotel in Burbank, I shuttled them back and forth from meetings at MCA to meetings at Warner Brothers with a waiting Russell and Lyor at every stop. This was the first time I had seen a bidding war up close, and it would not be the last.

MCA signed them to their subsidiary called UNI, and right after the signing, Eric B. and Rakim hopped a flight to Tennessee to do a show with Public Enemy. Someone got trampled to death at the after-party, which was a food drive of sorts, meaning anyone with a can of food could get in.

Six thousand cans of food and one dead person later, the food drive was officially over.

Public Enemy got the blame for the violence.

Somehow, I never saw Eric B. & Rakim's name mentioned in conjunction with the negative press that surrounded that day.

BRING THE NOISE

I continued to toil away at my gig at Rush. Lyor, whom I deeply respect, could be a real dickhead at times. Working for him had really started to wear on me. I mean, the guy yelled and screamed day and night. After a while, I had finally had enough of getting shit on. I had a blowout with Lyor, and I got relegated to work at Norby Walters, the booking agency, to protect his interests.

For the last two months of 1987, I worked for the legendry Cara Lewis, a sexy Jewish chick from the Bronx who talked liked Bobbie Fleckman but who was a pioneering rap-booking agent. Cara is a legend. She also went through assistants like people change socks. She's the one Eric B. & Rakim were rolling with, and if you recall there was even in a line in the song, "Paid in Full" that goes, "Cara Lewis is our agent…word up." Cara was, and is, a boss bitch. Like her or not, you *have* to give this woman her props.

I started booking advance dates and was putting holds on big arenas for prospective tours. I knew right away that being an agent was not for me. There was an air of datedness to the operation as a whole. It was a cutthroat environment dominated by guys who drank a lot of coffee, wore bad suits, and smoked cigarettes—kind of like a music biz version of *Glengarry Glenn Ross*. I wasn't into it and started plotting my next move. I had no idea what that would be, but at least I started thinking about it.

One night out on the town, I bumped into Monica Lynch, who ran Tommy Boy Records along with co-owner Tom Silverman. She mentioned to me that they were looking for an A&R person who would be responsible for talent scouting and overseeing the artistic development of recording artists. I immediately threw my hat in the ring.

Monica had fire-red hair, green eyes, and a beautiful smile. Originally from Chicago, she spoke in a Midwestern accent mixed with NY hip-hop slang. She lived near the rundown Tommy Boy offices on First Avenue, in the same building Stretch Armstrong did many years later, coincidentally.

Monica set up the interview, and it seemed to go well. She told me she had asked Daddy-O from Stetsasonic, a Tommy Boy act, about me and that he'd backed me up, as did a few others. She set a follow-up with me shortly after the Christmas holiday in January 1988, and we chopped it up for a little while. At the end of this meeting, she played me a cassette tape by a group that would change my life. As I heard the magical sounds waft out of her boombox, I was entranced. It was the weirdest coolest thing I had ever heard. She asked me what I thought.

"That's the best shit ever," I said.

"Glad you liked it," she responded.

"I love it," I said. "It reminds me of Ultramagnetic crossed with Slick Rick. It's so dusted."

She laughed. "The group is called De La Soul and the song is 'Plug Tunin'.' They're produced by Prince Paul from Stetsasonic. You know them?"

I told her what I knew of Paul and Stetsasonic, but admitted I hadn't heard of this group.

"Tommy Boy is going to sign them," she said. "You'll probably be their A&R guy."

"Wait," I said. "I got the job?"

I started working at Tommy Boy two weeks later, and I dove right into working with the De La crew. I clicked with them right from the get-go. We were almost the same age and had similar tastes in music and clothes. I was impressed by how unbelievably talented Prince Paul was.

De La Soul hailed from Amityville, Long Island. The three highly creative kids linked via music class. Prince Paul connected with Maseo via

DJing and became their big bro and producer. His band mate, Daddy-O, had brought the demo of De La to Monica Lynch for Prince Paul originally. There were several labels vying for the group, but Tommy Boy eventually inked the band.

When I first met them, I was confused. They were three Black guys from way out in Long Island, which might as well have been another planet to me back then. But they dressed way out, even by my downtown standards. They rocked paisley shirts and Africa medallions. Maseo was a big kid, broad chested with a booming voice. He was the hooligan of the crew, and we bonded instantly. Posdnuos was a tall, dark-skinned brother with a flat top and a cool, colorful shirt, glasses, and a wry sense of humor. Dove, a.k.a. Dave, was the quiet one, contemplative in a sense, seemingly very poised. They were progressive cats, and we clicked right away.

After meeting with them, I took them to the underground club, Milky Way, which was located at the legendary Irving Plaza, which would later be the site of their first show. The night is kind of blurry, but I remember getting drunk and me and Maseo almost putting our hands on some kids, which was, I'm guessing, my fault. We made a little scene of sorts, and this sealed our bond.

In the early days, I doubled as their road manager and booking agent. Basically, I was trying to supplement my Tommy Boy income. I took them to LA for their first West Coast shows, which was also their first time in LA ever. During this trip, Pos and I almost got arrested for jaywalking on Hollywood Boulevard prior to us playing a show at World on Wheels. We were literally jaywalking in front of a cop car, paying it no mind, when we hear over the car's megaphone: "You, the white guy with the stripped shirt, and the Black guy, get against the wall." We kept walking. Initially, we didn't know they meant us—until they made it very clear. They then berated us and only let us go after we explained we were from New York and didn't know the jaywalking rules in LA.

We also stopped by the legendary all-rap radio station KDAY and met then the most important program director and DJ in LA, Greg Mack. This same gig is where we first saw what real live Crips and gangbangers looked like. I clearly remember seeing Crip walking that night for the first time as well as cats in Dallas Cowboys and Georgetown Hoyas gear throwing up Crip signs. I also met DJ Muggs (then of 7A3, later he would produce Cypress Hill and House of Pain), Ice-T, and a very young Everlast, who was with us when we witnessed a huge gang-related fight break out at the venue that led to us being locked in the club while gun shots were going off outside.

That night, we got an upfront view of the emerging LA rap scene.

Later, we bumped into the Beasties at an afterhours club in Hollywood. We concluded our trip with a BBQ at DJ Muggs's pad the next day, where we ended up meeting a pre–Cypress Hill B-Real and Young MC, who was made to leave the party under duress by Mellow Man Ace and his brother, future Cypress Hill member Sen Dog.

Why? I don't know. But if Sen Dog was barking at me and I was Young MC, I would have left, too.

When I got a hold of the promo copy of "Plug Tunin'," I immediately sent it via messenger to DJ Red Alert. He hit me on the horn later that day and told me he dug the record and that he was going to give it some burn. Red had great ears and was the most progressive cat they ever let have a commercial radio show. Red had a crew he worked with called the Violators, which included a young hoodlum and future music biz mogul, Chris Lighty. These guys were no joke.

Chris and I ended up becoming good friends years later. He took his own life in September of 2012, something that will never sit right with me. The guy was a real mensch. He was a strong person and a good friend. One day I wouldn't be surprised if we found out foul play of sorts played a role in his much-too-early departure.

Chris, or "Baby Chris" as we called him back then, also oversaw a group called the Jungle Brothers that was on the same wavelength as De La. They, along with Monie Love, Queen Latifah, A Tribe Called Quest, and later Black Sheep, formed an Afro-centric crew called Native Tongues. At the time, the Jungle Brothers had a record out called "I Got it Like That."

We also grooved on their other gem "Jimbrowski," which was a euphemism for a penis.

Uncle Red was the slangologist of the day, always inventing new slang that would quickly be adapted by his loyal listeners. He was everyone's "uncle" and a really nice guy. He also bigged me up, so to speak, and started to really give the "Plug Tunin'" record some serious love. I was psyched that the first record I had been involved with at Tommy Boy was now on the radio. I thought, *Hey, man, this isn't so hard. I might actually be good at this.*

De La and I ran together like crazy at this point, and I felt like the luckiest guy in the world. Sure, I didn't make a bunch of bread at the time, and to make ends I was slinging weed out of the office and road managing on weekends for some pocket change. Money was tight, and Tommy Boy were cheapskates, always crying poverty.

Still, I loved my gig.

Meanwhile, I was still going to the LQ, but a lot less frequently. That scene was slowing down and a lot of the artists I would see there started getting booked into the downtown clubs, like Payday and The World.

I basically ran roughshod over the cats that did the Payday party. I was a real schmuck back then. Patrick Moxey ran the club. He would later end up being one of the most important DJ managers and the man behind Ultra Records, as well as the person who guided most of Gang Starr's career. I loved busting his balls, and I would show up at the club with my thugs in tow and be a real nuisance.

When I think about it, the way I acted worked well in my chosen profession during that time. New York was a tough place back then. This was before Giuliani, when AIDS and crack were taking out thousands of people out every year. The city was filthy, and the clubs were rough. This was before people filmed fights with their phones and posted it on Worldstar. I don't want to make excuses, but I was a product of my environment, and my behavior was usually fueled by booze.

"Plug Tunin'" connected and was a regional hit, getting burn on every East Coast mix show and club in the tri-state area. In the interim, De La had teamed up with the Jungle Brothers and their young protégé, a kid from Queens by the name of Jonathan Davis, a.k.a. Q-Tip. They would show up at each other's sessions and vibe. The exchange of energy was vital to the growth of all of the bands involved, and I believe hip-hop as a whole. The Jungle Brothers dropped their first album, *Straight Out the Jungle*. It was an amazing debut full of rare samples and clever rhymes. It was a street friendly record at the time. It was also one of if not the first example of alternative rap, which evolved twenty years later into trip-hop and neo-soul, as well as other sub-genres. I don't think it would be out of line to say that Kendrick Lamar is the bastard child of the Native Tongues and NWA. That's one of the things about great art. Even if an album doesn't sell ridiculous numbers right off the jump, chances are it will still be relevant, on some level, generations later. The whack shit may sell records but will be quickly forgotten, holding no cultural cache. How many kids do you think are playing Tone Loc these days?

As great as *Straight out the Jungle* is, it was mixed kind of strangely. I have always wanted to get someone competent to remix that whole record— it deserves it. Nonetheless, it was a beautiful piece of art that college kids and hoodlums both rocked out to.

As much as I enjoyed being around these cats, I wondered when De La would get the green light to make their first album or even record their second single.

It was out of my hands, but I knew I couldn't sit around and wait.

One night at the LQ, while watching the dance floor and hoping nobody kicked my ass, a slightly chubby, brown-skinned cat walked up to me. He had headphones around his neck, so I assumed he was some sort of a DJ.

He was a little bit older looking then most of the crowd at the LQ and a lot less grizzled around the edges. As a matter of fact, he seemed like a nice cat, which was unusual at the LQ. It kind of freaked me out actually.

"You're Dante Ross, ain't you?" he said, smiling a little.

"Yeah, man, who are you?"

"I'm Mark The 45 King. You ever hear of me?" he said.

I had indeed. He was a serious beat maker and digger, a term that wasn't really even in vogue at the time. His name indicated he was a King of digging for 45s, the rarest piece of vinyl. Being a digger means you're serious about diggin' in record store crates, looking through obscure records for hours at a time just to find just one sample-friendly piece of music. This can be just one bar or a sound. It can be a horn blast or a drum loop, there are no rules to what you can find or use. I still love digging for crusty records to this day.

Red Alert played Mark's instrumental promos and productions on his mix show and at the LQ. Mark the 45 King had a name in the streets. He was the head of a groovy rap crew from Jersey called the Flavor Unit and would become best known for a cut "The 900 Number," which was later sampled by DJ Kool for the song "Let Me Clear My Throat." He also had an artist signed to Wild Pitch Records, Latee, who dropped a track called "This Cut's Got Flavor" that Red played religiously. I dug the song, which featured a hip Fatback Band sample. I was secretly sweating the guy; I just didn't want him to know it.

He asked, "You wanna hear some flavor, Dante?"

"Okay," I said, fronting like I wasn't excited.

Out of his coat pocket he pulled a Sony Walkman and preceded to hand me his sweaty headphones before he pressed play.

What Mark played me that day blew me away. Dude had some of the funkiest beats I had ever heard. I quickly gave him my homemade business card that announced me as "Director of A&R"—an entirely self-appointed title. Technically, I wasn't lying since the entire A&R staff consisted of just me, and I was definitely directing myself.

Mark The 45 King called me that Monday with Fab 5 Freddy. Freddy's a character: He's an old-school hustler, a fine "artist," and a part-time actor who had credits in the film *Wild Style* and a cameo in the Blondie video for

"Rapture." He helped bring hip-hop downtown back in the day, and for this, and his role in the early days of hip-hop, he is a real New York City legend.

Freddy and Mark played a track—which I would later find out was called "The Wrath of My Madness"—over the phone by a female artist. I immediately asked Mark to meet me at my office with her, and he did two days later with most of the Flavor Unit in tow. For some reason Freddy didn't come with him, and to this day I don't know why.

I recognized some of the guys, but when this one young woman walked in, everyone else faded to the rear. She had an aura to her that said she was special. She had that "it" factor you hear about all the time but rarely see. Her name was, and is, Dana Owens—though she's better known as Queen Latifah.

After the introductions, Mark proceeded to play me music from several members of the Flavor Unit, including Lakim Shabazz and Apache. They were good, but when he played me Latifah's stuff, I went crazy. She could sing, she could rap, and she had dancehall elements going on in her music. I had wanted to sign her over the phone the first time Mark played her for me. Meeting her in the flesh just doubled this want.

I grabbed Monica Lynch and pulled her into the meeting. She was always good with talent, and this was no exception. She listened to Latifah's demo and shot me that knowing look before the first verse had even ended. Tommy Boy Records, Queen Latifah, and Mark The 45 King were about to be in business.

Tommy Boy was in an awkward place when we found Latifah. Stetsasonic had dropped their LP *In Full Gear*, and although it was a great record, it had not met its sales expectations. Their peers were going gold and platinum while their record had stalled at around 200,000. Other than De La Soul, the label was cold. Finding Latifah, coupled with the buzz surrounding De La, gave Tommy Boy a bit of fresh air. I believe my energy was also changing the perception of the label a bit, and things seemed to be heading in the right direction.

After we chitchatted for a bit, Monica asked me to come into her office. She told me we needed to sign her. I told her I was already there. This was one of the few no-brainers I have seen in all the years I've been doing this.

It wouldn't be the last, but it's amazing to me that it happened so early in my career. I got the demos and the lawyer's info from Mark, and as they say, the rest is history. I had officially found my first artist. This demo became the foundation for her first single and the cornerstone from which she built her amazing career.

Stetsasonic, or Stetsa as they were often called, has been called the first hip-hop band. It's a little bit of a stretch, since they only occasionally had a keyboard player and drummer. Still, no one could deny they were a talented bunch of dudes. "Go Stetsa I," from their 1986 debut album *On Fire*, was known to start a fracas in a heartbeat.

We can't, however, blame it all on BK. Through Eric B. and his crew, I got to know a quandary of Queens cats who were a problem. These cats used to sneak guns into clubs around Christmastime wrapped up in presents and whatnot. They would tell the security it was for the coat check girl, go upstairs, open the present, and bang—they were ready for the evening. These factions, plus Harlem cats like the murderous figure named Alpo, a legendary flamboyant dope dealer, were a permanent fixture at the LQ. Add Chris Lighty and the Violators from the Bronx, along with the KRS/BDP crew, and the depth of violence went far beyond rap music. Plain and simple, any night at the LQ, Union Square, or the Red Parrot could erupt into an outbreak of violence with deadly ramifications.

The entire scene had this dangerous air to it, but the vitality of it all was, for me, attractive and exciting. The amount of talent on display at these clubs, particularly the regular performers at the LQ, meant that on any given night you were possibly catching the birth of a major rap star or group. I had a job that could empower me to help some of the talent I was witnessing make it. I may have been living in a shitty railroad apartment with a bathtub in the kitchen on the Upper East Side, but I was happier than a pig in shit with my burgeoning career.

I was the luckiest guy ever. I was working with De La Soul, Stetsasonic, and Queen Latifah, and getting paid for it. "Plug Tunin'" was an underground hit. Red Alert ran with it from day one, and other DJs quickly followed suit. In the span of a few weeks, the so-called "Others from the Brother Planet" were on the map.

For the record, I gave them that name.

In turn, they gave me the title of "Scrub." I think they won.

I had a nice little industry buzz going. By early spring of 1988, De La Soul's record had gone wide. It was big coast-to-coast, and people wanted to see them live at this point. They had a pending gig at Irving Plaza, where the Payday party had moved, but there was one problem: De La had never done a show before, and I'd have to prep them for the rigors of the stage. Which raised another problem: I had no experience prepping jack shit. Thank God, they had a mentor. De La had Prince Paul in the wings, and he had done a ton of shows with Stetsasonic.

The event was a two-for-one marketing ploy by the label. They wanted to placate Stetsasonic with an album release event at Irving Plaza while simultaneously showcasing their rising stars, De La Soul. To say Tommy Boy's relationship with Stetsa and its dynamic leader, Daddy-O, was strained would be an understatement. Still, Tommy Boy had booked Stetsasonic to do a performance/record release show at Payday, and despite being at odds with the label over various issues, Stetsasonic agreed to perform.

In preparation for De La Soul's first show, I booked them into Rocket Rehearsal Studio on West Thirty-Seventh Street. They rolled up with their little crew, which consisted of dancers China and Jet, and their homie, a kid who was nicknamed Granny. The dudes had the crazy idea of having the dancers hold up cue cards with the lyrics written on them while De La performed in syncopation, which were hand drawn by Plug Two, a.k.a. Trugoy. It was pretty funny and original, just like their music, even if it was copped from an old Bob Dylan video.

Meanwhile, Stetsa were having major behind-the-scenes issues with the label that kept escalating. They felt Tommy Boy was under promoting them as they watched their contemporaries like Salt-n-Pepa, Eric B. & Rakim, and BDP sell records. Couple this with all the buzz surrounding the new kids on the label—De La Soul—and tensions were high. Things only got worse when Tom Silverman turned down Daddy-O's impassioned plea to make a video for "Sally." Silverman told him, "I don't believe it will help sell your record," and that "rap videos are an unproven entity." He may have been right about the video; we'll never know because the video never got made.

Daddy-O carried the weight of this decision around with him and had become pretty difficult to deal with at this point. I loved the guy, and I understood his angst about the situation and the label. He had a major chip on his shoulder the night of the event and proceeded to have a big beef with the sound man during the afternoon sound check. It was more about the video not being done, De La Soul being on the bill, *In Full Gear* not selling like he had hoped, and dealing with the ups and downs of the hip-hop game than what was actually going on during the sound check.

Meanwhile, I was a rookie A&R guy watching the headliner of De La's first show tell my boss, Monica Lynch, "We ain't doing shit tonight" and that "the label sucks" and "the sound is whack." It was a freaky thing to watch unfold.

I tried to soft peddle this to De La when they showed up, but the tension in the room was evident. The memory banks are a little fuzzy on this one, but if I recall correctly, they sound checked quickly, and we went and got some pizza. We then killed some time, which included me smoking some weed and calling Daddy-O's SkyPager in hopes of convincing him to perform that night. I was still freaked from what had transpired earlier. The last thing I remember from it was Daddy-O storming off screaming that Tommy Boy should "go get fucked."

Two hours before the curtain call, I was still hopeful Daddy-O was going to come back. One thing I knew for sure was that I had to get De La on stage and then the rest would take care of itself. Looking back, I laugh at how naive I was. When we returned from getting a few slices, Pos, Dave, Maseo, China, Jet, Granny, and I posted up adjacent to the stage in a tiny dressing room. I began thinking, *Damn, I had seen the Circle Jerks and my friends Frontline play here just a few years ago.* It was a bit overwhelming. I guess shit done changed for me, right?

It was getting late, and Stetsa was still nowhere to be found.

I did a few crowd checks, walked around, soaked up the vibe. It was hot and sweaty inside, even though it was the dead of winter. There were some heavy industry heads in the house like Russell Simmons, Lyor Cohen, DMC, Fab 5 Freddy, and Corey Robbins, the owner of Profile Records, but I wasn't worried about those guys. I was more concerned with some of the other guests. I grew up a stone's throw from the venue and a bunch of my cronies/crimies were in the spot. Nobody bricks you like your own people, so I was extra tense.

After conferring with Monica Lynch and a few of the Tommy Boy staff, it was time for Pos, Dave, and Maseo to rock. As they went out on stage with their dancers in place, Granny introduced the boys and they broke into a routine for "Freedom of Speak (We Got Three Minutes)," the B-side of "Plug Tunin'."

They did a half-song version of the joint and then went right into "Plug Tunin'." As the girls started pulling out the lyric laden cue cards in syncopation with Pos and Dave, the crowd started losing its collective mind. By the start of the second verse, the house was more or less rapping along with the cue cards, and I knew right then and there that these guys had something really special, worthy of even the mighty Latin Quarters stage.

De La received a serious ovation and the industry people all hovered around them, showering them with props. After the backstage scrum had died down a bit, we walked around the venue. Years later, Pos related that DMC told him they should go on again. And when he told him that the group didn't have any other songs, DMC told him to just do the same set again.

I honestly don't remember it, but I've got to believe Pos.

What I distinctly remember, though, is that around 2:00 a.m., an hour after De La rocked, the venue manager started sweating me about the next performance: the headliners. I spent five bucks in quarters blowing up Daddy-O on his SkyPager throughout the night. It was the first time I ever got stood up by a rapper, and I couldn't believe it. Unfortunately, working with the likes of Grand Puba, it was something I would eventually get used to.

In the spring of 1988, Tommy Boy sent me to the studio to go and help make Latifah's fabulous demo "Wrath of My Madness/Princess of the Posse" into a real record. The project was masterminded by Mark The 45 King, who was no rookie, having made several records over the last few years. Mark, always an outside-the-box thinker, got Tommy Boy to set up a purchase order at Sam Ash in Midtown for an Akai S900 sampler in lieu of his production advance. That's a real artist. This new and game-changing piece of equipment was his want—not cash. He was investing in himself, something I highly respected. I met him at Sam Ash where we picked up the sampler, and we then headed to the Port Authority to catch a bus to his home studio digs in East Orange, New Jersey.

His house was a beat head's dream. Records and collectible memorabilia were stacked against every inch of the walls. Dude even had a subway turnstile. Mark played me a ton of beats and records, and we smoked a gang of dirt weed. A few days later, I trooped it back out to Jersey and witnessed Latifah redo her hook on "Wrath of My Madness" and then the vocals on "Princess of the Posse" while her Flavor Unit partners hung out and encouraged her performance. She nailed 'em both easily. Like I said, she had the goods from day one.

Later, we would recut Latifah's vocals on both tracks at Calliope, the spot where just about everyone recorded in those days. Although Mark worked hard at Calliope with Latifah, I swear the demos were better. Regardless, when I played the final vocals for the Tommy Boy staff, they were ecstatic. We rushed the burgeoning Flavor Unit star into the studio to record and mix those songs. Mark did a great job bringing the record home. I felt in my bones we really had one here.

The end results were better than I could have hoped for. I had test pressings of the twelve inch just in time for New Music Seminar, which was an annual New York–based music business convention coincidently owned by my boss, Tom Silverman. The New Music Seminar commenced in 1980 with 220 industry insiders gathered together in New York City to discuss the changes and challenges in the music industry. By the time I brought Latifah there in the summer of 1988, it was the most important music business convention in America.

I'll never forget the heat that Latifah generated. Her buzz started at the convention and spread like wildfire. Once again, Uncle Red Alert was championing the record like nobody's business. There was a rising new star in the hip-hop world, one like no other.

In July, we officially dropped her first single, "Wrath of My Madness." It was a double A-side release, along with "Princess of the Posse." That summer, Latifah hit the road to push the record, with me occasionally doubling as road manager/A&R guy. We went to LA twice, and the second time there I got into a little fracas in the parking lot of a club. I cracked someone in the face while wearing a cheap three-finger ring that folded around my hand like a tin can. Immediately, I knew my shit was broken. Despite having a broken hand, I hung around LA two more days before we all went back home. The day after I returned to New York, I had three pins put in my hand and had to wear a cast for six weeks. It still hurts a little to this day. My temper, combined with liquor, has always been my downfall, and this was another example of it.

Nonetheless, I was back in New York, straight grinding, cast and all. I remember feeling great because Latifah was rapidly on her way to become a breakout star, De La Soul was bubbling, and Stetsasonic was doing pretty well, in spite of label politics.

We finally got the green light to make De La's second single. Prince Paul masterfully crafted an amazing tune based mostly on Eric Burdon and War's "Magic Mountain" sample of a dusty Jew harp. He added a yodeling loop from Parliament's "Little Ole Country Boy" combined with the breakbeat classic "Midnight Theme" by Manzel underneath it, resulting in the song "Potholes in My Lawn." De La Soul took their abstract song crafting up a notch, creating a secret metaphor-filled rap language with their cryptic rhymes. A lot of people still don't know that the lawn in the song is their lyrical style and that potholes were a metaphor for what's left behind when you bite. This tune was a message to the biters. I thought it was brilliant.

The B-side to "Potholes in My Lawn" was "Jenifa Taught Me (Derwin's Revenge)," a kind of playful message to the Jungle Brothers' "Jimbrowski," which helped cement the bond between the groups. The record was then mixed down in Long Island and mastered at Frankford Wane in Manhattan.

Mastering was a technical process I really didn't understand at the time. Later, I came to realize how vital it was in making a record knock. The test pressings came a few weeks later, and we were right on schedule for our September release.

I'll never forget the photoshoot we did for the record, which was shot by my pal Ari Marcopoulos, who would later go on to become a notable photographer known for documenting New York skateboarding culture, in particular the kids affiliated with the emerging brand Supreme. We trooped out to Amityville and set up a crazy little scene in the woods behind a local high school. The cover turned out better than I could have hoped for, and the record clicked right away.

The tune was a hit from the jump and now there was serious talk of getting an album started. Monica Lynch was feeling good about hiring me, but truth be told, Tom Silverman and I never really vibed. Since I had come to Tommy Boy, the label had been on a good run, and I was a part of that energy. If Tom realized it, though, he certainly didn't acknowledge it. Even if he wasn't, I was feeling myself. I was a complete knucklehead; humility was not my strong point during this phase of my life. Booze and weed didn't help my public persona one bit. Still, I was able pay my own bills, and the future was bright.

We had a real song on our hands and a real artist. The magnitude of this was beginning to dawn on me. Russell Simmons, my early mentor, started to give me real props at this point. He started telling me I was "a real record man," which I would learn was the highest compliment he could give to someone in our business.

During this time, I also had a hand in getting 3rd Bass going, and if I had been a little smarter, I would have pushed to get credited as their A&R person as well. I guess I just didn't properly understand the hustle back then. Fuck, I was still only twenty-three.

Regardless, "Potholes in My Lawn" was bumping in the clubs. In fact, almost wherever I went, I would hear a mini–Tommy Boy set, consisting of Stetsa's "Sally," Latifah's "Wrath of My Madness," De La's "Plug Tunin'" and "Potholes in my Lawn." I was proud of what I had accomplished in less than year at Tommy Boy.

Then, during one of our hangs, Russell hipped me to the fact that I was getting paid dog shit for my efforts. I've never been driven by money, and I tried not to think about it, but I knew deep down I was getting screwed. I may have been young still, but I had found and developed astonishing talent, made hit records, and helped turn around Tommy Boy. Still, I had to sling trees on the side just to make the rent.

During this time, my pops came in from California and spent a weekend with me. I was living on Eightieth Street and York. We spent an afternoon watching basketball and drinking at some bar on Third Avenue. I think we caught a fight as well. He was boozing a bit and ended up locked out of my house while I was at a lady friend's place for an adult sleepover.

I stumbled home early in the morning, and he was outside my apartment, furious. I couldn't help but laugh, which enraged him even more. I let him in, and he hit the couch for a few hours. He overslept and almost missed his plane. Of course, I got the blame. It had been an awkward little visit. Other than being at that bar and watching a game, we didn't hang much. My father and I weren't particularly close at this point. We would rap on the phone periodically, but we didn't really talk about much except for basketball. I got a few postcards and letters from him, and he seemed to be doing well. Still, there was tension, and I think it was the intersection of me becoming a grown man and him trying to figure out where he was headed as he entered middle age.

My relationship with my mom and sister had gotten a bit worse, too, as they moved from Rhode Island and were now living in Washington, DC. My sister was undergoing tests for cancer, which she would eventually be diagnosed with some time down the road. To make matters worse, they were both boozing heavily. Keeping in line with my family heritage, my sister had become a full-fledged alcoholic, much like my mother. I would battle alcohol addiction later in my life as well. It is, I believe, in some ways transferred down genetically and socially.

I took the train to DC and spent Christmas with them. It wasn't pleasant. In fact, it drove a chasm between me and my sister that still exists to this day. I was attacked for my views on life and commerce after I mentioned that someday I wanted to save up to buy a BMW. For the record, I never did buy that BMW. (Since finishing this book, I did in fact get my first ever car—a Lexus, not a beamer, though. I am now driving car number two: a Tesla.)

My sister had a child with Tommy Ford, the guy who helped my mom and me when we were homeless. I found this a bit I odd since they weren't even together at this point. Nonetheless, my niece Honore was cute as a button, and she is a strong young woman today. Unfortunately, I have missed out on participating in most of her life due to my strained relationship with my sister. Family dynamics can be a real bitch.

It was about this time I started to put distance between my mother and that side of my family, though with years of therapy and self-exploration I have made peace with my mother's shortcomings as a parent. I am still working on making peace with my shortcomings as a son. It is not easy to admit that your mother did you a disservice as a child. She handed me many of her worst qualities. She also passed on several of her better ones as well. She was a very complicated woman. She had endured a lot of personal torment in her life: from her own mother's death while she was just a young girl, to being a single mother in the fifties, to the dysfunctional relationship with my father. After her death, I would learn more about her pain and torment, which explained more of why she was so complicated. Still, as I became a young man and made my way through life, I'd come to this realization: My mother was not a great parent. She may not have even been a good one. She had the disease of alcoholism. She subjected me to her manic-depressive outbursts. She was emotionally unavailable for months on end, usually coupled with a drunken binge. She did not protect me in the ways a parent is traditionally supposed to nurture and care for a child. I was exposed to a lot of her mental anguish. We struggled financially, ending up homeless twice during my teen years, and ultimately, after the age of fifteen, I had cashed in any hopes of life getting better in my house. I disregarded any hope of a normal home life. This was a survival mechanism, and if nothing else, I have proven myself to be a master survivalist. I guess I can count that as an odd blessing from my mother.

The end result in all of this was a chip on my shoulder that I still carry with me. Most of my teenage friends had, and have, no idea what my childhood was like. Being vulnerable is risky, and as a teenager you don't really share these things. It led to a lot of my anti-social behavior as a young man, and in writing this, it's the first time a lot of my friends will find out the depth of my familial dysfunction. Maybe this will explain some of my behavior over the years.

Regardless, I made peace with my mother many years before her passing, I can't say the same for my sister. In the wake of our parents' deaths, a deep wound was reopened. Any chance of us having a relationship, or really being anything more than civil to one another, seems impossible. In therapy, years later, I finally began to unpack some of the reasons and accept some hard facts I'd been uncomfortable facing and that I still have a hard time acknowledging.

The demise of my relationship with my sister started when I was thirteen and I was spending the weekend in Brooklyn with her and her boyfriend. She was working at a bar in the Wall Street area frequented by cops, and she took me to her Christmas work party that year—in and of itself a questionable move. Why would you take a thirteen-year-old to a Christmas party with an open bar and a bunch of drunks? My mother didn't know about this, and for my part, I wanted to go. They had pinball machines, and being given a pocket full of quarters at the age of thirteen is like being given candy only better.

My sister got loaded, per family tradition, and we ended up going with a cop friend of hers who knew her boyfriend—a cop as well—to the Rainbow Room in Midtown, where they proceeded to get even more loaded. On the way back, much later, I was sitting in the front seat of her friend Bobby's car while she was passed out in the back. Meanwhile, her friend, who was a NYC detective, repeatedly tried to grope me. I resisted and resorted to yelling at him, including calling him a not very nice word for a homosexual, while attempting to wake up my sister several times. He kept coming at me. It was terrifying, but like I said, I am a survivalist. I am very lucky he didn't rape me, and I believe if he had the opportunity he would have. I do not believe this was the first time he had done this with someone. I am convinced he was a predator.

When we finally got to my sister's house, I darted out of the car and started crying. I explained to her what happened and asked her why she didn't do anything. She was three sheets to the wind and the only thing she asked was that I didn't tell her boyfriend or my mother. I never did tell my mother or her boyfriend. Many years later, after my mother had passed, my sister asked me why we never had a relationship. I explained that this was one of the reasons why. She denied this ever happened, losing her temper and calling me a liar. I believe her memory in this case, or her lack of memory, is borne of convenience. I have since tried to make amends, but she told me to kick rocks.

To be honest, this wasn't the first time someone had tried this stuff on me as a kid. At the Boy's Club, a similar incident occurred—one I never shared with my mother. I think getting molested as a child is a lot more common than people think. It took me over forty years to be comfortable enough to talk about it publicly, and even now it is a subject I rarely care to delve into. I have been very lucky that nothing beyond attempted groping ever happened. A lot of young people are not that lucky. That said, these incidents still left a cloud of darkness in my adolescent psyche. The most painful part of it all, though, was that my sister wanted to sweep it under the rug for fear that she would catch the wrath of my mother or her boyfriend. Apparently, she still wants to sweep it under the rug. My sister was supposed to protect me. Most of the time she did; however, she failed in this instance.

Idalis DeLeón, a gorgeous model/singer/bartender who would later be an MTV VJ, who happened to be one of the hottest ladies on the scene, somehow took a liking to me. Light skinned with light brown eyes, standing a sweet 5' 7", Idalis was intense, enthralling, and totally out of her mind. We soon became quite the item, making out all over town. To this day, I still rank it as one of my most passionate relationships ever. It wasn't all good though. We fought almost as much as we fucked, and that's saying something.

As much as I dug Idalis, I kept my eye on the prize and went harder than ever at work. I was babysitting the De La's at the studio most days, as they were busy putting together *3 Feet High and Rising* with Prince Paul. I was also busy trying to find new groups and preparing Latifah's second single, "Dance for Me."

I was gassed, and I wanted to interject a little something into that record. I didn't hear a big hook at the time we were making the song, and I felt it needed one. I badgered Mark The 45 King into adding a sample from Sly and the Family Stone's "Dance to the Music," which in retrospect was kind of whack. The record hit, but the beautiful Alvin Cash "Keep on Dancing" sampled groove was somewhat hampered by my contribution. The 45 King, as cool as he was, never got mad about it.

These were the days before rap music had encountered sample clearance hell. I wonder how much publishing my nonsense cost them on that one. Sly Stone samples don't come cheap, and we actually shot a video for the song. MTV had started a rap show called *Yo! MTV Raps* and Fab 5 Freddy was the host. He also hustled his way into the director's chair for Latifah's video and assured us that *Yo!* would run it. True to his word, the video got lot of play. Latifah's record also hit big out west, leading us to run out to LA for her first West Coast show.

The LA clubs were different from the ones in New York. At this point, much like today, rap had two separate circuits. Hollywood clubs like Water the Bush and Funky Reggae, owned by my friend Matt Robinson, were akin to the downtown clubs in Manhattan. The clubs we played at in LA at the time were more the chitlin'/brown paper bag circuit, where you got paid in cash and anything could go down, much like the LQ or the treacherous joint in the Bronx I had ventured to with De La. World on Wheels and Skateland were the two most notorious LA rap venues, and like the LQ, real violence could erupt at any time. Also like the LQ, it was the place to go if you really wanted to feel the pulse of what music was hitting in the streets.

The main difference, however, was that LA hip-hop was completely gang related. In New York, we had yet to see the rise of Bloods and Crips. We had crews, not gangs. LA had gangs, and to me that also made it more dangerous because the bangers really repped colors. Back home, people wanted your money or jewelry; in LA you could get fucked with for simply wearing the wrong shit at the wrong time or for being from the wrong hood.

If I had to say which city was more dangerous, I'd have to go with LA, and that's saying something since New York was clocking almost 2,500 murders a year in those days, compared to a little more than three hundred now. LA always had that Wild West mentality, and adding to that: almost everyone had cars. In New York, we didn't drive places, so it was often hands or razor blades inside the clubs if shit jumped off. In LA, you could transport guns easier and leave them in your car in case a violent after-party was brewing in the parking lot.

At this point in time, a lot of LA rap was still emulating New York. Rap was small still, and most of the music being made was coming from New York. Sure, Ice-T, NWA, and some of the Delicious Vinyl groups were emerging from Los Angeles, but there was no East Coast / West Coast rivalry in the 1980s. Even when NWA's *Straight Outta Compton* went platinum, it failed to get virtually any radio play in New York. Snoop and Dre would shift the balance in the nineties, but at this point it was mostly about New York, which would lead to coastal tensions down the line.

To its credit, even though hip-hop was born in New York, LA did manage to start the world's first all-rap radio station. It was an AM station called KDAY, though it still played mostly New York music for the simple fact that there was more of it, and they did support hometown talent. They had a bunch of amazing mix shows on air. The mix show DJs were called "The Mix Masters," and they were extremely talented. Many of them were extraordinary at scratching at fast tempos, I believe due to the fact that a lot of West Coast hip-hop at the time was based on electro-style beats. Several of the Mix Masters had been members of Uncle Jamm's Army, a pioneering group of funk-based DJs assembled by Uncle Jamm, a.k.a. Roger Clayton (RIP), a music biz street promoter. These DJs and parties influenced a young Dr. Dre, who was also the first Mix Master at KDAY. It could be said that outside of Dr. Dre, the foundation of West Coast hip-hop comes directly from Uncle Jamm's Army.

Latifah was booked to play a World on Wheels show sponsored by KDAY. We showed up at the radio station fresh off the plane, and coincidentally, Latifah's record was rocking on the radio. KDAY played all the Tommy Boy records back then; I think they were on the payroll. The station itself was a small operation located near Dodger Stadium on a hilltop at 1700 N Alvarado Street. This was not a glamorous location, to say the least. The whole place was only about 1,500 square feet, and it had a mammoth broadcast antenna outside. When I think about it, it's mind boggling that such an important entity in the culture of West Coast rap music was such a small, homespun, and accessible operation.

We were there about fifteen minutes when we heard an ad for a Saturday show at Skateland, in which Latifah was supposed to perform. Latifah and I looked at each other—it was the first either one of us had heard about it. Apparently, Uncle Jamm, being the slick motherfucker that he was, knew we were in town to perform at World on Wheels on Friday and somehow learned we weren't flying back until Sunday, so he took it upon himself to book us for a Saturday gig.

Latifah started her interview with the legendary Greg Mack and shined like the LA sun. A few minutes into it, I got a call at the station from Uncle Jamm himself, which I took in the other room. While I wasn't happy with him, I kept in mind that he was an LA legend and definitely gang related and that I was a long way from home. In other words, I couldn't scream on this guy—I had to handle him with diplomacy.

I picked up the phone and jumped right into it. "What's going on with this Skateland show, man? This ain't cool."

"Ah, homie, I knew y'all were out here, and I wanted to put some extra change in your pocket," he said.

"How much you talking, OG?"

He kicked that West Coast hustler shit and blurted, "A thousand dollars."

"Man, I was already getting that on Friday," I said. "And they're paying for our flights and hotels on top of that. You gotta come better than that, big dog."

"Eleven hundred, my man," he said.

"Yeah, we gonna pass on that. Sorry, Roger."

"D, the best I can do is twelve."

I wanted fifteen, at least. I mean, this cat might have been a G, but he was running game on me. He knew it, and so did I. "That's light, Roger, you gotta come better."

"Twelve-fifty is the best I can do, G," he said. "I'll throw in a limo and a driver for the whole night, too. Let y'all cruise around in style."

I told him to call me back in ten minutes.

I consulted Latifah and she asked me to hit him up for fifteen. Shit, she had game. I said I already had and that this was the best he was coming with. She smiled and said, "Fuck it, let's do it."

That Saturday night our limo showed up around ten thirty to take us to our show. I wasn't sure if it was a limo or a demo, I just hoped it would make it to the show and back. We walked into Skateland to a stench of angel dust, dirt weed, activator, and gangsterism like I had never smelled before. World on Wheels was a trip. I had been there before with De La and Latifah the previous night, but Skateland was a full-on Blood club, plain and simple. I had a look out at the crowd and got a little shook. I honestly had never seen so much red in my entire life, and being from New York, that shit was both terrifying and exciting as hell. There was no gunplay during the show, though, and Latifah won over every gangsta in the building with her short, three-song set.

Right before the gig, I was paid in messy five- and ten-dollar bills. Uncle Jamm provided us with our own shotgun-carrying Samoan bodyguard, who escorted us around and made sure we got to our car and out of the spot intact. I also met Ice Cube and Dr. Dre briefly that night and stayed in contact with Ice Cube for a bunch of years later. This is surprising, in retrospect, since NWA seemingly had Crip affiliations. Go figure?

I was moving at a fast pace and working hard. De La Soul's *3 Feet High and Rising* was almost done, and people were hollering at me from other labels about taking a gig. I wanted to finish the record before I went anywhere. I had an obligation to my dudes, and I was confident that we were going to hit a homerun.

Around this time my friendship with Pete "Nice" Nash had started to blossom. I had moved to 108th and Broadway, and Pete was attending Columbia University. He lived in the dorms and played basketball. I had linked him up with Sam Sever, who helped him with his first demo, which lead us to connect him with MC Serch and the eventual creation of 3rd Bass (who were first called "3 the Hard Way" until running into legal issues with the name).

Serch, Pete, our friend Marc "Sake" Pearson, and his boy Bobbito "The Barber" Garcia, and I often hit the clubs in Serch's Ford Granada, which we had dubbed "The Think Tank." At our urging, Bobbito would eventually get a job at Def Jam, and later, with Stretch Armstrong, he'd create one of the most important hip-hop radio shows ever at Columbia University's own WKCR. "The Think Tank" was our cruiser mobile, where 3rd Bass wrote a lot of their lyrics for the first album and where Serch and Pete battled in front of Sam Sever and me. The battle is what eventually lead them to become a group, I believe. I tried to get them signed to Tommy Boy based on a demo that Lyor had financed. Several songs were initially Serch solo songs, in fact. Tommy Boy wouldn't do the deal, but Def Jam eventually did.

A bit later, they dropped their first single for Def Jam called "Steppin' to the A.M.," which was produced by my old sparring partner, Hank Shocklee, and the Bomb Squad. This added to my growing rep as a guy in the know, as many saw me running around with them and just assumed they were my group. As I said, if I had been savvier, I could have parlayed the relationship into an A&R credit—and more importantly a check.

Oh, well. We were all making it up as we went, right?

HOTEL AMAZON PLAYLIST

Public Enemy—"Bring the Noise"

De La Soul—"Plug Tunin' (Last Chance to Comprehend)"

Smith & Mighty—"Walk On"

Queen Latifah—"Wrath of My Madness"

3rd Bass—"Steppin' to the A.M."

Chill Rob G—"Court is Now in Session"

Jungle Brothers—"The Promo (Ft. Q-Tip)"

LL Cool J—"Doin' It"

JVC FORCE—"Strong Island"

Stetsasonic—"Sally"

Junior Reid—"One Blood"

Run-DMC—"Beats to the Rhyme"

Eric B. & Rakim—"Paid in Full (7 Minutes of Madness mix)"

9

DOO WHATCHA LIKE

At the beginning of 1989, I was still Tommy Boying while waiting for De La Soul's *3 Feet High and Rising* to drop. As we prepared to unleash their unique sound on the world, Prince Paul and De La stumbled upon a song that would change the game. It was called "Me, Myself, and I," and it borrowed a sample from the P-Funk track "(Not Just) Knee Deep" from the 1979 album *Uncle Jam Wants You*. Paul masterfully added a Loose Ends sample and the drums from the Edwin Birdsong classic roller-skating jam, "Rapper Dapper Snapper" to the mix. (Years later on his NPR podcast, Ali Shaheed confirmed the legend that Tribe had also hooked up the same Knee Deep sample but decided not to use it when they heard the demo of "Me, Myself, and I.")

The guys thought the finished product sounded like something, and to Monica Lynch, me, and everyone else we played the record—it certainly did. I had a hunch this one might just blow wide open. The construction of this tune showed how savvy Prince Paul and the De La's were. By incorporating a classic P-Funk sample in the tune, they won the entire funk-loving West Coast over, opening the flood gates at West Coast radio. How they knew this would work is anyone's guess.

3 Feet High and Rising dropped on March 3, 1989, and connected right away. It didn't hurt that the two previous records had created a big buzz for the kids from the Isle of Long. The song was a hit out the gate.

The video was a great satire on the state of hip-hop at the time and got heavy rotation on MTV. Both De La and the Beasties were quite possibly the first rap groups to point out the absurdity of the macho trappings of hip-hop, albeit in totally different ways.

Almost immediately, the vultures started hovering, and before we knew it, my mentor/nemesis, Lyor Cohen, had started managing the group.

I was pistol hot on the heels of De La's breakthrough and took a ton of calls and meetings inquiring about my services. Two that stuck out: First, Ed Eckstine, a groovy music business impresario and the son of the famed blues singer, Billy Eckstine, wined and dined me a little something. Then Tim Carr, the A&R dude who had signed the Beasties away from Def Jam and put them on Capitol Records, made a big push for me, telling me he would pay me sixty thousand my first year. I balked at his initial offer, thinking he was joking. He misunderstood my reaction and quickly offered sixty-five—which adjusted for inflation is more than $150k in 2022. He also implied Tommy Boy was the little leagues and that it was time for me to move up to the majors. I believed in myself, and I realized so did some other people, ones who were willing to put their money where their mouths were.

If you were to ask those around me during this time, they would probably say that I was reckless and arrogant. I don't doubt I came off that way, but the truth is that I was still a somewhat awkward kid who felt like he didn't really fit in anywhere. As a child, I was too white for the LES, but I was too rough around the edges for the West Village. My family was poor but still stressed art and culture. I had evolved tastes, yet non-evolved funds coming up. I knew I was the shit but didn't really believe I would be compensated for it. I also knew I couldn't go on making bullshit money and that I was going to have to pull Tom Silverman's card and stick him up if I could. This was my word and bond to myself. It had been validated that I was worth something, and I was going to get paid my worth—by hook or by crook.

In all honesty, I didn't want to leave the fold. Tommy Boy was the first place I truly felt empowered in the music industry. I loved Monica Lynch. She was a mother figure to me in a sense, and one of the many women in my life who was a great friend. It has never been a problem for me to be friends with women; after all, I had been raised by two of them—my mother and sister. (Dating women? Now, that's another story.)

Besides being gun shy, I was still hard at work on Latifah's album. I believed in her and didn't want to walk out in the middle of it. I was also involved with a few marginal groups and was on the hunt for something better. I dipped my hand in the production well for the first time, coproducing an underground classic by an artist named Uptown. The record was called *Dope on Plastic,* and it opened with a shout out to me, which was pretty cool. I can remember Marley Marl cutting it up on his show and feeling like I had made the big time. The irony of this is endless.

I linked up with my LQ alum and weed-smoking pal from the short-lived Masters of Ceremony, Grand Puba Maxwell. They had a few regional Latin Quarters hits: "Sexy," and another song I dug called "Cracked Out." I felt like this cat was a diamond in the rough, a true talent. The De La's did, too. I found out early on that rappers are natural A&R people. They usually have great ears, and I can't remember too many times when I played a demo for a talented rapper and he would pick a lemon.

I figured the best way to get into biz with Puba was to get him to produce a track for Latifah or maybe even do a song with her. They were both down with the dance hall vibe, which was popular at the time. Puba being Puba, he missed about eighteen appointments, which was annoying as hell, but he would always call to reschedule. It got to be so regular that when he finally showed up, I was actually surprised.

Almost as soon as he got into the office, Puba played me a joint called "Ain't Going out Like That" by his new group, Brand Nubian. The song, which featured a prominent James Brown sample, floored me. I told Puba that I was interested in signing Brand Nubian. I could have left it like that, but I respected Puba, and even though I knew that it could jeopardize the deal, I wanted to be totally transparent with him—so I took a risk and told him I might be leaving Tommy Boy. I told him if I left, I would get him and his group a bigger advance if he could be patient.

Puba paused for a minute as I braced myself for the worst. He said, "Dante, I wanna roll with you no matter where you end up." I'm going to say that the money had a lot to do with Puba's declaration, but still,

I was honored. I never did get any beats for Latifah that day, but I did find a future project that I would be linked to forever.

I reached out to my friend, Andy Tavel, a seasoned veteran of an entertainment lawyer who had done a bunch of work for Def Jam and later worked at Grubman, Indursky, & Schindler—one of the top entertainment law firms on the planet.

Andy dug me from the time I worked as a messenger at Rush. He took a meeting with me and let me know he had watched my ascent in the business and was happy for me. He also let me know Silverman would be a tough cookie to crack in terms of getting my real worth. Regardless, Tavel said he'd try. He arranged a meeting with Tom Silverman and Monica Lynch. I waited with bated breath.

I never wanted to leave Tommy Boy, but I had come to the realization that I could make some real bucks. I didn't have a trust fund or a family co-op or parents who were supplementing my income. I was a blue-collar kid whose highest paying job at this point was waiting tables. I was tired of hustling on the side to make ends meet.

It took me a couple of days to get up the courage to confront Monica. I was confident that she wanted me to stay at Tommy Boy, too, but I knew she didn't have the final say (even though she should have). Silverman was the moneyman.

I sat down in her office.

"Mo, I know you're hearing things," I said.

"Yeah, D, I wanted to ask you about that," she said. "You know I think you're doing a great job, right?"

"Thanks, Mo" I said. "And no matter what happens, I'll always respect you. You gave me a real shot."

She smiled. "So, what's the deal?"

"I need to make paper," I said. "I got a bunch of cats in my ear from Russell to Ed Eckstein. I don't wanna go nowhere, but I gotta eat. I've got the hottest record out there, and I'm about to have another, and I'm still hustling weed to make ends meet."

"I had no idea," she said.

I doubted she was that naive since she once caught me moving a bag in the office.

"Dante, what do you want me to do?" she asked.

"Can you pull Tom's coat and set up a meeting?"

"Sure," she said.

I got up. "Thank you, Mo," I said. "Just give me a little notice so I can get Tavel here."

"Tavel?" she said.

"I hired Andy Tavel," I said. "I figured it's about time to get a lawyer, right?"

Monica's face said it all. I didn't think I had done anything wrong. I still don't. But this was one of the first times I realized how true that old *Godfather* adage is: "It wasn't personal, it was business."

I asked her if she would please be present if and when the meeting took place.

She nodded, and I left her office feeling shitty, but knowing I had done the right thing. My mother taught me when I was seven years old to stand up for myself, and that's what I was doing.

About a week later, a meeting was arranged with Tom Silverman, Monica Lynch, Andy Tavel, and me. A few days prior, Benny Medina, who had worked out a distribution deal with Tommy Boy via Warner Brothers, stepped to me behind their backs after I met him at Nell's with Andre Harrell and casually asked me if I was happy with my current gig.

I felt like I had Silverman by the balls.

We entered the meeting and my lawyer quickly got down to brass tacks. He explained to Tom and Monica that I was grossly underpaid, yet my loyalty was above and beyond. He reiterated what I had said—that I didn't want to leave for greener pastures, that I felt like I was part of something that was important to me. I'm almost positive Silverman saw this as a sign of weakness. I listened to Silverman as he explained that he would get me a company credit card and bump my salary by a whopping five thousand bucks.

I was pissed.

My lawyer chuckled and told Tom point blank, "I can walk Dante over to Mercury Records right now and get him $75,000 in a heartbeat. This kid is helping save your record company. You need to do the right thing, Tom, or we are going to have to pursue other options."

I saw Monica flinch. I felt half-bad but held my ground. I was instructed by my lawyer to say very little, and I followed his directive—until Tom pushed me too far.

"You'll never make it at a major label, kid," Tom said. "It's all politics. You're white, in case you haven't noticed. You can't work in the Black music department at a major label and sign rap acts. It doesn't work like that."

"Not according to Ed Eckstein or Tim Carr," I said.

Tom looked like he got sucker punched, and I wasn't mad.

Andy gave me the high sign to shut up and asked if we could go into my makeshift office to discuss things one-on-one. Tom, with that condescending tone of his, told us to take our time.

When we got into my poor excuse for an office, I thought Andy was going to rip me a new one. Instead, he turned to me and said, "Don't let it get to you. This is what I expected."

"Really?"

Andy said. "He's as cheap as they get. What would it take for you to be happy here?"

I thought about it for a moment. "Not sure, Andy," I said. "But I liked that sixty-five thousand dollar offer at Capitol. You think they'll match it?"

"They should, but that doesn't mean they will."

"I would take even a bit less," I said. "I love my groups and I…"

"Never take less," he said. "Your groups wouldn't do it for you, trust me. There's no room for feelings in this one."

Andy was right. Emotions will fuck with you if you're talking money and the guy on the other side of the table knows this.

I nodded.

"Dante, as I said, I doubt very much that this guy is going to do the right thing," Andy continued. "I'm going to work him as far as I can, but if all he is going to offer you is thirty-five grand, then you better be ready to move on. There's more Ed Ecksteins out there for you to work for. Let me see how many, cool?"

I nodded.

Andy went back to Silverman, who offered $34,000 and no employment contract—meaning there was no royalty incentive for me. (Traditionally, when you sign an artist, you are given one point as an A&R royalty). I decided I would stay for De La's album release and work my ass off finishing Latifah's record, and then I was out. I didn't care if I had to go back waiting tables at Tortilla Flats. I wasn't going to take Tom Silverman's shorts. It wasn't cool then, and thirty years later, it still bothers me. I knew it wasn't Monica's decision—she was too smart to lose the best set of ears Tommy Boy ever had over chump change.

Tom, on the other hand...

10

THE BUSINESS

Looking back, I still can't believe how much heat I had at twenty-three. I met with Chris Blackwell, had dinner with my friend Andre Harrell (RIP) a few times. Gary Gersh, Tim Carr's then-boss at Capitol, also courted me. Of course, I took council with Russell, leaving Lyor out of that conversation. As much as I love Lyor, he can be a treacherous person. I believed, and still believe, Russell had my best interests at heart, but I'm not sure I could say the same about Lyor at that point in time. While working at Tommy Boy, I had met a cat named Raoul Roach, who is the son of the legendary drummer, Max Roach, and a former employee of the mighty Quincy Jones, who was then the head of urban music at Elektra Records. He was a good A&R person and a lovely guy. He was a friend of Russell's and we hit it off right away. In many ways, Raoul and I were total opposites. I was arrogant, brash, confident, crazy, reckless, and totally connected to the pulse of the streets. He was sedate, laid back, and contemplative. Some would say he was evolved. Me, I was still a neanderthal. The guy was good money in my book. He had an air of grace about him.

We both knew I could fill the gaps at Elektra. I also knew if I went to work for him, I could do whatever I wanted because Elektra needed me in order to become a player in the rap game more than any other label except possibly Capitol.

I started plotting.

Raoul set up a meeting with Bob Krasnow, a music biz legend and a man of class and style. In his legendary career, he signed P-Funk and Richard Pryor, which was more than enough for me. He had also recently signed both Keith Sweat and Anita Baker, two of the biggest acts in Black music at the time. He was larger than life, full of piss and vinegar, which I found appealing. He was the genuine article and a straight shooter.

When I met him, he quickly became interested in my flashy new four-finger ring. He asked if he could try it on. I quickly obliged, and I asked if I could try on his gorgeous big diamond ring, which he passed to me. We admired each other's jewelry for a moment, and I asked him if he wanted to trade. He laughed at my moxie and quickly handed me back my Canal Street classic. Bob was my type of guy. Underneath it all, he was a blue-collar cat just like me. By the end of our initial meeting, I had decided I would go work for Elektra Records, the label that couldn't get a rap record played for payola. It was a risky move, but one I wanted to take.

I was impressed by Bob's diverse musical knowledge. I remember him telling me the label had just signed the Pixies, who were one of my favorite alternative bands at the time. I was impressed. The label also had Metallica, another rock act I was a fan of. The label was eclectic, to say the least, and Bob seemed to be involved in all of it.

In the 1960s, under the watch of Jac Holzman, Elektra was home for The Doors, the brilliant Arthur Lee and Love, the Paul Butterfield Blues Band, the legendary MC5, plus Iggy Pop and the Stooges. In 1972, Elektra merged with Asylum Records, which was home to bands like The Eagles, Jackson Browne, and Joni Mitchell. As time progressed, David Geffen and Joe Smith came and went. Bob Krasnow, who had been with the Warner Music Group at Warner Brothers Records since the early 1970s, was promoted to chairman/CEO in 1983. He had helped bring in metal acts such as Mötley Crüe and Metallica. The Cars were also signed under his watch, as were alternative superstars like 10,000 Maniacs. Bob had taste, and he was on a hell of a run when I got there. Best of all—for me, at least—is that he had a rep for hiring risk-taking A&R people and making big artistic statements.

The thing that impressed me the most about him, besides the fact he had worked with James Brown and George Clinton, was a record he played for me that day. It was by an artist I had never heard before. It was beautiful and haunting; it made a big impression on me. He played "Fast Car" by Tracy Chapman. When he told me she was Black, I was floored. I remember him handing me an advance copy of the album when I left his office. This, I believe, was a major factor in me wanting to work at Elektra. I saw how cool Kras was, and I thought he would get my taste in hip-hop. I have to say, in my many meetings with various label heads, that meeting was the best to this day. My mind was made up: I wanted to work at Elektra Records.

I had to figure out how to moonwalk out of Tommy Boy with the minimum amount of damage due to my respect for Monica Lynch. If she hadn't been in the mix, I would probably have socked Silverman in the mouth and kept it moving. But I didn't, thank God. In retrospect, Tom was just doing what he thought was best for Tom, and I honestly can't blame him—that's just his way. As we all witnessed in his hassles with De La Soul, Tom's gonna do Tom.

I told Andy I wanted to work for Bob Krasnow and he asked me why. I told him my reasons. He was a bit apprehensive, explaining that Kras was hot and cold, a bit like me. Andy made sure I knew I was taking a chance, one that could negatively impact my career and leave me buried. He was also pretty confident that he could get me at least seventy-five grand because Krasnow got what he wanted.

That was music to my ears.

I told him I would reach out to Raoul Roach and see what the play was. Andy asked me to sleep on it, and I told him I already had the night before along with my girlfriend, Idalis. He just shook his head and said he'd check into it.

Andy was dead on: they offered me $75,000 and covered my legal fees. I took the job. I had no idea I was about to become the first rap A&R person to ever work at a major label strictly with the purpose of signing hip-hop artists. At the time, I put zero importance on this paradigm and didn't even realize it until Dan Charnas pointed it out in his book *The Big Payback*. I guess, in retrospect, maybe it was.

Tavel worked out the deal and I started to set up shop at Elektra, unbeknownst to Monica Lynch and Tom Silverman. The end was near, and I decided to just go for it. Beyond the finances, I wanted to leave in order to sign higher-profile groups, to be competitive with the big boys. I had been shut down by Tom on signing The D.O.C. for 175,000 bucks and A Tribe Called Quest, both of whom had seasoned managers and wanted deals that were much bigger than Tommy Boy was accustomed to doing. Tom wouldn't budge; he was as cheap as Tavel had suggested. It was well known within the industry, and it was endlessly frustrating. I figured at Elektra I would be competitive financially.

I will never forget the day I told Mo I was moving onto greener pastures and the animosity it created between us. The riff between us healed long ago, and I still consider her a friend and mentor. I want to be crystal clear: Monica Lynch is the most underrated person in the history of the hip-hop music biz. She understands music, marketing, branding, people, and the fabric that connects us all, no matter what and where we come from. She also signed De La Soul, not me. I have never met someone who so openly showed me the gift of knowledge all while being a good friend. I miss her, and writing these pages makes me realize how big of an impact she had on my life. Monica was like a big sister to me. I learned a great deal about the business from her, and along with Lyor and the Captain, she was my most important mentor in my formative years. Monica was the first woman I had seen in the rap game who understood branding and the importance of iconic logos and great talent. She helped make Tommy Boy a real entity, rivaled only by Def Jam in its prime. I don't understand why she isn't held in the same regard as Russell Simmons, Lyor Cohen, and Rick Rubin. If I were to guess, I'd say it's because Tom Silverman took a lot of credit for her brilliance, along with the fact that the music industry was, and still is, a boy's club. The woman is a cultural icon.

There were grumblings from the Black music department at Elektra to be heard down the line, but I ignored them to the best of my ability, knowing I came from the culture of hip-hop, and like it or not Corey Robbins, Tom Silverman, Lyor Cohen, Rick Rubin, Barry Weiss, and others were all white Jews like me and were all key players in the early days of the business

My sister Carla and me, San Francisco 1970
Photo by John Ross

My godmother,Louise, baby me, my mother, and older sister Dylan
Photo by John Ross

My mother and me, age four, Long Island 1969
Photo by Susan Gardner

My father, John Ross, and me, Humboldt County 1979
Photo by Sid Dominitz

Skating on Ave A, LES 1983
Photo Hillary Snyder, courtesy of Laura Cox

Skate Rats: Jeremy Henderson, Ian Frahm, and me, NYC 1985
Photo by Jessica Bard

Jules Gayton, Dominic Chianese, and me, Tompkins Square Park 1984
Photo by Bennet Breen

Monica Lynch and me, NYC 1988
Photo by Rod Huston

Me, Jessica Rosenblum, Jill Revson, and Paul Moore outside Soul Kitchen, 1992
Photo by Brooke Williams

Carla, me, and my dad in San Francisco on his sixtieth birthday
Photo by Pauline Takahashi

1986
Portrait by Alice Arnold

1992
Portrait by Jill Revson

Lysa Cooper, Jill Revson, Yves Brewer,
and me, NYC 1992
Photo by Brooke Williams

This is the first ad in the history
of streetwear, shot in '87.
L–R: Paul Mittleman, Jeremy
Henderson, me, Jules Gayton,
Kevin (last name unknown)
Photo courtesy of Stussy Worldwide

Me and the squad, NYC 1994
Photo courtesy of John Base

My Stimulated Dummy partners
Geeby Dajani, John Gamble,
Zev Love X a.k.a. MF Doom, and
Subroc Chung, King Studios 1990.
Sadly all the people in this photo
have passed
Photo by Dante Ross

Geeby Dajani and John
Gamble, Calliope Studios,
NYC 1989
Photo by Dante Ross

Old Dirty Bastard
Photo courtesy of 4 Screens Entertainment

Me in the Hamptons. I had my socks on because I had poison ivy on my feet. Don't ask…
Photo courtesy of Brooke Williams

Me and Public Enemy. This was for a proposed cover of the PE song "Sophisticated Bitch"
that was never used, I think my white socks were the reason why
Photo by Glen E. Friedman

Lysa Cooper, Keith Haring, Dreena Deniro, me, and Pilar Maschi at Florent Restaurant, NYC 1988
Photo courtesy of Tina Paul

Portrait at SD50 Studios, 1998
Photo by Jill Revson

Portrait outside of Tramps, NYC 1993
Photo by @david.corio

Me and Adam Yauch at the Palladium, 1995. Note: Adam is wearing Harold Hunter:
Old Dirty Harold American Dream T, designed by my friend Aly Oasha Moore

Photo courtesy of Sue Kwon

MF Doom
Photo by Cognito

Me and Daryl Jenifer, the bassist for the first group that changed my life, Bad Brains, Brooklyn 2018
Photo by Mimi Majgaard

Clark Kent, Ricky Powell, me, and Bobbito

Posdnuos, me, Dan the Automator, unknown woman, Maseo, Trugoy, and Del the Funky Homosapien
Photo by Damion Siguenza

Me and my big brother, Dan Cuomo, who I didn't meet till I was forty-nine years old
Photo by Susan Cuomo

Rakim and me, NYC 2017
Photo by Matt Kemp

Me with a very fat face, Dash Snow, Harry Jumonji, and Aaron Bondaroff, 205 Club, NYC 2006.
This was when downtown was in full swing again. Rest easy Dash.

Photo by Josh Fishel (with my camera)

My dad in all his glory. I miss him every day
Photo by Peter Murray

Me, Michael "Kaves" McLeer, and Everlast, Brooklyn, NY 2017
Photo by Operator Emz (with my camera)

of hip-hop. I never felt that I was a descendent of those guys, though. First, I'm not technically Jewish. My dad was a non-practicing Jew, and my mom was a nonpracticing Catholic. I was baptized, for Christ's sake. I also came from a much more working-class inner-city upbringing. Me and those guys simply were not the same, and I doubt any of them would ever invite me over for a Passover dinner.

Elektra Records was located on the eighteenth floor of 75 Rockefeller Plaza, a swanky locale if there ever was one. My office was nondescript, but it looked like Gordon Gekko's compared to my hovel at Tommy Boy. I had a decent sized desk, two chairs, and a window that overlooked Fifty-First Street. Best of all, I had a real stereo. No more boom boxes for this kid.

I was ready to go to work. Day one at Elektra, I jumped into the middle of a bidding war trying to sign A Tribe Called Quest, who I had wanted to sign to Tommy Boy but was shot down by Tom Silverman's short pockets. Tribe was managed by my friend Chris Lighty and was being pursued by my other friend Sean "Captain Pissy" Carasov, who now worked as an A&R guy at Jive Records. Needless to say, after offering $300,000 plus, a huge amount of money for a rap group at the time, I eventually lost the band to Jive. Tribe gave up half their publishing in signing with Jive, though I understood why: Elektra had no track record in the rap game, and Jive did. I have to admit, losing Tribe still stings more than missing out on any other group in my entire career. They were, and still are, one of the best rap groups of all time. Since then, I have lost a plethora of bands—but this was the first time for me, and honestly, it felt like my heart was broken.

There were more hassles to come at Elektra. My friend Nelson George had a column in *Billboard* called "The Rhythm and Blues." At this point in his storied career, he was basically a music business gossip columnist. He ran a mention stating I had signed De La Soul and Queen Latifah and was off to new digs at Elektra and wished me success.

I was happy with the plug, but my happiness was short-lived.

Tom (along with Monica) took it upon themselves to demand a retraction from Nelson George and *Billboard*. It stated, "Dante Ross, while working on the De La Soul record, was not responsible for their signing to Tommy Boy Records. In fact, Monica Lynch and the Tommy Boy staff were responsible for signing and nurturing De La Soul." When I saw this, I was spooked but hoped no one would notice. It was true—De La had landed in my lap. I do, however, believe my appreciating them prior to their first single being released led Tommy Boy to hiring me at the label in the first place. While I did not technically sign them—something I've never claimed to have done—I worked very closely with the band and indeed did help nurture them creatively. To undervalue my working with the group was spiteful and a direct sabotage attempt.

I'm pretty sure Tom put Monica up to it. Regardless, the word was put out there. An Elektra publicist who shall remain nameless alerted several executives. One of those was my boss and friend Raoul Roach, who sat me down to discuss what was going on. He was obviously displeased, and I couldn't blame him. He also knew I didn't lie my way into the job. I reiterated exactly how it all went down—how Mo played me the demo, how I got the gig and went to work on the record, which was my first project for the label. Raoul, being a stand-up guy, told me he had my back and he proceeded to defend me to all who inquired, including their legendary A&R man/drunk genius of a prick, Howard Thompson, who was then the head of our department.

Howard called me into a meeting to discuss this. He told me my situation was problematic and he did not mince words. He told me that this could end up costing me my job. He intimated that he didn't like rap music and that if this was the way I operated, then maybe Elektra wasn't the right place for me. He also threw the Tribe debacle in my face and asked how I could lose a band to Jive Records. For once, I kept my trap shut. To his credit, Raoul Roach defended me, explaining to Howard what my connection was to the success of De La Soul, Queen Latifah, and the intricacies in losing Tribe.

I didn't lose my job, but Thompson made my first year at the gig a living hell whenever he could. He was an interesting character and he intrigued me. He was drunk or high half the time and hyper-opinionated, but also brilliant in his own snarky way. He once got mugged for his bicycle and showed up at work the following Monday with a black eye, telling people that that some kid who looked just like me mugged him. I sucked it up. I saw right through his elitist bullshit.

Thompson was a bigot, though he wouldn't consider himself one. (What bigot would?) He thought Black people, or I should say "hip-hoppers," were beneath him. He talked down to me all the time. He rode me hard. Down the line, I would eventually win his respect, but at the time, it was clear that Howard didn't respect what I was doing. He was even trying to discredit me among my coworkers. At one of my early A&R meetings I played the Brand Nubian song "All for One" before it was released. Thompson quipped, "Why is that kick drum so horribly loud? I don't understand."

"Because it's all about that 808 on the one," I said.

He smirked and said, "It sounds like rubbish."

"That's aight," I said. "I would be worried if you actually liked the song."

The peanut gallery snickered.

"Do explain, Dante," he said.

"It's like punk rock, Howard," I said. "Were your parents into the Sex Pistols?"

"Not particularly," he said.

"Neither were mine," I said. "If they were, punk rock would have never been cool."

He looked bewildered, and I added, "Rap is just Black punk rock, Howard."

The room laughed out loud, and Howard moved onto the next topic. The song, of course, would later be hailed as a classic.

Several years later, during an Elektra A&R summit week, a few of us were drinking at his house. Howard made a homophobic remark to me about a gay coworker, the brilliant Michael Alago, who was responsible for signing Metallica and who happened to be one of my closest friends at Elektra. Howard referred to him as "the little Puerto Rican Mary." I let it slide, which of course, gave him permission to keep it up. As he got drunker, he remarked about how much time I had spent with the wogs (a British racist term for Blacks) and how it really had rubbed off on me. I think he thought he was giving me a compliment. I let it slide. He was drunk, still I knew the score. He wasn't fooling me.

I watched Howard go through it at Elektra. He went from being the mean head honcho to being demoted and eventually shown the door. I can't say I felt particularly bad for the man, as he was a prick half of the time. But to be fair, Howard Thompson had amazing ears. He signed some of the best music of his day, and you can never take away the visionary aspects of his career. I mean, the man signed Bjork, amongst others. You could never take that away from him.

I felt his distaste for rap music may have had some form of racism or classism attached to it. Or maybe he just didn't like it. Or maybe he just didn't like me.

Who knows, and who gives a fuck?

In the end, I learned a valuable lesson from Howard. Well, not from Howard, but from Howard's downfall. It doesn't matter how talented you are—once the hits dry up and you lose touch with what the youth is listening to, it will only be a matter of time before you're handed your walking papers. Thank you, Howard, for letting me learn from your mistakes.

It's a lesson I'm still learning. Let's just hope I stay teachable.

The playing field at Elektra was filled with potholes, and they "weren't in my lawn." Raoul was busy fighting his own battles and my getting thrown under the bus by a publicist didn't help his cause. He was concerned for the both of us. I took a meeting with Russell at Def Jam, and he offered me a gig there for less money. Giant Records and that loveable nut job, Gary Harris (RIP), who was up for the Elektra gig before I was (though he missed two meetings with Krasnow), offered me a gig for equal money. I thought about it. My friend, Brian Koppelman, the whiz kid behind Tracy Chapman, who was unhappy at Elektra, walked me over to his dad's new label—SBK Records—and Brian and I were offered a label deal there that we almost took. I ended up staying at Elektra, mostly because I believed in Kras and wanted to make my mark there. Brian elected to eventually join his father.

De La Soul, and before them Sam Sever, had borrowed a few records, so I thought that maybe I should try making my own beats since I might get fired anyway. The record I had made with Uptown (CJ Moore did the programming on the record) called *Dope on Plastic*, had been well received, so I thought maybe producing could be a good side hustle for me. I had signed a female rapper named Shazzy and decided to produce her first record with two of my friends—a questionable decision. *Attitude: A Hip-Hop Rapsody* was convoluted from the start. The artist and I didn't get along while making it, and there was an obvious conflict of interest at play. I was the A&R man and had given myself a production gig. That wasn't kosher. Obviously, if the record had turned out to be a hit, it would have been moot point. But making the record got ugly.

I reached out to Krasnow for a sit down. Kras liked me. I asked him about the *Billboard* retraction. He gave two shits. He asked me about the Shazzy record, and I told him it was a horrible experience. He told me women artists could be particularly difficult and to get used to it, and to do myself a favor and try not to work with divas and kid acts because it would put me in an early grave. He also told me to put some numbers on the board and everything would go away. He hadn't given up on me despite the rumblings from down below, and for that, I was appreciative. I knew the clock was ticking. I have felt that clock ticking on some level for most of my career. It's just how the game goes.

A few months earlier, along with my two production partners, I had produced the B-side of 3rd Bass's single for *Product of the Environment* titled "3 Strikes 5,000." Red Alert started playing it on his show, and it was getting some heat. With my production partners, I had also done a D-Nice remix for *Crumbs on the Table*, which also got some play. All of a sudden, I was getting gigs as a producer/remixer.

I had linked up with Geeby Dajani and John Gamble, two of my boys from the Westbeth crew, the punk rock posse I ran with a few years earlier. They had converted the former punk rock rehearsal space where I engaged in drunken shenanigans with John Berry into a groovy if not cramped hip-hop production studio. In early 1990, we did a session with the newly signed Busta Rhymes and the Leaders of the New School, and all got very stoned. Busta blurted out mid blunt, "You cats are a bunch of Stimulated Dummies."

When Busta spit out that gem Geeby immediately asked if we could use that name. He laughed that infamous Busta laugh and said, "Use it? You are it!"

That evening, we officially became the Stimulated Dummies, a.k.a. SD50. (Our studio was #50). We also worked with my then-boo, Idalis, and her group, Seduction. We remixed their song "Heartbeat," which was a remake of Tanya Gardner's classic and something right up my alley. I have to say we killed the remix, and Fred Buggs started to play it daytime on KISS-FM, every time announcing it as a Dante Ross remix. That wasn't entirely accurate, because John Gamble and Geeby Dajani had helped a great deal on that mix. My preexisting A&R job at times negated my partners from getting their just due. As a result of these various remixes and productions, my name was buzzing outside the office, and I used this to my benefit at Elektra.

Geeby Dajani had been someone I looked up to since I was fifteen or so. He was charismatic and funny, but also one of the toughest kids I ever knew. I thought of him as an older, bigger, stronger, funnier version of me in a lot of ways. John Gamble was a studious, neurotic sort who was immensely talented—even if he didn't realize it. Me, I was just a schmuck with a lot of records, a new SL-1200 turntable, and some connections—more or less. I also understood the way the business actually functioned. We worked nights while another friend of ours from the punk rock days, Miles Kelly, worked days in the same studio.

We started innocently enough, just looping records and trying to mix and match loops together while we drank beers and got stoned. There was not a lot of science to it in the beginning. Gamble was the de facto engineer. Geeby and I were the diggers, so to speak. He showed me his rare finds and I shared mine in return. This meant Gamble would help hook shit up while we unearthed the loops. We eventually grew tired of this and started to program our own stuff while Gamble took to mixing. This was before automation would make its way into our set up and fifteen years before digital recording came into the mix.

The equipment we used was basic, maybe even below basic. We had an Akai S900 sampler, an MMT-8 Alesis sequencer, a basic Alesis drum machine with stock sounds, and a FZ-1 Casio sampler. The FZ-1 had more sampling time than the S900, which came in handy, and a great low-end filter for bass lines, which became a real sound during the boom bap era. We ran it all through an eight-track Soundcraft board, often going right to cassette and ¼" 2-track tape simultaneously. This was before DAT players became the norm. We also had a ½" 8-track tape machine that we would mix down to, at times often bouncing multiple samples to one track. We used the ½" 8-track tape machine sparingly being that the tape was expensive. We later started using an Atari computer and a sequencing program called Creator/ Notator, which Gamble excelled at. We also had an assortment of old, beat-up compressors, an Avalon mic pre that I bought, and several vintage microphones left from the boys' punk rock days in the band Frontline. I also had a shit ton of records, and Geeby had some real gems as well. Later on, we would upgrade our equipment to fit our needs and wants. It was a primitive setup but one I grew to love, its limitations often forcing us to become more creative.

All my nights hanging out at the LQ and Payday weren't for naught. By soaking in the sounds of the moment, I had a sense of what was funky and what was whack. Add that to the time spent in the trenches with Sam Sever, The 45 King, and Prince Paul, and I had picked up some tricks of the trade. I was skilled when it came to mutes and drops—a B-boy flavor my former punk partners were lacking. I also found out that I had good arranging skills and could run the board pretty well, doing manual punches on the fly. This is before any sort of automation came into the picture unless we were working in a real studio.

As much as I may have had excelled in certain areas, I cannot undervalue Geeby's or John's contributions. From the beginning, Geeby was our leader, and I learned a lot from him specifically what artists to look for when digging and how any part of a record no matter how unorthodox it may seem could work. He had an outside-the-box diggers mentality and would find some off-the-wall shit. He also knew classic soul as well as anyone I have ever known and had a great sense of pitch, something he passed on to me. Unfortunately, over time, Geeby proved to be the most preoccupied of us and not a good fit for the role of boss. He was a free spirit and enjoyed life and creating on his terms. Being responsible was not his strong suit. He was a groovy, happy-go-lucky stoner. As a result, I started to take the lead. I was the first to show up and the last to leave and the only one of us who had a full-time A&R gig. I was painfully focused—some would say obsessive and controlling—when it came to making beats and digging. I was fortunate because I could go on big record buying sprees and write it off for work. This was a huge advantage over my partners, who were struggling to pay the bills a lot of the time. I was also driven beyond control to make an impact, to sell a beat, to become a producer, and there was no way I was going to be denied. My ego had a lot to do with my want to succeed as a producer. It was also my worst enemy at times, especially when it came to working with my crew. I found it hard to play nice with others at times.

My record buying sprees had me digging everywhere from the Bay to LA, and especially New York. I eventually found my way to the revered record conventions at the Roosevelt Hotel, the Mark Ballroom, and the Fourteenth Street Armory. It was during these digging exertions that I connected with some of the greatest beat makers in the history of hip-hop and learned a great deal about finding breaks and gained an infinite amount of knowledge in regard to sample sources. I would dig side-by-side with characters like the Beat Miners (Black Moon and Smif-N-Wessun's producers), Buckwild, T-Ray, and Q-Tip. We would exchange "secret" info on breaks and beats we were looking for, complain about the high prices of records, and spend money trying to find that special ingredient we all wanted for the magic track we hoped to create. These exertions allowed me to become a prolific digger and provide a lot of sample material for our careers. I have to give Geeby a lot of credit in this area as well. Dude kept pace finding obscure and price-friendly gems on the regular. I still love digging for records—the rush I get when I discover an old-school record or break never gets old.

Sampling is the art of looking backward in order to go forward and create something new. This formula can be seen in graphic and fashion design. I believe the world woke up to the idea of recycling and innovating existing ideas and concepts, basically recontextualizing/remixing, due to this era of hip-hop. It's not an accident that my favorite hip-hop producers today are still sample- and break-beat heavy, like Kanye West. Too bad more record companies don't see the value in this. When sampling became too cost prohibitive, hip-hop lost some of its funk and soul.

In addition to my digging excursions, I was also hanging around guys who were producing records, and I was picking up production tips from the likes of The Beatnuts, Prince Paul, Pete Rock, and the legendary Paul C. This gave me an insider's knowledge that would prove to be invaluable. To be fair, my partners had day-jobs that didn't allow them the same opportunities. In fact, my job encouraged me to dig and to be in the studio, which turned out to be a blessing. But like many blessings, there came a curse. The process of producing hip-hop records during the boom bap era was fueling an unspoken internal resentment between my partners and me. I blame my arrogance for a lot of it.

John Gamble had very little interest in digging for beats. Having been a drummer, he was intuitive when it came to drum programing and seemed to be able to figure out anything technological, yet he was also a bit of a sad sack, prone to catering to his own pity party. He lacked the confidence that Geeby and I possessed. He was also one of the most talented cats I have ever worked with and was hands-down the most talented of us from a technical standpoint. To this day, I wonder if Gamble's talent and my drive created one pretty good two-headed producer, or if I pushed him so hard because he was so passive by nature and I was so competitive. I don't know if I will ever get to the bottom of that.

The three of us had a lot of fun, particularly early on. But as time progressed, we also fought like brothers. I have a terrible temper and Geeby's rivaled it. He was my mentor in the early days, but over time my commitment would alter that dynamic.

Being partners with anyone is hard—end of story. It's especially hard when some form of childhood pecking order is in the mix. I loved Geeby like a big brother, but I eventually came to a place where I didn't want to discuss and debate what loops or drums we were going to use. I believe he also no longer wanted to answer to my demands. I wanted to do what I wanted to do, as did he. We both wanted things to be on our terms, and in a working relationship that is often impossible no matter how close you are. Two alpha dogs usually don't mix, and I could see the writing on the wall.

WAKE UP

My first record for Elektra, Shazzy's *Attitude: A Hip-Hop Rapsody,* dropped on October 3, 1990, and died a quick death. I figured this would be the final word but then the unexpected happened: *The New York Times's* esteemed music critic Jon Pareles wrote a glowing review of the album in an article spotlighting female rappers. He also put *Attitude* on his "Best Albums of 1990" list. *Billboard* also put it on their best of list, as did Robert Christgau, the dean of all music critics, who included it in his annual "Pazz & Jop Top 50 List" for the *Village Voice.* I honestly thought the record was a total frisbee, but what did I know?

I have been blessed to work on some great records in my career and some of them have even gone down as classics. Shazzy's *Attitude: A Hip-Hop Rapsody* is not one of them. Nonetheless, it was an important record for my career in terms of being a learning experience. The review in *The New York Times* alone got Howard off my back and allowed me to get more funding down the road when I needed to support my artists internally.

I had been speaking to Grand Puba since I was at Tommy Boy, and true to his word he and his group, Brand Nubian, signed with Elektra. The first single "Feels So Good" was met with a decent reception, nothing more. I was a bit surprised. I thought these guys were going to make a bigger initial splash. We got stuck with a video for "Feels So Good" that was so whack the band and I refused to back it, which didn't win me any favors with the video department. If you can find it online, you will understand exactly why we refused to support it.

Brand Nubian were part of the Five-Percent Nation, a radical offshoot brand of Islam that incorporates street knowledge into the equation. The Five-Percent Nation as a religion prospered in prisons, particularly on the East Coast, and was created by a mysterious figure named Clarence 13X. The religion centers on the belief that the Black man is a God on Earth and that ten percent of the world has knowledge of this and tries to keep eighty-five percent of the world—the general population—in the dark and ignorant. The five percent (Gods) are the ones that see the true mathematics on Earth and are chosen to carry the message of Clarence 13X.

I thought then, and still think now, that despite its positives as a religion, it incorporates separatist ideologies that at times can be used to justify hatred and overtly sexist rhetoric. I am all for Black empowerment; I am not for separatism and sexism. That said, I have many close friends who call themselves Gods, and I respect every person's right to connect with their chosen faith. I have the utmost respect for the true word of Islam. I have seen Islam and the Five-Percent Nation of Gods and Earths guide many Black men to positive spiritual places, so I celebrate the many positives I have seen in the Five-Percent Nation's teachings. It is an interesting faith to say the least.

Whatever brings us to recognize something bigger than ourselves, for me, is a positive. As a kid going to high school in Brooklyn, I saw the rise of the Five-Percent Nation of Gods and Earths. Several people I knew had become Five-Percenters, so working with the Brand Nubian seemed par for the course. The Gods were a strong part of the early so-called golden age of hip-hop. I had years prior developed a friendship with Rakim Allah a.k.a. The God MC. He and a plethora of other artists I considered friends were Five-Percenters. I believe the influence of the Five-Percent faith helped elevate hip-hop in countless ways.

Still, it bothered me early on that Brand Nubian would direct their rhetoric toward me when I was trying my best to get them off the ground. DJ Alamo was the worst. He seemed to really enjoy busting my balls. To be honest, it was occasionally intimidating. In retrospect, I like to think he was testing me to see what I was made off. I eventually won him and the band over through my unyielding dedication to the band's music and messaging—one of my true duties as an A&R person. They eventually saw that I sincerely would fight for their voices to be heard. Alamo and I would later became close friends. To this day, I love the guy like a brother. The early days, though, were rough. Respect is often earned and seldom given. This was one of those times.

It would be an understatement to say Brand Nubian's first album was not easy for me to make. I was unproven to the band, and on the run at work. Brand Nubian were young, angry Black men challenging the establishment, a.k.a. the label—me included. One incident that sticks out is when Lord Jamar, the group's most militant member, swiped a booklet of car vouchers off of somebody's desk. Unbeknownst to me at the time, he and his crew rang up sixteen thousand dollars in car service bills at the label's expense before getting caught. In retrospect, it's kind of funny, but at the time I found it disrespectful. I'm not sure if stealing from your record label was a revolutionary action, particularly when it made my gig harder.

We hunkered down mostly at Calliope, the studio where I had worked with De La and Shazzy. Almost immediately, Puba started pushing the boundaries of irresponsibility. He figured out how to finesse the petty cash from the studio manager and pocket it, which would end up on the studio bill. He didn't show up half the time, and when he did, he was usually a good three hours late. It was becoming a headache.

Much like myself, Puba was also an egomaniac with low self-esteem. He felt he was too good for the band he had created, while the third member, a wide-eyed quiet young man named Derrick Murphy (a.k.a. Sadat X), was a huge talent in my eyes. He had a completely unorthodox style of rhyming, one that Puba readily incorporated into his own rapping dialect. Simply put, Puba didn't sound like the Puba you are familiar with until he linked with Sadat X. That's the God's honest, no pun intended. If you don't believe me, go back and listen to the Masters of Ceremony album.

In spite of all this craziness, the Brand Nubian record was off to a good start creatively; Puba and the cats had come up with some great tunes. One in particular, which was helmed by Geeby, was called "Step to the Rear."

It was definitely one of the best records the Stimulated Dummies have ever made. How this record came to be is an attribute to being adaptable while in the studio.

Puba had picked a beat I slid to him based on a loop from a song called "Corey Died on the Battlefield" by the New Orleans funk band The Wild Magnolias. We went to Calliope and tracked out the beat. Puba showed up three hours late as per usual. When he got there, he sat around for a few before declaring that he couldn't fuck with the beat. This has happened to every producer before. We were stuck for a few, so we started playing him samples, not wanting to lose the opportunity to make a song for him. I was ready to throw in the towel when Geeby pulled out a S-900 disc and played him the loop and Puba started vibing. We then added a kick and a snare under the soul loop. I found a piano hit from an old soul record, and we added that on top of the loop. Puba proceeded to write, then lay down, his rhymes. Afterward, Puba, Geeby, and I found a bunch of records to scratch in the chorus, including a wild vocal sample Geeby found that made the chorus really work. Puba laid the scratches, and the record was more or less done. The whole thing took all of eight hours to make and this was the basis for the best pure hip-hop song my partners and I have ever been credited with. I give major props to Geeby for this song, he was the main force behind it. It's a testament to his brilliance and adaptability.

During the making of the record, I did also see the genius of Grand Puba several times. Watching him assemble *One for All* was one of these times. The fact that he found the loop for "All for One" on the slept-on James Brown tune "Can Mind" and was smart enough to only take one side of the stereo recording is an example in ingenuity. He also taught me more is less countless times. "All for One" is a classic example of this. There are no drums in it, just an 808 kick and a drum fill. His ability to incorporate Jamaican influences over a James Brown loop on "Who Can Get Busy Like This Man…" was fantastic, and I still think it's one of the best cross pollinations of rap and reggae ever. His voice and his ability to simply entertain were uncanny.

As I plugged away on the Nubian record, Howard Thompson was lining me up to get my head chopped off. I was going over budget due to

Puba's constant no-shows. I had $65,000 in the budget, and I needed $15,000 to finish the record. The label also added the $16,000 car voucher debacle to the bottom line, pushing me over the top. I had to reforecast my budget, not realizing at the time that every A&R person does this. They ended up giving it to me. Puba started to jump on tracks solo ("Step to the Rear" and "Who Can Get Busy Like This Man...") and he started doing songs with Positive K, whom he probably should have been in a group with in the first place.

To add insult to injury, Puba started telling me and everyone else that Jamar wasn't up to snuff and that he wanted to go solo, or "to the head," as he called it. I personally liked Jamar's contributions to the record. I could see bad shit up ahead, but for the time being I just wanted to get this record to the finish line. I knew I was going to die trying, at the very least. That, or Puba was going to kill me by stressing me to death with the constant disappearing acts.

That's not to say it wasn't fun sometimes. While we were rerecording the vocals to "Who Can Get Busy Like This Man...," Melle Mel, the great old school rapper, inadvertently came into the session and saw Puba in the vocal booth. They knew each other and exchanged pleasantries. As Melle Mel left the studio, Puba did his first verse in a classic Melle Mel flow, complete with an old-school deep voice, ad-libs and all. It was hilarious and the rest of the night Max kept doing Melle Mel's trademark "rahhh," which made me laugh my ass off. Puba could be a lot of fun when he showed up. His sense of humor was totally off the wall, and he brought that humor to his records—something that's really missing in rap music these days.

I made a demo tape of the rough mixes from the album and they leaked to the streets. This, in turn, had people interested in the record just based on word of mouth. This was the internet before the internet. Somehow, if you were in the know, you ended up with every group's album months before it came out. This was how it was if you were a rap fanatic back then. The kids at the *Source*, which at the time was the rap magazine of merit, called me up saying they had the demo and wanted to review it. I begged them off and asked them not to review it until I had a firm release date. How they got it I have no idea. They agreed to hold off as long as I gave them a proper album copy first. The project leaking early may have hurt a bit sales-wise, but it helped Brand Nubian create an organic and loyal fan base.

There is a song on the demo called "Where is Puba?" that is unreal. (There is a version online that incorporates the Meters Hand Clapping song, but it's not the version from the first demo.) I have no idea why it didn't make the final cut. The song featured an R&B singer named Jetta and sampled Lafayette Afro Rock's "Hihache" years before Mary J. Blige and Puffy used it in a similar fashion. Back then, Puff (before he was Diddy) and Puba were friends. Puff and Andre Harrell managed Brand Nubian for a brief spell, and there's no doubt he was influenced by Puba's work.

The tape had been heard as far away as California, Virginia Beach, and somehow London. I had people coming up to me telling me what songs they liked, and I still didn't even have a release date. I did, however, have a mastering appointment with Herb Powers, then the don of Black music mastering and a total gentleman. I explained to the company at our A&R retreat that we really had one here, and if we could figure out an innovative marketing plan, we could break this band. They nodded their heads and laughed at me behind closed doors. After all, we only sold 20,000 copies of the single "Feels So Good," and even that may be stretching it. We had no retail history, the band scared white people and the bougie Blacks who worked at the label as well, but fuck it, I knew I had one and I stood by it.

Thank God Krasnow had my back. He was, after all, from the mean streets of Cleveland and had logged a lot of years in the trenches as James Brown's road manager. He supposedly once body-slammed the Godfather of Soul, and if you met Kras, you wouldn't find this hard to believe. He was one of the architects of Warner Brothers Records, and the rumor was that they gave Elektra to Kras so he could bury himself. Instead, he was wildly successful for a number of years. He was a tough motherfucker, with hands like baseball mitts and an appetite for destruction. He was a colorful cat who had a lot of flavor, and like most flavorful gents, he recognized taste and style in others. I like to think I was one of them.

Even with Kras on my side, Elektra was still treacherous waters for me. It seemed like I had a new promotion boss in Black music every month.

Most of them didn't like me off the jump. They didn't want to know about a goofy, rap-loving white kid who wore baggy jeans and carried around a skateboard. I was everything they detested.

The first cornball to go was Primus Robinson. He hated me from the get, seeing me as the changing of the guard. He was correct. Robinson was toast somewhere around Shazzy's first pringle. (Geeby use to refer to singles that flopped as pringles.) Next up was a stiff named Joe Morrow, a nice enough guy, but ancient. He bit the dust early on, then we got a real winner, Doug Daniels. This guy was a trip. Rumor was that Doug had a serious cocaine problem, as did half the staff at Elektra and I suspect the music industry in general in the early nineties. I heard tale of him in his office blowing lines with artists several times. The guy also had a gang of side hustles. He was a crafty dude and a worthy adversary.

We had lunch one afternoon early on in our coworking days. He broke it down to me.

"Dante, I hear you're not connected to the streets," he said. "You're not in the mix."

I was stunned. If nothing else, I was in the mix. Maybe too much in fact. "Where did you hear this?"

"Shazzy's manager," he replied.

I laughed. I swear, I saw him hiding the blow when I was summoned to his office one morning when he was hanging with Shazzy's clueless manager.

"Why not ask Red Alert or Russell Simmons instead?" I said.

I figured they would both vouch for me. Red had love for me, so did Uncle Rush.

"I'm gonna do that," Daniels said.

Later on, Russell told me he set him straight and then some when he called to check my resume. He was toast before the Brand Nubian album hit the streets.

One for All was a slow burner released on December 4, 1990. The record bubbled for a few months and really hit its stride in late February on the strength of Red Alert and his mix show. This was when mix shows actually broke records, much like Soundcloud does today. The first single,

"Wake Up," was a politically charged banger with a beautiful Roy Ayers sample (later co-opted by Puffy for Mary J. Blige's "My Life").

A few years later, Puffy would also use a significant portion of Puba's mojo in creating Mary J. Blige's epic first record *What's The 411?* Puba cowrote the title cut and rapped on it as well. I don't believe Puba saw any publishing, just a quick ten grand advance brown paper bag style, possibly the biggest blunder of his whole career. The publishing check on that song would have been major, but Puba was always a short money guy. He never saw the big picture, and he got swindled on that one. I'm sure he didn't run this by his then manager, Lyor Cohen.

The Stimulated Dummies and I did the original version of "Wake up," which was also on the album. I actually walked in when the new version was being created. I was furious and had serious words with Lord Jamar over it. We almost came to blows, though in all honesty, I think I might have caught a beating. I couldn't believe that they weren't going to use my version. The irony is the version they were working on that day, which combined Ray, Goodman & Brown's "New Day" sample with the Roy Ayers sample is now considered a classic. My ego had almost gotten in the way of a great record.

I wonder if Jamar even remembers this.

Fab 5 Freddy directed the video for "Wake Up," which was initially banned from MTV due to the devil character in it. The video had to be reedited several times and saw limited play. Despite the video hassles, the record still got played on New York mix show radio.

By early 1991, the LP had started selling. It had five consecutive weeks where the retail went up. We started pushing a steady 5,000 to 10,000 records a week for several consecutive months. By April, we had a minor league hit on our hands. Rush Productions ended up managing Brand Nubian. At this point, Chris Lighty was very involved with Rush, which bode well for me. We worked well together, and he is to this day my favorite manager I have ever worked with.

My reigns at the office had loosened up a bit. I was let into the executive circle. I bonded with another OG A&R man, Peter Lublin, a crotchety genius with a great ear who signed the Pixies, one of my favorite alternative bands at the time. Rock music was in a slump pre grunge, and only a handful of alt groups were of any merit to me. The Pixies, along with Dinosaur JR, Jane's Addiction, Sonic Youth, Fugazi, and a handful of other bands, were some of the only games in town in the face of hair metal. I believe this had a lot to do with young white kids identifying with rap music so deeply. Peter somehow understood this, hence our friendship. In the business, we often talk of "record men," the highest compliment you can give an A&R person or anyone in the music biz more or less. The A&R staff at Elektra had several real record men. Amongst them were Sue Drew (record woman), Raoul Roach, Bob Krasnow, and of course, my friend-emy, Howard Thompson. This team of A&R people are to this day the most well-rounded group of record men and women I have ever worked with.

While I was knee-deep in the world of the Gods, my relationship with 3rd Bass came deeper into play as I signed KMD, who were managed and signed through Serch and Pete's R.I.F. Production Company. I forget who actually brought them to me, but I'm pretty sure it was Serch. They were buzzing after Doom had a stellar verse on 3rd Bass's "Gas Face."

KMD was, at its center, the Dumile brothers: Daniel (Zev Love X a.k.a. MF Doom) and Dingilizwe (DJ Subroc). Doom was born in the UK, but his family moved to New York before Subroc was born. The brothers went to elementary school in Manhattan before the family moved to Long Island. Even though Doom was two years older, they seemed more like twins. Their childhood friend Alonzo Hodge (Onyx) completed the group, rapping on several songs.

Doom and Sub were both amazingly talented in everything from art to music to social observation. The group itself was pretty self-contained and had a concrete vision. They did most of their demos with John Gamble in my studio, and I heard them every step of the way. I thought they were brilliant. One of the craziest things about doing all that preproduction back then is you would have to virtually recreate a lot of it when you went to a bigger studio. In fact, the album was more or less tracked twice, once to an

1" 8-track tape machine we had in our studio and again at Chung King on a 2" 24-track Studer tape machine. This was often the creative process back then. It's hard to believe in today's Pro Tools home studio-friendly world, but in 1990, this was how we did things.

The snap sessions we had in my basement studio were hilarious. Listening to Doom and Sub's sarcastic bickering was hilarious. Doom was a great artist, and his nonstop drawings of Subroc and his various nicknames associated with the drawings were ridiculous. He christened him Sub Roach in one of them, drawing Sub as a cockroach that was being stepped on by a big foot that was titled Doom. Another had him as bread roll about to be eaten and was titled Sub Roll. Doom and Geeby also collaborated on a few X-rated drawings on my record sleeves. Imagine pulling out a break beat record mid-session and the sleeve has a cartoon of a giant penis with your name on it. Whenever I think of making *Mr. Hood*, I end up chuckling to myself.

Mr. Hood, for all of its laborious twist and turns, is genius. It's filled with crazy vocal snippets that narrate the entire record, telling a story of a misguided youth in a material and spiritually lacking society, all with a firm tongue-in-cheek vibe, as only they could do. The band also created all the artwork for the project, which I thought was brilliant. Being around Sub and Doom was special. They had an almost ESP-like quality to their working relationship. Sub, in fact, did a lot of the production, which is lost on some people. Doom would often start ideas and Sub would finish them. He was the more technical of the brothers, and don't forget that he was only sixteen years old when we started recording the first record. They were honestly some of the smartest young men I have ever had the pleasure of working with. Ironically, a lot of MF Doom fans are not even aware of Subroc or KMD.

While Doom and Sub were working on the *Mr. Hood* demos in my studio, KMD had free reign on my record collection, which was stored in the studio for the most part. What they did with the few records they borrowed from me was so outside of my way of thinking, it was mind-boggling. I was inspired by their abstract way of looking at samples. Specifically, I loved the way they used "Me and Mrs. Jones," the Billy Paul classic, on "Figure of

Speech," a predecessor to Kanye's chipmunk soul vibe. I rarely cared that they used my records, except for what transpired on "Humrush."

I showed up at Chung King to check in on a KMD session, see how the fellas were doing. When I walked in, I heard "Humrush" and was like, "Hold up, those are the drums I have in a beat I just made, slowed down in the same exact way." I asked Doom how he came up on them and why he slowed them way down like that. Doom turned to me and said, "I don't know, ask Gamble, he gave 'em to me."

I got kind of pissed, I can't lie. I wondered why Gamble, who could call me to ask me my Chinese food order or what pair of kicks I was wearing that day, neglected to ask me if it was cool to give my drums to Doom. I was kind of tight and suggested we go take a walk and get a sandwich at the Italian food center on Mulberry Street, our favorite deli.

Doom being the wiseass that he was, in an effort to defuse the situation, offered to buy me lunch—a first in my A&R career. This is a rare thing for a rapper to do. In fact, it's never happened again since. As he paid for our sandwiches, he explained to me that my producer "advance" was the lunch he just bought me. I started cracking up, but not before I demanded a Manhattan Special soda as additional payment. To his credit, he later gave me coproduction on the song, which I didn't really deserve. Every time I think about *Mr. Hood*, the goofy grin he had on his face when he bought me lunch pops in my head. It's just an example of how irreverent Doom was.

I loved the record, and in a case of history rewriting itself, it is now hailed as a wonderful piece of art. The reviews when it came out in 1991, though mostly favorable, didn't attach the value to the record it has since gathered. As much as I loved the record, it wasn't an overwhelming success commercially. It only sold around 170,000 copies, enough to warrant a follow-up record. If I have any regrets in signing them, it's that it would have been much easier business-wise if I had signed them sans 3rd Bass, who in all fairness had been taught the lay of the land by Lyor Cohen and Russell.

Lyor and Russell got half of 3rd Bass's publishing as part of their record deal more or less for free. This was the way they learned the business and they exercised these life/business lessons upon KMD. I don't believe they were being malicious; they just didn't know any better. In particular, Serch could be a huge pain in the ass to deal with. He has apologized to me about his behavior then—still, he stepped over the line of friendship way too many times for my liking. The guy was just extra.

Business being business, 3rd Bass had KMD signed to a production deal, reaping a generous share of the advance as most production deals tend to. When it came to business matters, things occasionally got uncomfortable when I was dealing with Serch and Pete. I am sure I didn't make matters any easier. Serch in particular tended to live over his means—I mean, he is a rapper, right?—which led to some arguments that I believe were financially driven. The guy would harass me to get the label to release cash to the production company throughout the entire making of *Mr. Hood*, something I was unable to do. It could have cost me my job.

At times, we mixed up our various business dealings. I remember one particularly harsh argument during the final mixing stages of *Mr. Hood* when Serch, with Pete Nice on the phone, was looking for the backend payout. Serch was particularly abusive this day. When I told him he would have to wait a few more weeks, until the record was mastered, to receive his back end, he berated me, telling me he had "made more moves in a year than I had made in my entire life" and that "he made me" before adding, "You're a joke." It was insulting, especially considering our relationship. Add to the fact that my partners and I had been in the studio with him and Pete only a few weeks before, working on his sophomore album, and had delivered what would eventually become the bands biggest hit, "Pop Goes the Weasel." The sting of his words that day still bother me. As my career progressed, my relationship with Serch disintegrated. I may have missed out on a chance to sign Nas because we just could not get along. I believe he changed dramatically once he became successful. Our relationship certainly did.

Eventually KMD's debut record came out, and it was followed less than a month later by 3rd Bass's sophomore record *Derelicts of Dialect*, which went gold within three months. The Dummies and I had several songs on it, including the previously mentioned platinum-charting "Pop Goes the Weasel," the Vanilla Ice diss song that would end up being 3rd Bass's biggest hit. The album got a lot of good ink; many of the reviews compared it to De La Soul's *3 Feet High and Rising*. I could see the connection. They were both smart, inventive, and creative records. Prince Paul worked on both of them and I am grateful to have been a small part. Funny thing is, Pete Nice got the idea for "Pop Goes the Weasel" when he saw EPMD open their set with "Sledge Hammer." Pete suggested I hook it up, so the SD50s and I did. The rest, as they say, is history.

As much as I liked having a hit song, I winced whenever I heard "Pop Goes the Weasel." I hate the way the drums sound on that record. A lot of that was my doing. I'm honestly not sure why we used those drums, but I know I provided the drum loop for it. The sounds just are off; the snares sound like bongos to me. There's just too much going on, in my opinion. Still, despite my sonic misgivings, it was a massive hit.

The other reason I cringe to this day—for that song and the others we did for 3rd Bass—is that I have never seen a royalty. While I don't blame 3rd Bass, I do blame Def Jam's funny-style bookkeeping. Not getting paid for work you do can really take the enjoyment out of hearing a hit song you helped make. Most producers I know can identify.

For what it's worth, hanging with 3rd Bass could also be a lot of fun. We were wild kids out for a good time. Before money or success entered the picture, we were tight. My bond with Pete Nice remains to this day.

One of those misguided adventures almost cut my career in the music business short, however. We were all at the Gavin Convention in San Francisco, an annual industry event put on by the now defunct *Gavin Report*. We'd been invited to a St. Ides Malt Liquor-sponsored party in the St. Francis Hotel, where we were all staying. We got bombed after guzzling a few 40s each. We drank enough of that garbage to make the beer muscles really start to act up. They didn't call it liquid dust for nothing. Some college skater dorks who were with a band called Alice Donut started trying to clown us. It was me, DJ Richie Rich, my former neighbor Sam Sever, Bosco Money from Downtown Science, Pete Nice, and Serch.

One of the skater dorks started to ask Pete Nice what was up with his cane and if he could see it. He was out of line, and we checked him. He and his crew might have been as wasted as us. I vaguely remember Pete Nice telling the dork, "Step off, Alice Donut, you don't want this." Pete wasn't a tough guy, but he wasn't a punk either. None of us were. Being the resident knucklehead, I stepped to the dude and he backed up. We had the numbers and he didn't want to get a beating, so he bounced and headed to the lobby with no worries.

We were milling about, drunk and talking to Russell and a few other industry folks. At this point, I had mended fences with Russell and Lyor. Shit, I had delivered them a hit song. The day before Russell and Lyor had taken me to dinner in Chinatown. They proceeded to offer me a gig at Def Jam—and it wasn't as a messenger boy again. I politely declined, but I really felt like I was the real deal after that dinner.

The lobby was crammed with a who's who of the music industry circa '91. Out of nowhere, the skater dork and his crew of clowns rolled into the lobby. Apparently, the kid we had punked had rounded up his posse. They surrounded Pete Nice and started harassing him. I was playing the back, and dude saw me. The biggest dork, who wasn't even that big, tried to shove me. I grabbed Pete's cane and proceeded to bonk the kid over his head with it, much to his and half the lobby's dismay.

The next few seconds were a blur. I know he put his head down and charged at me before I unloaded a shot to the side of his jaw. I dropped him, but also put myself off balance. I was swarmed by a couple of dudes, but they hit like girls, and no damage was done. Out of nowhere, a friend/ A&R guy named Jeff Sledge who was built like a fire hydrant appeared and clobbered, and I do mean clobbered, one of the dorks who was on top of me. He hit the kid with a haymaker and a half.

I spun, and the other kid who was trying to hit me looked freaked. I two-pieced him, which dropped him quickly, and then I kicked him upside the head for GP. He was lying under a free-standing restaurant sign, which I proceeded to slam onto his head, which split him wide open and made the entire lobby gush. Yep, it was a cheap shot, but I never did fight fair.

Next thing I knew, hotel security was everywhere, and they hemmed me up as the cops were soon on the set. An ambulance was called, and I was put in handcuffs in front of half the music industry. I was standing there cuffed when Elektra's VP of rock promotions, Ray Geminor, a legendary record business weasel, approached the cops and asked what was going on.

The cop said, "This kid busted the other guy's head open. He's going to jail."

I was shitting bricks but not about going to jail. I did central booking in New York a few times, and it sucked, yeah, but it wasn't scary. Being blackballed was a much scarier prospect.

"Well, I work with this young gentleman. I'm sure it's just a misunderstanding. Is there anything I can do to make this go away?" Ray had subtley tried to bribe the cop.

Nice try, Ray.

"There isn't shit you can do here," the cop said.

Ray stepped aside and slid his card in my back pocket and told me to get in touch and that he would bail me out. Wherever you are, Ray, I love you for that move.

I looked for a way out. I tried to talk to the cop, a young Black man who wasn't being a total dick like the others. I think he figured it's a college kids' brawl and those kids lost. Back in those days, you usually didn't get locked up for fighting. Nonetheless, I had fucked that kid up pretty bad. And San Francisco wasn't New York.

I looked for a life preserver, and I saw one in the form of Uncle Rush. He approached the cop, who obviously knew who he was. "What's going on here?" Russell asked.

The cop explained. Russell nodded his head. He knew what had gone down—he had seen the whole thing. "Officer, this is my artist, Dante Ross—he's a very talented young man," Russell said. "I'm sure this is a big misunderstanding, just some kids having a little fun that went too far. You're not going to arrest him, are you?"

The cop stammered. Obviously, he was impressed with Russell. "We may be able to let him go," he said. "It's up to the victim." He then turned to me and asked, "You staying in this hotel?"

I nodded yes. Russell jumped right in. "He has an important show this evening. He's here all the way from New York," Russell said. "He had a little too much to drink, but he's a good kid. What do you think, officer?"

Russell then handed the cop his card and smiled. The cop looked down at the card like it was glowing or some shit. Russell then took the officer to the side and had a one-on-one with him. What Russell said to the cop is a mystery to this day. Whatever it was, it worked like pixie dust. The cop then returned and took the cuffs off and told me to go directly to my room and stay there until I heard from hotel management.

I nodded again. Russell and the cop walked me to the elevator, and then Russell took me to my room. He wasn't mad. In fact, he thought the shit was funny and gave me props for not getting a black eye for once. He told me to keep it chill the rest of the night—which of course didn't happen. I ended up going out, getting more wasted, and went home with one of the shortest women I ever finessed in my life. The 3rd Bass guys ended up calling my room repeatedly asking if there were any munchkins that needed to be returned to Oz.

Those fucking guys.

Despite everything, I love the adventures we had together, particularly in the early days. It's sad to see them go at each other publicly over the last few years, but I get it. As we get older and we lose more and more friends, I tend to just want to let things go and remember the good times. With 3rd Bass, the good outweighs the bad immeasurably. Tomorrow's never promised, and with the passing of my two production partners and both Doom and Subroc, this is even more clear. I hope one day Pete and Serch can hug it out. They made too much great music together not to. As for me and Serch, I choose to love my brother from a long distance.

While I was in the midst of finishing up the Brand Nubian record, I had stumbled across a trio of rappers from Uniondale, Long Island, named, oddly enough, Leaders of the New School. I had heard of the band because they had a vague Bomb Squad affiliation. More importantly, I had seen them live at the Ukrainian Hall on Second Avenue.

The Ukrainian Hall has some history for me. It was a place where I saw both Johnny Thunders and Misfits play. It was also the spot where Tommy

Boy celebrated De La Soul's *3 Feet High and Rising* going platinum. The night of the De La event, I wore a fresh three-piece Brooks Brothers suit only to be upstaged by Big Daddy Kane, who rocked his purple pimp suit. Sometimes you can't win for losing. The event felt like a personal coming out party of sorts. I felt like I had finally made it. I will never forget Keith Haring being there and giving me a hug, congratulating me that night. Keith was an early De La Soul fan and a great person. I had sent him the De La singles that preceded the album as he had gifted me a bunch of cool stuff over the years. It's pretty obvious the album's cover artwork was on some level inspired by his work. Him being there and being a fan made me realize De La had hit a significant cultural tipping point.

The night I caught the Leaders, I walked in just as they were about to start their set. The three kids on stage—Charlie Brown, Dinco D, and Busta Rhymes—were just that: kids. They had one microphone that they shared, but they still managed to keep their routines and vocal trade-offs over the classic drum break from "Impeach the President." The tallest of the three was a monster of a MC, controlling the tempo and flow as well as the microphone. One mic or not, they straight up murdered it. It was one of the greatest performances I have ever witnessed by an unknown rap band. That was the one and only time I have ever wanted to sign a rap group solely based on their live show.

After the performance, I approached the crew and asked them where they were from and what their deal was. Charlie Brown, who seemed to be the self-appointed leader of the Leaders, knew exactly who I was. I was wondering why he was doing all the talking. The tallest kid was the one who had the most charisma, yet he remained silent for the most part. I gave Charlie a business card and expected him to hit me right away because he seemed pretty eager. A week went by, though, and I hadn't heard from these dudes.

In the interim, I did a background check on the band, and I would come to learn they weren't only affiliated with but were actually conceived by the Bomb Squad. Hank Shocklee and Chuck D. had put the group together in a hood version of an *American Idol* casting call of sorts. In fact, Chuck gave Busta and Charlie their stage names. Unbeknownst to me at the time, they had an expiring production deal with the Bomb Squad, which Brown told me about a few weeks later.

When Brown finally came to see me, I wondered why he had taken his time. I would find out later the group had in fact "broken up" in the time between my seeing them live and our meeting. Apparently, they had patched things up. I believe that Brown had used my interest in them as a reason to try to work out their differences.

When we met at my office, he pulled a book report folder from his backpack. In it was the blueprint for Leaders of the New School's entire record, complete with all the members' names, their descriptions, various video ideas, and very rudimentary storyboards. The layout was crude and loaded with misspellings, and the drawings were raw to say the last, but the concepts and presentation were nothing short of brilliant. I wish I had saved that thing. It was truly priceless. I asked about the tall kid. Brown told me he was Busta Rhymes. Other than that, Brown was a bit evasive about him.

Things were already starting to get complicated. Charlie Brown was a masterful hustler. He was a great rapper. Keep it a buck, he was also a complete pain in the ass. Brown was competitive with everyone under the sun. Most of all, he was a hater of the highest order. Brown was also brilliant in his own way. I developed a serious love/hate relationship with him.

I asked Brown to assemble his copilots and have them come to my office for a meeting. I wanted to sign them, but they didn't even have much of a demo. I met them and was immediately taken by Trevor George Smith Jr. a.k.a. Taheim a.k.a Busta Rhymes. When I had seen the group perform, Busta seemed like the ringleader of sorts, though Brown firmly took the reins when it came to politicking with me.

I was surprised by how at odds these two were, even that first day in my office. They got into an argument—over what, I didn't know. I could see there was tension in the ranks with the Leaders, but in all honesty in music, a little tension can make the music more exciting, as fucked up as it sounds. At times, dysfunction motivates amazing art—it had with my own production crew—and I was crossing my fingers that this was going to be one of those times.

The group was rounded out by Dinco D (James Jackson) and Cut Monitor Milo (Sheldon Scott). Dinco was the nicest kid of the bunch, totally stoned most of the time but always pleasant with a sweet demeanor. Busta could be a handful, but around the fourth member of the group, Cut Monitor Milo, he always fell back. Milo was his older cousin, a bit rougher and older than the rest of the crew, and basically checked them behind the scenes, as I would come to find out later.

Down the road, due to his insistence on rapping on the second LONS record, Milo altered some of the group's chemistry. It never made any sense to me. I didn't think he was a great MC by any means, and him being on the mic just made the group's whole approach more confusing to me. Why nobody shut him down, I have no idea. I still don't get it. I will never know if he sincerely wanted to be an MC, if he was just flexing his ego, or if he was just trying to get over.

The "get over" mentality was, and is, rampant in the rap game. I have seen hundreds of careers shot down by what I jokingly refer to as the "homeboy management/producer network." I have seen cats who have no business being rappers decide they were now MCs because of their proximity to real MCs. I have heard artists tell me, "My boy's my new manager," and, "My man's producing my new shit," only to watch it all go down the drain. Rappers seem susceptible to hangers-on in a way that does not exist in other genres of music. Maybe it's the perception that rapping is easy, or the fact that cats feel the need to bring their entire clique into their business world for comfortability factors. I've seen it happen to many great artists. To this day, there is no shortage of "weed carriers" in the rap game. That said, I have also seen a few street guys turn into great managers.

The rap business was mostly lawless at this time. We made it up as we went along. There were no established protocols, and it's hard to believe it has become such a huge business today. More often than not, executives and artists alike were just a stone's throw from the streets and had no real grasp on business other than selling drugs, the business rappers often site as their life/business experience. Shit, I wasn't any better. I was making it up on the fly, too. Without guidance from good mentors, how can you figure out right from wrong? It's a constantly shifting playing field with rappers, managers, and, at times, executives changing the rules as they see fit. It can be an ugly scene, and attempting to negotiate with a thugged-out rapper or manager can be pretty difficult, and potentially dangerous. The only thing worse is dealing with a rapper's yes-man.

I was only twenty-four-years old when I was figuring this shit out with the Leaders, and they were much younger. Charlie Brown was nineteen, and Busta wasn't even legal yet. In fact, he had to bring his mother when he signed his contract. Collectively, they could be extremely difficult. They were also capable of making incredible music at times.

They had a chemistry that was missing in rap music at the time and were one of the first groups to look to Cold Crush for inspiration. Live, they were one of the best groups in their day. Still, the tension was always palatable and capable of derailing the LONS train. I literally saw Brown and Busta have a fistfight at Chung King Studios in the middle of recording "Transformers," early in their career. My partner, Geeby, had to get in the middle of it and literally drag Busta away from beating up Brown. This would foreshadow a lot of the groups inner turmoil that was yet to unfold.

Recording the first record was intense. They each had several solo songs on it—a sign of things to come, I suppose. One of those was "Feminine Fatt," a showcase for Busta Rhymes. It became a fan favorite and a highlight of the early shows. Brown's solo song, "Show Me a Hero," did not receive the same response.

Watching them do vocals was a trip. Young Busta had yet to fully master his delivery, and initially it was hard to record him. I would end up having to compress his vocals a bunch as well as stress him to pronounce his words. He figured it out pretty quickly. Brown, on the other hand, had his mic technique figured out early on. He was a very good MC who reminded me of a baby Chuck D. at times. Unfortunately, he started to rely on his high-pitched ad-lib squawk a little too much, which grated on me and the listening public a bit, too, I think. Dinco was always somewhat overshadowed by his bandmates, and while a competent MC, he lacked the charisma on the mic the other two possessed.

I had high hopes for the Leaders' debut. They had a nice buzz going as they worked toward finishing and releasing it. There were a lot of cooks in the kitchen, as well as a lot of samples flying in and out. The music reflected the studio atmosphere a bit. It all felt somewhat chaotic. As we started rapping it up, I felt the record was very good but not great. It was one or two fantastic songs short of being a grand slam and paled in comparison to their live show. Still, I was proud of the record and the band. I knew that if they didn't self-destruct, they would eventually find that illusive hit song. I also knew their self-destructing was a real possibility.

Charlie was always at the center of those concerns. He was an ace manipulator and would inspire the band to stage mini revolts at times usually directed at the label but on occasion directed toward Busta. One of the worst was the "International Zone Coaster" remix debacle. This incident eventually made me change my home phone number after fifty-plus late-night calls from various members of the band.

The Leaders agreed to hire the SD50s to do a remix for them and then proceeded to torture me over it. I turned in two mixes to appease them. I thought I was done, but then they all decided—rightfully so—that they were producers, each submitting versions of their own. I basically told them to use their own remixes and throw mine in the trash. One of theirs was actually really good, and I believe one of mine was as well. Brown went berserk at my suggestion of shit-canning my mixes. I didn't really care. I was over it by this point. This situation led to one of the worst things I may have ever done as A&R person.

A few days after switching my phone number, the Leaders sans Busta showed up at my office. Charlie, their de facto leader, was carrying a large African walking stick. He continually gestured that stick toward my face while he barked at me. He was on some half-assed tirade about how I wasn't shit. He went on to say that I was more supportive of KMD than LONS. Keep it 100, I was more into getting a root canal than hearing Brown and his bullshit that day. Finally, he demanded that the Leaders use my remix since they had paid me half up front. I offered to give the money back. No harm, no foul.

He was caught in a lurch with no argument left, so he started inventing shit. He once again accused me of favoritism, of being a devil and a biter, and he demanded a meeting with Bob Krasnow for the hundredth time. Knowing the last thing Kras wanted was an audience with a bipolar rapper named Charlie Brown, I told him flat out, "That ain't happening."

What Brown failed to realize is that he had a good manager. He should have had Chris Lighty meet with Krasnow. It would have made him seem way more professional and would have gotten him taken more seriously by upper management. I could just imagine Krasnow's face if he'd ever had a one-on-one meeting with Brown.

Brown retorted, "Why? Cause n****** can't meet the president of the label?"

I laughed. "Come on, man. Keith Sweat and Anita Baker meet Bob all the time," I said. "You're bugging."

"Oh, so we ain't important n******, only Keith Sweat and them other n****** get to meet Bob Krasnow? Fuck that!"

Brown was wilding out. He kept pointing his stick within inches of my face, which I did not appreciate. The whole thing was insulting. I ended up getting into a tussle with Brown before the rest of the Leaders pried me off him. He had asthma, and this led to him having an asthma attack. The whole thing was so fucked up. I was completely wrong in losing my temper. I'm lucky the rest of the Leaders didn't jump me. I probably deserved it. I will say this: It did not make Brown any easier to deal with down the road. In fact, it may have made him worse.

It was pretty clear from early on that Busta was the star of the show and that LONS was going to end up being the "Busta Rhymes Show" sooner or later. This was the real crux of the Leaders's problems. Brown was ultra-competitive and made things difficult on Busta. It was wearing on him. I know he wanted to make the Leaders work. I suspected it wouldn't. By the time the second album was being recorded, everyone knew the end was near. I have a built-in crystal ball, and mine said: "This won't work out—Busta goes solo." This happened, and as mean as it sounds, I felt no sorrow for Brown. He had a good thing going, he was very talented, but his ego and want for drama, combined with his envy for Busta, got the best of him. At the end of the day, it was his own doing. And it's unfortunate because the guy had the goods.

On the other hand, Busta's drive and determination helped make him the success that he is today. Busta shined on the remix of "The Scenario," and in the wake of this, while struggling with *T.I.M.E.*, the second Leaders's record, I asked Chris Lighty if Q-Tip might possibly oversee and executive produce the record for/with me. The first version of the record wasn't up to par, and with Chris's help, I wanted to send them back in to rethink the record.

It was the first time I had ever done this with a band.

I approached Brown and the rest of LONS with the idea. I remember Brown calling Q-Tip "a biter," claiming, "Tribe bit their stage show from us. We invented the East Coast Stomp, now they do it. I ain't fucking with Tip like that." The East Coast Stomp was a dance the Leaders did on stage. Tribe did do that dance, yes. But so did Cypress Hill, Naughty by Nature, and eleventeen other groups. It was what rappers did onstage in '91.

Busta, on the other hand, was open to the idea of bringing Q-Tip on board. To this day, I wonder what the end result would have been if I could have made that happen. Several years later, Q-Tip oversaw Mobb Deep's *The Infamous* to tremendous results.

I'll never forget this short-sighted decision. Later, after the sub-par performance of *T.I.M.E.*, the Leaders would disband. Less than a year later, the world would hear Busta destroy the "Flava in Ya Ear" remix, a precursor to his solo career. Busta was just too talented, too smart, and too dedicated to his craft not to succeed. To this day, he is the single most driven artist I have ever seen. The guy is relentless, as well as being a master politician.

When the Leaders initially caught wind of a potential Busta solo record, they stormed into my office led by Brown and called Busta, who was on the movie set of *Higher Learning*, and started beefing about his going for solo. It was an uncomfortable moment, what with the band he didn't want to leave accusing him of being a backstabber. I still don't know if all the Leaders felt this way or if they had been riled up by Brown.

It all culminated with their breakup live on *Yo! MTV Raps* after the release of *T.I.M.E.* in 1993. Charlie Brown's declaration that he was "getting to know myself and what my capabilities are and what I'm gonna do in life" sparked a meltdown within the group live on camera. It was literally moments later that Brown, off camera, declared he no longer wanted to be in the band. I remember my publicist calling me from the shoot with Busta explaining to me what had just occurred. I couldn't think of a worse way to break up. Brown, ever the drama queen, had officially sealed the band's fate live on TV. All these years later, watching the clip of it transpiring still makes my stomach hurt.

As for Busta going solo, lots of stories have been told about the behind-the-scenes dealings that lead to it. To be clear, the move was inevitable. I knew this, and so did Chris Lighty. Lyor Cohen, who was partners with Chris at Rush Management, did not have anything to do with Busta going solo, as has been claimed by Dinco D. The idea was brought to Busta by Chris and me. It was an obvious conclusion to the Leaders equation. It's what the people wanted. To Busta's credit, he was beyond loyal to the band. After some coaxing, Busta made the move.

I have no regrets for putting the offer in front of him. It just made sense.

I was trying to juggle Brand Nubian, Shazzy, and the Leaders. I also had to deal with a never-ending game of musical chairs in the urban promotion department. In the beginning of 1992, we finally got someone who could deliver—an OG named Ruben Rodriguez (RIP), who came over from Sony with his own attached production/label, Pendulum Records. Ruben had been Lyor's archnemesis at Columbia and knew me vaguely from the Def Jam/Rush connection. Ruben favored long mink coats and LVMH luggage, and he called everyone baby. He didn't dig me too much, and the feeling was mutual. He probably saw me as a threat, but he knew Krasnow was checking for me, so he played nice. I hoped the guy would break one of my records. He was capable.

More importantly, I was delivering. I remembered what Russell told me when he reprimanded me for getting into it with Hank: "Make a hit record and you can beat up anyone you want." *The Source* had given a five-mic review to Brand Nubian's *One for All*, which helped push the album over 150,00 records sold by the time Ruben came aboard. The record was still going strong, moving close to 10,000 a week steadily, which it would do for the remainder of the year. It peaked out at about 350,000 units—not bad for an underground record that cost $80,000 to make.

Of course, it wasn't going to be smooth sailing. There was dissension in the ranks with the Nubians. Puba was ego-tripping, and Jamar and X weren't having it. They were intent on being respected, and Puba was intent on being Puba. He missed gigs constantly. He was dismissive in interviews. He had his own DJ, Ron Stud (RIP). He was a wildly irresponsible cat. One day, I got a call from Pow Wow, the old Soul Sonic Force member, and Afrika Bambaataa, the head of the Zulu Nation.

They asked me in a not-so-nice way why LG hadn't gotten paid or received any producer credit for the songs, "Who Can Get Busy Like This Man…" and "Grand Puba, Positive and L.G." I was shocked. I thought Puba had done the beats—because that's what he told me when I created the final credits with him. I asked those guys if they were serious, and Pow Wow explained he was deadly so. I respectfully promised to get to the bottom of it. Apparently Puba had blamed it on me when questioned by LG and Pow Wow. It started to come to light that Puba had a habit of forgetting to give people proper production credit, something that would surface again later. I love him to this day, but I would never rely on him for anything, least of all part of my income. I feel badly that the other brothers in the Nubians have to continually deal with his shenanigans. I'm long done babysitting grown men.

Puba is a wild cat. I believe he is deathly afraid of success. One minute he is a man with a huge heart, and the next, a stone-cold hustler; I have seen him play his own people, only to have it come back to him. We used to joke that he liked to keep his peoples down. He shorted a lot of his inner circle on paper and the credit they had rightfully earned. He tried to jerk me several times and even succeeded once or twice. He was always on the hustle, trying to play every record label around, especially the ones that he was signed to. He was a short-money kind of dude. I don't know if he ever truly valued his artistry enough.

He only confessed under duress to playing LG. Still, I had to make amends to LG and square it with Bam and Pow Wow. I ended up paying LG $10,000 and created a producer agreement, which Puba ducked signing/paying for months.

The fact that the Zulu Nation almost tossed me a beating didn't sit well with me. Shit, in Puba's prime, almost no one could rap as good as he could. I've seen Puba play the piano pretty damn well in addition to make beats, DJ, and produce. He was a high-level natural talent. It came very easy to him—almost too easy. If Puba had been focused, I believe he could have been a Hall of Famer, remembered alongside his contemporaries like Q-Tip and De La Soul. Unfortunately, that wasn't the case. Most youngsters don't even know who he is.

In the midst of all this, I found an oddball of a kid with a deep baritone and a penchant for psychedelics named Del the Funky Homosapien. Ice Cube, whom I had first met at Skate Land in Los Angles a few years earlier, was riding high as a solo artist, releasing *AmeriKKKa's Most Wanted* and its follow up EP, *Kill at Will,* following his departure from NWA. He brought Del my way because I liked "that weirdo shit." It turned out that Del was Cube's younger cousin, and he said the kid was talented and bright—a child prodigy. He sent me Del's music, which had been created with the help of Sir Jinx, Ice Cube's then-musical sidekick. I listened and concurred.

I soon brought Ice Cube to NYC to meet Bob Kransnow, who was impressed. He liked marketable Black rage. Ice Cube had become a darling in the mainstream music press, which helped Kras understand his importance artistically. Del had very little to do with the Black rage Cube embodied; he had his own trip. Kras gave me the thumbs up, and we proceeded to sign Del via a production deal with Ice Cube's fledgling Street Knowledge label. Unbeknownst to me at the time, my life would be changing, and a lot of it had to do with Del and where he was from.

Del was from Oakland, California, the sister city of San Francisco, right on the other side of the Bay. Unlike San Francisco, Oakland is a rough place, one of the proudest and most politicized Black communities in the country, complete with a long history of militancy, gangsta rap, and all out madness. But it's even more complicated than that. Oakland is the hometown of both the Black Panthers and the Hells Angels. Go figure.

I like to say that Oakland is to San Francisco what Brooklyn is to Manhattan, at least before the gentrification and influx of hipsters. Oakland doesn't get the credit it deserves in hip-hop. Words and styles come from the Bay on the constant, yet many don't even know it. In rap music, nobody said "Beeeyyaaatch" before Oakland native Too Short did so way back in 1986. The terms "popping collars" and "player hater" are also originally Oakland slang. Referring to friends as "playboy," too. With its long history of Black empowerment, as well as hustlers and pimps, Oakland has a style all its own; the Blaxploitation classic, *The Mack,* was filmed there for a reason.

Del, a.k.a. Teren Delvon Jones, was certainly a unique individual. He and his crew, the Hieroglyphics, were one of the most skilled rap crews in early nineties hip-hop history, changing the perception of what Bay Area rap was supposed to sound like. Prior to Hiero (as they are known), the idea that Bay Area rap could be as lyrically and stylistically innovative as New York rap was unthinkable. With their innovative take on rapping, from styles to lyrics, Hiero changed that idea. They were as forward thinking creatively as any group from New York City or anywhere, for that matter. As a collective, they could hold their own with any rap crew around. They were masters of freestyling, which nowadays gets confused with dropping bars. Bars is simply stringing together rhymes you have already written. This has become known as freestyling, when in fact freestyling is improvising lyrics on the spot or going off the top of the head. I have never to this day seen a collective able to freestyle at the level of Hiero. At the time, actual freestyling was a coveted skill—and Hiero had that skill in droves.

I always looked at them artistically as an extension of what the Native Tongues had put forth, and I am proud I was able to help introduce the Hieroglyphics crew to the world. As great as they were as rappers, they were equally great as people, and I have remained friends with them to this day. One of the reasons may be that I also inadvertently introduced them to their longtime manager, sometime producer, and member of the collective, Damien "Domino" Siguenza.

I first met Domino when I was digging for records at a great record store in the Haight called Groove Merchant. I had become friends with the store's owners, Mike McFadden, and his wife, Jody. They had told me about a kid who rented the space behind the store named Domino that I should meet. Mike explained that he was a talented beat maker, a rapper, and a serious record collector, who was digging for a lot of the same kinds of records I was. I asked if he was around, and Mike said he was. We knocked on his door and he quickly answered. Mike introduced us and we started talking records. He had a little studio set up there and I noticed he had a FZ-1 like the one we used in our studio. We started talking about the sampler. I told him I was in the Bay Area meeting with Ice Cube's cousin Del, who I had just signed. Domino told me he rapped and asked me if I wanted to hear some beats.

He cued up a tape of beats and the first thing he played me was a beat with a sample I had just used for Grand Puba. I lost my mind. I had the tape with me and played it for him, and we started cracking up. He played me a gang of joints I was impressed by that day, and I don't impress easily. The kid *was* talented. We instantly became friends. I connected him and Del before I went back to NY, and they met without me one afternoon in Oakland.

About a month later, I was back in the Bay. I hit up Domino and told him I was going to meet Del and the Hiero crew that night and he was welcome to roll with me to Oakland if he wanted, so he tagged along. We met the Hiero crew at Opio's house and proceeded to sneak in the back of a local night club. We got drunk, then went back to Opio's house, where the crew rapped over my and Domino's beats till daylight. It was a hell of a night. Domino and the crew's beats fit perfectly. He likes to say this is the day he decided to retire from rapping and focus on producing after hearing Hiero's freestyling abilities.

Shortly thereafter Domino and the Hiero crew cemented their relationship. Dom, as we call him, became a center figure in their clique. He has worked with the fellas for over twenty years now and this might never have happened if I hadn't met him that lazy afternoon in SF digging for records. He remains one of my best friends. I like to think something bigger was at work that day we first met.

At this point, the rap game was consuming me on many levels. I was battling with the Leaders constantly. Brand Nubian was headed for disaster, with Puba's ego and irresponsibility finally getting the better of him and the band. After 3rd Bass had my crew and I produce "Pop Goes the Weasel," which subsequently provided both them and us with the biggest hit record that any of us of had experienced up to this point, they hit the skids. At twenty-six years old, I was starting to learn that nothing lasts forever.

I escaped a lot of this confusion by digging in deep and working closely with Del. It was a wonderful form of escapism. We also shared a love for groovy loops and funny lyrics. He started making his record in LA with Ice Cube, DJ Pooh, and his squad, the Boogie Men. Pooh was Cube's main producer on the classic *Death Certificate* and a West Coast legend in his own right. Pooh, as a junior member of the LA Posse, produced "Jack the Ripper" for LL Cool J and would later helm *Tha Doggfather* after Dre and Snoop went their separate ways. Pooh and Cube would also cowrite *Friday* and their subsequent sequels. My job was made easier by the fact that Ice Cube was the executive producer of the record. He had a game plan, and for the most part the guy knew what he was doing. He was hot as a pistol, and being in business with him was a smart move.

Del had a lot of ideas, and Ice Cube, Pooh, and his team would help him with the execution. The record was called *I Wish my Brother George Was Here*. The title is a reference to George Clinton, who we brought in to narrate the record. I will never forget him smoking crack right in front of me in the studio like it was nothing, then with his back to the engineer while on the phone telling him to turn down the reverb on his vocals and pan them rabbit ears. After smoking crack the next day in the studio, JD from the Da Lench Mob lost it and screamed at him, forcing George to get high in the studio parking lot. Even on that shit, George knew what was up in the studio. Still, it was a thrill to work with George Clinton, one of my musical heroes.

Del's debut record was one of the first records to base its sound on P-Funk, a few years before Dr. Dre's *The Chronic*. It was supposed to be Ice Cube's version of Digital Underground, and I guess it was in some ways. The record was fun to make. I got to travel to LA, where Cube was located, to hear his forthcoming masterpiece, *Death Certificate,* before it was released and to watch Pooh and Del craft the record at Echo Sounds, one of the go-to hip-hop studios in LA at that point in time. I thought *I Wish My Brother George Was Here* was great, though I still question why Ice Cube picked "Sleepin' on My Couch" as the first single. For me, though, the real prize was getting to spend time in the Bay with the burgeoning Hieroglyphics crew.

At this point in my life, I was in constant touch with my dad. Traveling to the Bay often reinvigorated my relationship with my pops to a large extent. I'll never forget my dad coming to Del's album release in SF and the humongous Samoan bouncer buggin' out that he was my dad, since they were neighbors. It was a trip. Spending so much time in the Bay also opened the door for a series of friendships and relationships that were vital in the chemistry of my family's dynamic and helped in some ways bring to light one of my favorite West Coast rap music movements of the nineties.

Somewhere in the midst of all the madness, I was involved with another great group. My erstwhile boss of sorts, Raoul Roach, had created a friendship with Eddie Ferrell, a.k.a. Eddie F, the DJ/producer for Heavy D & the Boyz. Eddie was an intelligent, likeable cat from Mount Vernon, New York. Eddie had a young protégée named Pete Rock, who was also from "Money Earnin'" Mount Vernon. Pete, who coincidently was Heavy D's cousin, was busy making a name for himself as a DJ and had a slot on WBLS Marley Marl's *In Control* show every Friday and Saturday. He took it upon himself to play demos of his own group, Pete Rock & CL Smooth. Pete had a different sound—horn laden and soulful, with bright cracking snares that drove the entire track, incorporating filtered bass lines way before they had become the norm in hip-hop production. He had a soulful, somewhat psychedelic sound, and I dug it. When Raoul asked if I wanted to meet with Eddie and listen to Pete Rock's stuff, I was eager to get involved.

Raoul was already sold on signing Pete Rock and CL, even before I met with him and Eddie F. All he wanted from me was to cosign, which I gladly did. At Eddie's suggestion, we decided to release an EP tilted *All Souled Out*. Soon after, I remember being delivered the band's first photo shoot. Not sure who the stylist was, but the shoot was comedy. CL had on a pair of beige Hammer pants and Pete had on an extremely questionable paisley shirt, an Afrocentric wooden necklace, and some crazy shoes with buckles on them.

I called a meeting.

Fortunately, Pete and CL weren't attached to the shoot, and neither was Eddie. In fact, we all laughed at it. We agreed to do another less "fashion forward" one. We quickly fixed the photo shoot and dropped the EP, and then something unexpected happened. We initially went with a song called "Go With the Flow." It was a cool tune, very trademark Pete Rock, with a sample of S.O.U.L.'s "Burning Spear"—a break I always dug. Pete had a way of using breaks that was unfathomable to me at that time. The way he layered drums, EQ-ing parts out of them and accentuating others, it was mind-boggling, as was his sample digging. I listened to Pete's demos often, getting ideas for my own music such as flittering and chopping bass lines, layering snares, what breaks to use, and a myriad of other ideas.

While we were working "Go With the Flow" to moderate success, the B-side, "The Creator" surfaced as the more popular tune. Pete, an unlikely MC as there ever was, with some help from Grand Puba's pen, rapped on it, which fans really liked. The song is based around an awesome Eddie Bo tune "From This Day On," and some heavy Pete Rock drums. The record took off in part to Funkmaster Flex playing it during his daily mix show and soon enough it became a sleeper hit. I wasn't complaining, and neither were Pete and CL. The irony of their first hit song being rapped by Pete was wild. There was a reason the band was Pete Rock *and* CL Smooth, I suppose. Pete was always the headliner in retrospect. Raoul, my senior copilot in signing them, had left the company by then, unfortunately, and never got to join in on the group's success with me.

We shot a questionable video set on a boat with Pete and CL acting like pirates. I'm still not sure that was really the way to go, but *c'est la vie*. Pete and CL had proven themselves the hard way and had caught a break with "The Creator." Subsequently, they were green lit to start making their debut album, and by then, the hip-hop nation was waiting. In the interim, Pete became a very sought-after producer, which made getting him to focus on his own record difficult. During this time, he did one of the best remixes ever for Public Enemy's song "Shut 'em Down." Pete, who also had grown more confident in his rapping ability, spit a short but very well-received verse on it. It was amazing to watch a youngster from Mount Vernon blossom right in front of me. He was on his way to becoming the go-to-guy when you wanted a remix or a hit song. He also blessed House of Pain's anthem "Jump Around," as well as spitting a hot little verse on it, at Everlast's urging. To this day, it is still my favorite remix ever done by Pete Rock. I would love to take more credit for Pete Rock's ascent, but it was all Pete and his talent. I was just lucky enough to be in the right place at the right time.

Pete and CL were about to embark on a musical journey that would change the sound of rap for the next few years. The first record, *Mecca and the Soul Brother,* sold well and featured a poignant hit song, "They Reminisce Over You (T.R.O.Y.)," which was a monster right out the gate. It featured a beautifully crafted Tom Scott sample that, legend has it, was given to Pete by Large Professor, a story I can neither confirm nor deny, though Large Pro did use the horns from it first on a Slick Rick remix of "It's a Boy."

The song was dedicated to their close friend Trouble "T-Roy," a dancer for Heavy D & the Boyz, who died tragically while on tour. To me, it was CL's brightest moment on the LP; he really raps his ass off on that one. It was not, however, an obvious choice for the first single, as it lacked a huge chorus, but the fellas and Eddie F were convinced, and I rolled with it. I do know this: That when I first heard it, with its constantly moving offbeat snares, I was blown away. I incorporated this exact idea on the biggest hit song I ever made in my career, Everlast's "What it's Like," which came a few years later. Pete's album contained a zillion mind-blowing samples, some cracking kicks and snares, and some of the best interludes ever put down on wax. His use of the SP-1200 sampler was mind-boggling. The production on *Mecca and the Soul Brother* set the hip-hop production bar. The way he constructed his records was artistically, in my opinion, comparable to people like Miles Davis or painters like Picasso. I consider it high art.

Puba helped Pete with his rhymes and appeared on the record with Heavy D and a few others. The record was hailed as a classic and still is thought of one to this day. The biggest stars in rap music today, including Kanye West, got a part of their sound directly from this branch of the Pete Rock and CL hip-hop tree. Sampling, which Pete and most of the hip-hop producers I really admire did a lot of, really injects a dose of much appreciated soul into the equation. When rap music moved away from this kind of sound, rap production became less interesting to me. I'm not sure if it's the generic keyboard sounds or the fact that most trap records have the same fruity loops drum kits or the lack of any form of lyrical content for the most part, but the rap music of today is not the rap music I came of age to. The music of the Pete Rocks and DJ Premiers is.

Maybe it's generational, who knows?

One of the tenants of hip-hop is braggadocio. Here I go: My track record during that time period is one of the most incredible runs of any A&R person I have ever known. Puffy had his moment, as did my man Matty C at Loud. I'm sure a bunch of other people I'm forgetting had serious runs, too, but in my eyes, my level of artistry was rarely ever matched, as I had helped put together one of the greatest rap rosters in the history of the golden age.

I was lucky as could be, but I also understood what made rap music good, from MCing to producing and everything in between. I really dug my groups because we all related. I was lucky enough to be put in the position to help expose great music to the world and to help my acts get their individual messages out there in an un-compromised way. I always say I was lucky but not responsible for the talent I helped share with the world. Only God can be given this credit. I was taught growing up to trust my gut, and I did with all of these signings. I was not fearful. I was not scared to fall on my face. I did with Shazzy and learned a valuable lesson, one I took with me on every project thereafter. It was an honor to work with all of these great artists. I believe I showed the proper respect by empowering my artists to express themselves as they saw fit. I felt it was my duty to protect their chosen point of view. To this day, me and my artists, minus Charlie Brown, have a mutual love and respect for each other. I like to think it's because I honored their creative visions.

A few years ago, Pete Rock was performing at Summer Stage in Central Park. His brother, Grap Luva, was performing with him. Grap spotted me in the VIP section and in between songs told the audience that I was the man responsible for helping bring his music to the masses and that I was the greatest A&R man of all time; Pete joined in and told the audience that I stuck my neck out for him, Brand Nubian, Busta Rhymes, and ODB, time and time again. He told the captive audience that I helped bring all these great acts to the world and for that, the audience should all salute me. And they did. It's not an accident he deejayed my fiftieth birthday party. I love Pete Rock, though I may not agree with some of the things he says on social media.

Busta has done the same multiple times, as have Grand Puba and Del. It's moments like those that make it all worth it. Any time I bump into any of the artists from my days at Elektra, I realize I really did something positive and helped raise the consciousness of some people through music, if only just a little. I also found within these experiences a feeling of worth and vitality that I may have never quite captured again at any other time of my life.

Had I known what I know now, I would have plotted to take over the world.

Elektra Playlist #1

Leaders of the New School—"Case of the P.T.A."
Leaders of the New School—"The International Zone Coaster"
Brand Nubian—"All for One"
Brand Nubian—"Slow Down"
Pete Rock & CL Smooth—"The Creator"
Pete Rock & CL Smooth—"Go With the Flow"
Del The Funky Homosapien—"Mistadobalina"
Del The Funky Homosapien (Ft. Hieroglyphics)—"Burnt"
KMD—"Peachfuzz"
KMD—"Humrush"
KMD (Ft. Busta Rhymes and Brand Nubian)—"Nitty Gritty (Remix)"

12

NITTY GRITTY

Long before YouTube, the first viral video came courtesy of an Argentinian immigrant plumber named George Holliday who, from his balcony, shot a blurry black and white videotape of a Black man being beaten viciously by four of LA's finest, as another dozen cops looked on. Holliday contacted the LAPD about the video but couldn't find anyone who was interested, so he dropped it off at KTLA-TV, a local station. They aired it, and a few days later, CNN put it in rotation. The video would go on to become the most famous home movie since the Zapruder film.

When I first watched the video, I was disgusted but not surprised. I had witnessed the police beat down people of color several times. I also saw them kick the shit out of white people—including my dad—but there is no doubt that if you are Black or Latino, your chances of getting a beating from Jake were, and are, magnified greatly.

I grew up thinking the cops will fuck you up if they got the chance most of the time. As I got older, and had spent a bit of time in LA, I came to know that cops in LA were way more apt to do so than the members of the NYPD. NWA, Cypress Hill, Ice-T (with Body Count), and a plethora of LA-based rappers, tackled this in their music with such songs as "Fuck tha Police," "How I Could Just Kill a Man," and "Cop Killer."

LA was a city with a serious gang culture and the LAPD seemed to take special offense to this. Anyone who was part of the culture of hip-hop in the late eighties or early nineties couldn't have been surprised by the video. I think I was more surprised by the fact someone actually videotaped the whole thing and didn't get his ass kicked for doing so. Similarly, I wasn't at all surprised when the verdict came down a year later. They had moved the trial from Los Angeles to lily-white Simi Valley, which was a telltale sign the fix was in. Remember, activists raised me. Growing up, I was taught not to believe much of what the media propaganda wants us to believe, and I still don't.

I was, however, surprised at the aftermath of it all. I was confused by images of Black people burning down their own neighborhoods, thinking: *Isn't this what the oppressors want? Doesn't this give cause to the police and to right-wing assholes to further take advantage of the rage they helped create in LA? Didn't it cause more friction between Blacks and whites, Asians and Blacks? Latinos and Blacks?* One of the more disturbing images was when Reginald Denny was pulled out of his truck and attacked; I was actually nauseated. As much as I was repulsed by this, I had to remember the images of Black men being lynched, the murder of Latasha Harlins, and the acquittal of her murderer, Soon Ja Du, that preceded the riots and the brutal beating of Rodney King. It was a literal cinematic version of the hate that hate created. In sorting out my feelings, I recall this Martin Luther King Jr. quote: "And I must say tonight that a riot is the language of the unheard. And what is it America has failed to hear? It has failed to hear that the promises of freedom and justice have not been met. And it has failed to hear that large segments of white society are more concerned about tranquility and the status quo than about justice and humanity." Rarely have truer sentiments been voiced about the rage and hate inflicted by centuries of systemic racism.

In New York, storeowners closed early on Broadway. There was tension in the air, but nothing jumped off. Instead, I had a front row seat to the madness on TV. I remember talking to DJ Muggs and my old crimie Jerry Dean, who had moved to LA. Jerry had been out looting, which I found kind of sickly ironic since Jerry is white and the son of a police officer. Then again, Jerry had been looting one way or another his entire life, so the riots were another excuse; he wasn't full of rage, he was just an opportunistic criminal like many who looted, I suspect. Muggs, on the other hand, on day three or four of the riots, was hanging with Da Lench Mob, Ice Cube's crew, watching that shit go down on TV, and they were bugging out. Years later, Everlast told me he was driving back into LA with Cypress when the shit first jumped off, coming all the way from Humboldt County, tripping on shrooms, and he could see LA burning while driving into the city. That must have been one hell of a trip.

During those six days of rioting, I remembered back to when my parents told me about the riots in Watts and Newark in the sixties. I also remembered all the looting that took place during the Blackout of '77 and how my mother had made me return the swag the Ortiz brothers gave me to Moe and how he subsequently lost his business. I wondered what the mothers in LA were telling their children and what that must have been like. I wondered about the collective trauma that was experienced.

To me, it all seemed inevitable. You can only fuck with people so much and expect them to take it. Black people had been handed enough bullshit by the LAPD over the years, and this was the day a lot of the world found out about it. The injustice done to Rodney King was the injustice done to thousands of people of color, not only in LA but all across America. Thirty-one years later, the shit seems worse than ever, and it will not stop as long as we have police officers that are disconnected from the communities in which they work. Only this time gangster rap foretold this story. Music has always been reflective of society. Rap music that is based on words even more so. This ethos continues to this day, albeit in a very nihilistic way.

Most cops tend to be Republicans, many of them conservatives, with an us-against-them attitude, whether Black, brown, Asian, or white. I also know a few cops who are good people. Still, I don't see it getting better any time soon. While we made progress during the Obama years, it's too bad Donald Trump and the legions of the alt-right dirtbags he inspired did and continue to do their best to make America more racist again.

To make matters worse, many branches of law enforcement in America are compromised by Oath Keepers, Proud Boys, and Three Percenters. Same goes for the military. Look no further than what occurred on January 6, 2021. How many former police officers, sheriffs, and former military personnel were there attacking democracy head on? How many militia members nationally have been in the military and may still be active police officers? How many times do cops look the other way in these situations because they have shared political ideologies? I believe the Capitol police didn't open fire on January 6 for one reason: Fire would have been returned. This would have created a plethora of martyrs for the far right in America and may have pushed forth a modern-day civil war.

Eric Garner was choked to death on video, and the cops got off. Trayvon Martin was shot to death and his killer, George Zimmerman, a wanna-be cop who was so whack that the police wouldn't even take him, got off. Michael Brown was killed in Ferguson and the cop got off. Philando Castile was shot and killed in the Twin Cities for reaching for his registration, his lady streaming it while she and her kid sat in the car and watched him die. Just a few years later, it happened again in the Twin Cities when George Floyd was choked to death by Derek Chauvin. Breonna Taylor was murdered in her own home for nothing.

What about all the murders we don't know about—the ones when there were no witnesses and no cameras? This shit seemingly never ends. The video of Rodney King may have shocked America in 1991. Now it is the norm. This shit is not new, only the constant documentation of it is. Much like the waves of hate crimes targeted toward Asian Americans, it's been here.

I find it disappointing that more rappers today, with a few exceptions such as Kendrick Lamar, Killer Mike, YG (who is a self-professed gang member), and J Cole, do not speak on or even seem to care about what's going on. Instead of rapping about Breonna Taylor or George Floyd, we are subjected to verse after verse about pussy, Lean, and materialistic bullshit. I wish a trap version of Public Enemy would surface. Lil Baby's "The Bigger Picture" gives me hope that the youth will speak out more. Unfortunately, kids often want nihilistic escapism today, not thought-provoking music, and whether I like it or not, the youth run this rap shit—not me or the guys I came up with. I can listen to PE and early Ice Cube on my own time.

Race has played a profound role in my life, and I have always felt honored to be able to experience things very few white people have experienced. No matter how I grew up, I am acutely aware that I am white and that being white grants me certain opportunities and advantages in life that people of color don't get. White privilege exists, and as uncomfortable as it is to say it, I have benefitted from it, every white person in America has. These days I remain very conscious of it. We have no time to play games. I constantly ask myself: If I recognize white privilege when I see it, what can I do to address it and attempt to change it?

When I think about systemic racism, I think of my childhood friend Ricardo Ortiz. Ricardo couldn't read in the fifth grade, yet he was an intelligent kid. The school determined he was "slow." He was put in remedial classes, which only increased his anti-social behavior. He acted out in school and would get violent when he was teased for being left back a grade. When he was in my house looking through comic books with me one day, my mom tried to teach him to read. She came to suspect he was dyslexic.

A few days later, she gave him a dyslexia test she had acquired and it confirmed her suspicions. She attempted to help get him into a special program to correct his dyslexia. His mother, for whom English was a second language, had great difficulty navigating the school's bureaucracy. Ricardo eventually learned to read, but by then it was too late—the system had failed him. Ricardo dropped out of school in seventh grade. By the time he was seventeen, he was serving ten years in prison for selling a bundle of dope to an undercover cop. If he were a white middle class kid, I doubt this would have happened. Being the child of an immigrant single parent, living below the poverty line, he never had a chance. I didn't realize this example until I wrote this book in all honesty. This is how deeply woven into the fabric of America systemic racism is. I simply wasn't conscious of this example for forty years. My mother saw it clear as day, though—another reason she was such a special person.

My upbringing has been a real blessing; it is why I have always been socially conscious. My parents were left of liberal political activists. My dad called Kwame Ture and Bobby Seale his friends. I was raised to respect Malcolm X and the ethos of the Black Panthers and the Young Lords. I was taught the war in Vietnam was unjust and that often the police were not your friends. I was raised with an understanding that Black, brown, and Asian pride/consciousness are valued principles, which were to be supported and revered. When I first heard Public Enemy, it struck a deep nerve because of these principles. I was attracted to Latifah, Brand Nubian, and KMD's music because of the same thing. I felt honored to be able to help them get their message to people.

Being raised and growing up on the Lower East Side in the early seventies, my closest friends were Puerto Rican. I felt more comfortable with Latinos than I did with people of my own race until I was in junior high school where I was turned on to skateboarding, white girls, that dude Led Zeppelin, and his boy, ZZ Top. Prior to that, my musical leanings other than The Beatles, and oddly Queen, were soul, disco, and funk. Most rock music was on the back burner. I was too busy digging Stevie Wonder, The Jackson 5, and P-Funk.

The fact that me, a half Ukrainian Jew/half Italian kid from East Second Street, could break bread and work closely with a militant group of Five-Percent Nation–affiliated rappers is a manifestation of my parents' life force at work. I also think it speaks volumes about the power of hip-hop culture and music.

Working with Brand Nubian, KMD, ODB, Pete Rock & CL Smooth, De La Soul, Latifah, and Busta Rhymes (many of whom are also Muslim) is an attribute to the environment and culture I was raised in. The fact that these artists trusted me with their music and messaging means a lot to me still. For the experience of working with these brothers and sisters, and for the values I was raised with, I have the utmost gratitude.

Because of my upbringing, I have always had an affinity for Latino culture. As a teenager, while spending a summer with my dad in SF, I became fascinated by *cholos* and West Coast Latino culture. The first time I saw low riders hopping on Mission Street, I was blown away. That summer, I was all of thirteen years young and beyond jazzed at what I had just witnessed. I remember going with my pops to the Mission Cultural Center to check out a low rider art exhibit and getting hooked on *Lowrider* magazine. I was infatuated by *esse* culture.

I had a few little *vato* friends running around the Mission. We would cruise by the McDonald's on Twenty-Fourth Street, checking out the gangsters with their hairnets, winos, locs, derby jackets, Dickies, and flannels. It was a mesmerizing site—a totally different, yet totally Latino gangster vibe, one that was nothing like *Boricua* culture, the dominant Latino culture I grew up around. I always wondered what my Lower East Side *Boricua* brothers would have thought of the *esses* from the Mission.

The fact that I spent time in the Mission in San Francisco as a kid and dug it always helped me appreciate the West Coast and the Bay Area in particular. This also helped me a great deal later on in life. I have always been comfortable in California, whether Los Angeles, San Francisco, or up north in Humboldt County. Shit, I have been comfortable almost everywhere really, whether in a strip club in Atlanta, at a car show in Oakland after the club, or in a freestyle club in the South Bronx. I have never been intimidated by these cultural differences, but quite the opposite: I am intrigued and respect these differences deeply. I have a lot of gratitude for the ability to walk through cultural doors. It's a real gift.

I have never been the victim of any direct violence or ostracized in any of these settings. I believe if you're comfortable with yourself and you're rolling with the right people, nothing is going to happen as long as you carry yourself right. I feel more uncomfortable in a room full of Orange County bros than I ever have in any of these situations. All that said, I know I will never know what it's like to be a Black, Latino, or Asian man in America. I will never know what's it's like to be trans or nonbinary, or a woman for that matter.

I appreciate that the younger generations have adopted the ethos of a more eclectic society as their norm. Don't get it twisted though: We do not live in a colorless society. It's a nice utopian idea—one only afforded to white people. Still, I love the open-mindedness the youth have today, particularly when it comes to LGBTQIA+ issues. They do not carry the homophobia, by and large, that my generation was steeped in. I remember when everyone wondered who the "gay rapper" was in the late nineties. Today, we have queer rap icons like Lil Nas X and Tyler the Creator. Personally, I think that's so punk rock, and I love it. This is the future of the America I choose to celebrate.

These days, it's fairly common for a Black kid to wear an Iron Maiden shirt and to skateboard just like it's common for a young white kid to be obsessed with trap music and such. I feel the birth of the obsession many white kids developed with hip-hop culture happened because white youth culture in the mid-to-late eighties, especially musically, did not appeal to us. Bands like Ratt and Bon Jovi held no weight for many white urban kids. Indie rock also didn't fit the bill for us—a lot of whom were attracted to the danger and power of bands like Run-DMC, PE, or NWA, and in turn helped pioneer a generation of kids who enjoy an eclectic perspective musically and culturally. I think the world is a better place for it.

I find it odd that when many white kids go through a hip-hop phase, they try on Black culture for a few years and discard it when it's convenient or when the next trend comes along. (Anybody remember EDM?) For me, it was never about that. Hip-hop has been the dominant culture for me my entire adult life. The other side of that coin is Bad Brains. Punk rock for me is the first sub-culture I found, and there's an element to it that's resonated with me in every subculture I participated in after. The irony that the greatest hardcore punk rock band of all time is made up of four Black Rasta's from DC is not lost on me, and that they spoke to me the loudest in my early adolescence. What could be more punk rock than being Black?

Race had never been as prevalent in my career as it was during KMD's second album. With the passing of my friend Zev Love X, a.k.a. MF Doom, reliving this story is now accompanied by a deeper sense of pain. I would be remiss not to preface this chapter by stating the myriad of emotions this evokes.

Following the release of *Mr. Hood,* things had changed with KMD. Serch was no longer involved, having had a falling out with KMD and Pete Nice. Serch being out of the picture was for me a blessing, he always made everything unnecessarily difficult.

Sub and Doom, Kurious, and their crew, the Constipated Monkeys, were experimenting with psychedelics a bunch. The amount of acid my friends were gobbling was significant. Doom and Subroc went all in. I had taken my fair share of psychedelics in high school and thought a little mind expansion within reason was probably a good thing. As KMD got ready to create their new record, Doom and Sub camped out at Kurious's house a bunch. The problems started when Subroc received his advance, which funded a long and intense acid trip. While under the influence, he gave away a significant amount of cash to a few of his cronies hanging at Kurious's house. He apparently thought he had access to a time machine that would allow him to retrieve his hard-earned advance from his group of friends. When I heard about this, I was a little concerned.

A day or so later, when he realized what he had done, he seemingly didn't care. I feared he was potentially on his way to becoming an acid casualty. I had a lot more experience with this type of thing than Kurious, Doom, or anyone else involved. I had seen a few cats never come back from acid trips before. When I raised these concerns, I was told not to worry. I wasn't anyone's parent here, so I fell back. I mean, who was I to tell anyone how to live? I was drunk or high six nights out of the week my-damned-self.

Doom and Subroc had a symbiotic connection. They were unusually close, even for brothers. They were inseparable. They made music together constantly and were so connected that one could not exist without the other—a dynamic that would soon be tested. They literally finished each other's thoughts; it was almost telepathic. In the weeks following the time machine incident, Subroc remained a bit spacey. I asked him about what had happened and he just laughed it off, which I took as a good sign.

The Black Bastards record was, in part, based on Gylan Kain's The Blue Guerilla record and incorporated sound bites from the record throughout the course of it as skits and backing tracks. Kain was an angry, hilarious, irreverent poet, as well as a founding member of The Last Poets. He used a wide range of techniques and sounds in order to rally against all that bothered him, especially stereotyping. KMD's fascination with The Blue Guerilla made sense. A transformation had occurred among KMD. They were no longer cute, cuddly, conscious rappers. While still quirky, they were now more mature, serious, and hardened. Onyx had opted out of the group and, overall, the influence of street life and psychedelics had infiltrated the creative psyche of the brothers Dumile. Things had taken a turn toward the real and the trippy by the time they made Black Bastards.

One evening after spending the night at rapper Cage's house in Washington Heights, Subroc headed to the Long Island Rail Road train to trek back home. When he exited the LIRR, he attempted to cross the LIE and was struck by a car and killed. The culprits were never found and many conspiracies surround his death. I still don't know what actually happened, none of us do. I do know this: What little innocence Doom may have had left went down the drain when Subroc was killed.

We, as a group of friends, tried to come to grips with the loss of a young brother we all cared for greatly. I was shaken, and I can't even imagine how his family felt. To make matters worse, Doom and his family didn't have enough money to cover the services. Pete Nice and myself ponied up some bread, and I passed a collection plate among my coworkers and friends and collectively we all came up with enough to pay for the services. Watching my little man in that casket, all of nineteen years young, broke my heart. I believe the spirit of the entire Constipated Monkeys crew was altered forever by this experience. I will never forget Doom putting a boom box next to Sub's coffin, playing the album they had been working on. It was heartbreaking. I will also never forget Serch being asked to leave Sub's service, such were the tensions by then.

Sub's passing had an effect on all of us. Some of the innocence we shared as young men was gone. I witnessed first-hand Doom slipping into alcoholism and becoming more and more cryptic, sarcastic, and somber. He was in pain. The yin to his yang was no longer with him, and this pain and anger quickly spread to his work. Some would say this cynicism and anger were integral parts of his forthcoming persona, the supervillain MF Doom. From great pain often comes great art.

Shortly after Sub's death, Doom hunkered down, spending a lot of time in Jersey City at the studio of Rich Keller, his engineer, crafting the remainder of the record. Rich contributed some live elements to the record in the process. Doom would stay at Rich's house for days, sleeping there and fine-tuning the project. I believe this was cathartic for him in some way. It was never spoken on. Doom was stoic and often whimsical when it came to the topic of his brother. He was in deep anguish, and the finishing of the record provided him, I believe, some form of healing from his loss. He did not, in my opinion, want people to see how much pain he was in. He played it close to the vest.

Doom turned over the record to me and Pete Nice in November of '93, and we really dug it. Doom handed in the cover art and credits right before the Christmas break, and I scheduled the record for release early the following year. Since Doom, like his brother, had been into graffiti and was a gifted artist, it made sense when he designed the cover. He had created all of the group's prior artwork. It was part of the band's ethos. For the cover, he had drawn a Sambo character being hung on gallows. In an ode to the children's game Hangman, the title appeared underneath: *Bl_ck B_st_rds*. I dug the record and the cover. I was feeling positive about the project going into the New Year. I believed they'd made their best record yet, and I considered the artwork thought-provoking. It had meaning to it, like much of KMD's rhetoric.

The album got mastered and the artwork went through the Elektra system without a hitch. In April 1994, we released the single "What a N***a Know?" (modified to "N***y" for the radio). It featured a crafty Jody Watley sample, "Looking for a New Love," and was performing well. Doom did a bunch of interviews. Advance cassettes were circulated along with Elektra's marketing materials, which included the release date of May 3, 1994.

We were good to go.

Or so it seemed.

Then, out of nowhere, the record was deemed offensive. The artwork from advance copies had caught the ire of several *Billboard* columnists, including two Black writers, Terri Rossi and Havelock Nelson. Rossi shot first, deeming the record racist. In her column for the *Monday Morning Monitor*, a radio trade zine published by *Billboard*, she attacked the record's artwork without ever listening to the record itself. She never asked Doom to explain his artistic statement. Instead, she vilified the young man's opus without having any direct dialog with the man himself.

The rap editor at *Billboard*, Havelock Nelson, in his weekly column "The Rap Up," called the record offensive and derided Elektra Records, calling them irresponsible for releasing the record, cover art and all. I don't think Havelock, someone I considered a friend, ever listened to the record.

He certainly had access to Doom and me and could have exchanged dialogue with us before making his accusations. To this day I am offended by his conviction without investigation. These attacks were supported by many high-ranking executives of color within the Warner Music Group, many of whom had been rallied by Terri Rossi personally. Not one of them ever spoke to Doom (or me) about the record.

The tragedy of all this was not only that Doom had recently lost his brother, but also that he wasn't given the audience he deserved in a forum where he could defend his messaging. The record is a powerful examination of race. The hanging of Sambo symbolized the death of racism and stereotypes. It could also be interpreted as a loss of innocence, which was a strong component of KMD's first album. The missing letters alluded to the fact that more work needed to be done in terms of where the world stood racially. How this was missed by a bunch of people, particularly educated Black people in the music industry, was beyond me. The perceived offense by people within the WEA (Warner, Elektra, Atlantic) system was also a comment on where rap music stood within the culture of the company.

It was a trying time for me. I needed my gig, but I knew Doom was getting screwed. I was called into my boss's office. I glanced at the Robert Longo and David Salle art that adorned the walls of his spectacular digs as Krasnow broke it down for me. He told me the record was in trouble and barring a change of cover art, it could not come out as it stood. I argued that it was an important political and artistic statement and that, the last time I checked, we didn't bow down to censorship. Kras, with patience and love, explained to me that politically he was on the ropes within the WEA structure and that he had to pick and choose his battles, and this was one battle he was going to pass on fighting. I pleaded with him to give Doom an audience and a chance to defend his artwork. He acquiesced and said he would, and he kept his word. A meeting of the minds was scheduled for the following Monday. We were to meet Terri Rossi, Sylvia Rhone, Dick Parsons, Gerald Levin, and Bob Morgado, who Kras had mockingly named the Lying Hawaiian. (Eventually, Morgado and Doug Morris were responsible for Kras's ousting).

When we showed up at 8:45 a.m., an ungodly time for both me and Doom at this period of our lives, Kras summoned me by myself to his office. He informed me that the meeting had been canceled and that a decision had been made. I saw that he was pained by what would come next. He quickly got to the point, and he didn't mince words. "Today just ain't our day. They're shooting this one down. It's a bigger issue than this record." I was pissed and responded with "'They owe Doom a chance to explain himself," I said. "This isn't Nazi Germany."

Kras looked at me like he wanted to rip my head off. He explained, "Dante, one day you will understand. I simply am going to have to let the band go." He took a deep breath and asked me to get Doom.

He wanted to explain what would transpire to him personally.

Doom sat there quietly while Krasnow explained the situation. Kras told Doom he would give him $20,000 and his masters back. He also apologized to the both of us. I could see Kras was conflicted about what had transpired. I was pissed as all hell. I lacked the maturity and experience to understand what the big picture was in all of this. The truth is, Kras may have not even listened to the record. I believed he defended it as best he could out of his belief in me as an A&R person. It was a defense of my intellectual sensibilities as much as anything.

We left Kras's office stunned and defeated. I had a case of wine in my office that someone had sent me for the holidays a year earlier. Doom quickly opened a bottle from the case of wine. He was the only person I can ever remember drinking any of the wine. Over time, he must have drank half a case of it while visiting me in my office. It was labeled sweet premium white wine, which was the name of a KMD track, no accident. I usually didn't drink during the day (this would change down the line) but I hit the bottle with Doom until it was all gone.

When we were finishing our first bottle, Doom turned to me and smiled before opening another. I believe he knew how much I felt for him, what he had gone through with his brother's passing, and being dealt the dirtiest hand I had seen up to that point in the music biz. Beyond the business, we were people. I loved my artists. I loved their art, and I felt it was my duty to defend it in as transparent and empowering a way as I could. This day was no exception to my ethos as an A&R man.

Doom turned to me and said, "Don't worry, man. Today's a great day. I got twenty grand to get dropped, and I get my masters back. I ain't mad. I should get dropped more often." Oddly, Doom did not seem angry. In retrospect, I can see now that losing a record deal paled in comparison to losing his brother. As terrible as it was, I believe it was a small thing to a big person. To his credit, Doom never held it against me. He saw that I fought for him, for his art, and for what was right. For all the fighting I did, we both took an L. One that has stuck with me ever since.

I tried to laugh as we continued to pass the bottle back and forth, I called his manager, Pete Nice, and told him what had happened. He was understandably upset. Drunk, I then took the rest of the day off. I thought I might get fired when I left the office, and frankly I was drunk enough not to give a shit. I left Doom at the train station on Sixth and Forty-Ninth, gave him a hug, and told him if I could do anything for him I would.

That day soured me on the music biz to some extent for the rest of my career. That cynicism never really left me. I realized it wasn't a fair playing field and that righteousness had little to do with any of it. It was a lesson well learned.

At that time, I couldn't let my anger go. When Jonathan Schecter, my friend and then the editor of *The Source* (who loved *Black Bastards,* incidentally), called me for a quote or two, I let it fly. Kras never read *The Source,* but he did two days later—at the behest of a coworker, I believe— and called me into his office. Apparently, the powers that be at WEA were out to get him behind one thing or another. Kras had an infamous "T & E" budget and didn't give a shit about protocol. He was a maverick, and his style had worn thin on his peers.

Kras broke it down. "The music business is not fair. I believe you when you say it's valid and important music, but I got sharks out to get me." The Ice-T/Body Count "Cop Killer" incident had transpired a year earlier. At first "Cop Killer" was defended by the powers that be at Sire Records (a Warner distributed label). Seymour Stein and Howie Klein vowed not to bow down to censorship. Gerald Levin, Time-Warner CEO at the time, backed them up publicly in the *Wall Street Journal*. A few weeks later, due to overwhelming outside pressures, including The National Sherriff's Association with support from Vice President Dan Quayle, Warner Brothers acquiesced, and Ice-T and Body Count were thrown to the wolves. Precedent was already there; I just chose to ignore it.

My beloved boss Kras then talked about a color even more powerful than Black or white in the music industry: green. He explained how a recent Metallica box set had flopped. That and a few other tankers like Dokken, an expensive signing of an over-the-hill Huey Lewis, and Mötley Crüe firing their singer had my boss on the run. Mostly, I remember wondering why the fuck would anyone sign Huey Lewis.

I had never felt the sting of censorship before *Black Bastards*. I believed in freedom of expression. Shit, my dad was friends with Mario Savio and was part of the Free Speech Movement. But this was not the first time rap music would be tested, and it would not be the last.

Black Bastards became a bit of a holy grail to some. Many consider it the great lost rap record, a hip-hop *Smile* so to speak. By the time my friend Bobbito Gaarcia would release *Black Bastards* in 1998, Doom had reinvented himself as MF Doom, a masked eccentric genius who sampled Bukowski and became a pioneer of "backpack" rap. Doom, for all of his trials and tribulations, was a testament to Black America. He took all the adversity heaped on him and turned it into fuel for his fire, ultimately becoming as important a figure in underground hip-hop as there has ever been. For me, he remained a trusted and dear friend—something I value eternally, especially in the wake of his death.

With his passing, he's been hailed as a genius by the same people who didn't recognize his genius when he was among the living. That's okay, as long as people discover the music and aren't just playing grief vampire. Seeing him celebrated is ironic on some level, though. I believe he would be laughing at some part of it and figuring out how to transfer some of the praise into money for him and his family. I also don't think he'd want people to be sad. He would want his friends to talk him up and laugh at his antics. I have a picture I took at Chung King that is of Doom, Sub, John Gamble, and Geeby. It's hard for me to fathom that all four of those people, each of whom I loved dearly, are no longer here—three of them passing in a twelve-month span, no less. I never thought I would be the last person in that picture still alive.

I cherish Doom and my experiences with him. That the world found out about his death in January 2021, two months after he'd passed, says a lot about his cryptic nature. A part of me hopes it's just another elaborate prank. The real me knows it isn't.

Till I see you on the other side, my friend, I will forever talk you up.

'93 TILL INFINITY

I was still making beats, but even that was starting to feel stagnant. My dynamic with Geeby, which had been strained for quite a while, would be tested that year while we were working on Kurious's *A Constipated Monkey*.

Two important acts I worked with were no longer, as both 3rd Bass and Brand Nubian disbanded. That, coupled with Subroc's tragic death and the *Black Bastards* fallout, had me on edge. My artists were working on new records at this point, but for the first time in what seemed like years, I didn't have a lot of projects going on. My groups were what is referred to as "off cycle." I came to realize that it was just a timing issue, but at the time I felt like I was slipping a bit.

Puba had decided he wanted to do a solo record and that he had to get his. I supported his decision based on his rapping ability and that his solo songs on *One for All* were very well received. Still, I did not think Puba had to break up Brand Nubian to accomplish this.

The second Leaders of the New School record, *T.I.M.E.*, came out and tanked. The Leaders blamed me and my lack of support for its failure; I blame the record. As an A&R guy, I only have so much control over my marketing team's spends and focus. After a record stumbles out the gate, no record company will spend on it—especially when the press coming back is lukewarm. No amount of money was going to make *T.I.M.E.* a hit. Its failure had very little to do with me and everything to do with the record.

Grand Puba was doing his solo thing while the two remaining members of Brand Nubian waited in the wings, plotting their next move. I green-lit them to make a second record without Puba while keeping the group's name intact. It was sounding surprisingly good, exceeding my expectations. Diamond D had done a remix for the album track "Punks Jump Up to Get Beat Down," which I thought was fantastic and sounded like a hit to me. At Lord Jamar's urging, Sadat X and I agreed this should be the lead single as opposed to being a remix. We included it on the LP, opting to use the original version featuring Diamond D rapping on it for the 12-inch, as well as the version that sampled the horns from *Rocky*. It was a club banger and to this day is still one of my all-time favorite Brand Nubian records. Diamond D did his thing on that one.

Sadat X also became an in-demand sideman. The streets were into what Brand Nubian was doing. The second Brand Nubian record was a stellar record from top to bottom. I had given Jamar and Sadat a shot against some people's advice, and they came through with a classic. I love that record to this day.

Puba on the other hand, had a hit song as well, but his expectations were much bigger, so his record seemed a bit underwhelming to me and many of the rap cognoscenti. In retrospect, his debut album, *Reel to Reel*, is thought of as a minor classic. Upon its release, I deemed it good not great. Artistically, I think I just wanted it to be better. On the other hand, the second Brand Nubian record (sans Puba) *In God We Trust* was a sleeper hit. I was proud of Jamar and X because they had overcome the burden of Puba and stood on their own. It was a bittersweet triumph, but short-lived. *Everything is Everything,* their third record, would be a flop.

Eventually they reunited with Puba and made a record for Arista, but sadly they never really hit their commercial stride again. I did have the pleasure of making a Sadat X solo record *Wild Cowboys* at Loud Records in 1996. The guys at Loud really tried to make the record click. We made four videos, including one for the title track that was a full-scale Hollywood production. The whole record had a Black cowboy theme, which proved to be a bit much for the general public, and the album was met with a mixed response. Still, I had an amazing time with X. We went on the road with

Mobb Deep, and then later with Xzibit on a promo run labeled "The X Men Tour." We didn't make a lot of bread overall, but we did have an amazing time touring the world and getting into trouble.

The highlight of working with X was a trip to Tokyo where he performed. I brought along a bag of promo T-shirts and pimped them for a few thousand bucks, which I promptly spent on rare records. X was always just a great dude; love him like a brother, always will. On our return flight, we were so desperate to smoke some killer weed we flipped our tickets to take us to San Francisco, where we were greeted with an ounce of greenery by my Hieroglyphics compatriot, Casual. We proceeded to smoke our brains out for two days then flew back to New York.

Right around my second anniversary at Elektra, Karen Schoemer featured me in an article for *The New York Times* called "'Indie' Rock Settles into the Executive Suite." The article, which was on the June 6, 1993, cover of the Arts & Leisure section, was important to me for two reasons: First, I got to speak my mind about the state of the music business in the most important newspaper in the world, and second, it connected me with my long-lost younger sister.

Up until that point, my sister spent the first twenty-two years of her life living in Oakland. My dad had not seen her since she was an infant. He had battled drugs, got caught in the fallout of the sixties, and had his ups and downs. I found out later that in 1971, he threw craze at her mother, Ellen, and was told to stay away from them. Carla's soon-to-be stepdad, a tough blue-collar bus driver named John Murray, made sure of it.

Pops was apparently on drugs at the time of this demand, and he took the message to heart and was subsequently absent from her life for the next twenty years. This was a huge mistake on his part. When the article was published, Carla was a college student and an avid reader of *The New York Times*. She had read the paper and saw my picture and asked her mom if she thought I was her brother. Ellen confirmed that I probably was.

One afternoon, I got a message from my secretary who told me someone claiming to be my sister had called. I noticed the name—Carla. I looked at the message for a pretty long time. Could it be? I remember spending a summer in SF with her, my dad, and Ellen, much to my mother's disliking. Carla was an infant, and I was five years old. I had pictures to prove she existed but separating memory from the photos was hard. I hoped it was her.

Dialing that number may have produced the weirdest, scariest feeling I ever had. I pondered a zillion things while dialing that number. Did she look like me? Was she cool? Did she hate our dad? Was she a well-adjusted young adult, or was she some psycho full of anger and hate misdirected at her absentee father? Thankfully, after a few minutes of conversing with her, I realized she was cool, sweet, and someone I felt compelled to meet. I arranged a call between her, my dad, and myself, in hopes of us all meeting soon.

A few weeks later, at my urging, my dad and my sister met up in San Francisco. My dad conveyed she was a sweet young lady, who looked remarkably like me. I couldn't take it anymore—I hopped on a plane to San Francisco to meet Carla face-to-face. Coincidently, I was working on Del the Funky Homosapien's *No Need for Alarm,* so I was traveling to the Bay frequently. I used this as an excuse to fly to SF to meet my sister.

My dad and I were to meet my sister in the lobby of the Pan Pacific Hotel. I am not a patient person and waiting those few minutes pushed my limits. My stomach was in knots. I kept looking around the room for her, as I suspected I could recognize her. I had never met anyone who resembled me as much as she did. When I was a kid, my older sister Dylan would tease me, telling me I was adopted. It used to drive me crazy because I didn't look like anyone in my household.

After ten minutes, I noticed a thin, ivory-skinned, attractive young lady walk toward us. She looked so much like me it was spooky. As we hugged, I experienced a connection to her that I never had with anyone in my life. I cannot explain it to this day. I guess it was our physical similarities or maybe it was because I had a fresh slate with a family member. All I know is it was one of the most powerful connections I have ever made. Some would call this a God shot.

We spent the early evening talking and then eating. It was never uncomfortable for one minute, which seems odd in retrospect. She expressed she had a void her whole life wondering if she really had a brother, wondering where her biological father was, and why she had no connection to either of us.

My younger sister coming into my life was one of the greatest blessings I ever received and another confirmation for me that there is something out there bigger than all of us. Call it what you will, divine intervention or a higher calling—after twenty years, I reconnected with someone who has continually given me strength and a deeper sense of family.

In the coming years, my sister would move to New York, get married, and became the glue that held me and my father's relationship together. She settled our squabbles and guided us both through our relationship with a steady hand, which was no easy task. She also acted as a mediator of sorts between my father and his sister Susan, whom he had an uneven relationship with as well. My dad was a cantankerous man and I'm no peach. My sister Carla has been a Godsend.

While I was in SF meeting my sister, I had to figure out how to handle one of my most gifted artists. Ice Cube had basically given up working with Del and the project by this point. I bumped into him one afternoon at Hit Factory in New York. We walked around Times Square for a few and tried to figure out what to do with Del and how to get him to deliver somewhat of a commercial song or two. Cube explained he wasn't up to the task of babysitting Del anymore, which made me more concerned about Del's future.

But I decided to dig in deep with Del. He was too talented to give up on. I tried to rearrange the existing tunes, make them more structured in hopes of landing something on the radio. While in Oakland, working on this record, one of the scariest moments of my life occurred. While hanging out with the Hiero crew and the rapper Saafir (before his feud with Casual erupted), we went to a nightclub right off Market Street downtown near City Hall. The club was on top of a Burger King, oddly enough. We entered the club and hung for bit talking to some honeys and grooving. The vibes were a little off, so we decided to hit the parking lot to smoke some dank. Saafir joined us with a few of his Hobo Junction partners. This was shortly after he had done his cameo in *Menace II Society*, in which he was murdered in a carjacking. He and I were both rocking some jewels. He had on a big chain, and I was rocking a brand-new Breitling watch and some big diamond earrings. We were basically flashing—not a wise move.

As the cipher started and the blunts were being passed, a van pulled up at the mouth of the parking lot. Out came a short, slightly built Black male who quickly pulled down a ski mask and pulled out a massive chrome 9. The gleam caught my eye from thirty feet away as I heard him bark out, "This ain't no fucking joke," followed by, "Get the fuck on the ground, I'm jacking all of y'all."

Me, I'm not one to take orders, so I turned my back and was ghost. I heard several shots go off. I didn't look back, cause that shit's for dudes who get shot. I wish I could say it's the first time I had a gun pulled on me and ran. Side by side with Tajai from the Souls of Mischief, we set a world speed record that night, eventually dipping into an underground parking garage and posting up until we heard police sirens. At this point, I turned to Tajai and said, "I think they shot Saafir. That fool might be dead."

Tajai shot back, "Nah, man, I think Domino got shot."

My heart sank. Just then Saafir and his crew rolled up in their ride, shouted for us to get in.

Saafir said, "Domino got shot, we gotta go see what's up."

As we drove back to the scene of the crime and entered the parking lot, I saw Domino surrounded by police officers. We approached them. He looked like he saw a ghost. I asked him what had happened.

Domino said, "Dude ran right up on me the second after you and Tajai bolted and pointed the gun right at my face and squeezed off. Somehow he missed me."

I could not believe it. Domino had powder burns on the side of his face. He was visibly shaken. He had just seen his life flash before his eyes. I turned to him and said, "You're here because you're a good person. That was God watching out for you. You're a lucky motherfucker."

He just nodded.

I asked him if it was the first shot that missed him, since I had heard several.

Domino said, "Nah, he shot at you and Tajai first when y'all jetted."

"Shit," was all I could muster up. Good thing I never looked back. Who knows what would have happened.

I gave Domino a hug and left. The fact that he didn't get shot and that we all experienced this ordeal together made the Hiero crew and me brothers for life. Our friendship is still as strong as ever, and I consider those cats family. No trip to the Bay is complete without checking in with my brethren.

The record that would come out that November, *No Need for Alarm*, was a weird one for me. Del was rapping at a very high level. His spit game was formidable, yet I felt at the time that the songs weren't as good as they were on the first record. The record became one of the crown jewels for West Coast underground rap fans, but for me at the time, it was a bit disappointing only because I had big commercial hopes for Del. I anticipated a follow-up to *I Wish My Brother George Was Here* and I got something completely different.

I thought he could make hits. I wanted him to make a better first album, but instead he went left. The first glimpse of this path was the B-side release, "Eye Examination." I still appreciate the record he made and love him like a younger brother to this day. I also knew the record wouldn't expand his commercial fan base. I suspect Ice Cube knew it as well.

As for Del, he didn't give a shit what Cube thought at this point; his journey into his own world was underway and he made exactly what he wanted. When I first got the demos for the album, there were very few real choruses. There were long intricate verses over boom bap beats, and it was missing the funk influences from the first record, which had seemingly disappeared when Ice Cube stepped off. The lack of song structure was a big problem I had to figure out. I determined after many listens that if Del added some choruses and shortened down the verses here and there, the record was salvageable. I made detailed notes on almost every song. Ninety percent of my notes were arrangement based.

One of the tricky parts about A&R is navigating relationships with both artists and management and gauging how much influence you actually have. I hoped I would be able to convince Del to follow my makeshift blueprint in hopes of fixing the record. I discussed my idea with Domino, Del's manager, in great detail, and he told me he would discuss my thoughts with Del. A few weeks later, I went to the Bay and we went over my game plan. To my surprise, Del was pretty agreeable. He came to New York a few weeks later and fixed the record's arrangements at Battery Studios. Del and Domino trusted me, and I believe this trust made the record much better than it was in its demo form. The rhymes were there from the jump, the beats as well, but it was assembled in a unfriendly way, commercially speaking. Even in its new form, it was not an overtly commercial record. Still, I felt it was now much more palatable while retaining its raw feel.

I didn't realize at the time that it would become a benchmark for underground rappers globally. It also has one of my all-time favorite beats my crew and I have ever made on it, "Boo Boo Heads," a song Del still performs to this day. I recently revisited the record, and it's only gotten better with age, like a fine wine. I am proud of *No Need for Alarm*; it's one of those times when I got really involved from an A&R perspective and accomplished what I needed to get done. My relationship with Del and Domino allowed me to do my job on that one.

I couldn't have been happier for Del when his independently released album *Future Development* sold 100,000 copies, or when he linked up with the British alternative super group Gorillaz and rapped on the hit song "Clint Eastwood." Del and the Hiero crew are some of a handful of artists who have been able to validate themselves independently after they were left for dead by the major label music machine, starting their own label and controlling their own destinies. Hats off to them.

The Stimulated Dummies and I produced two songs on *No Need for Alarm*. This was the project that would accelerate my eventual fallout with Geeby. John and I worked hard on the two tunes we had on the record. Geeby was largely absent when we created them. When I went over the credits with Del for *Catch a Bad One*, he asked me, "How come I never worked with Geeby?"

I didn't have an answer.

As much as I knew the relationship was becoming toxic, I didn't forget how much Geeby meant to me as a friend and a mentor. He had brought me into the studio he had with John Gamble. He had taught me about breaks and showed me how to use a sampler. And, as I stated, he was the funniest and most charming person I have ever worked with, which made him a hit with artists. On a personal note, I loved Geeby and looked up to him. He was like the big brother I never had. He was and still is a huge influence on me to this day. Our working relationship had soured, though. I blame myself, in part. I was combative at times, and Geeby was nonconfrontational. He only participated in things on his terms and, me, I wanted everything on mine. I believe that was the crux of our problems. As much as I was dreading it, I knew we would eventually have to end our partnership. I approached the situation like I was approaching a divorce. Our fifteen-year friendship was in a lurch. We worked on two more records together: Kurious's *A Constipated Monkey*, which we did a few songs on, and Hard 2 Obtain's *Ism & Blues*, which we produced ninety percent of, though on both of these records the collaborative process was somewhat nonexistent. Each of us was crafting our own individual songs, if you will. Regardless, the Hard 2 Obtain record contained some of our crew's best production efforts to date. The record, however, wasn't a hit. This would be the last project we worked on collectively as a production trio. To be frank, by this point we were both over working with each other.

As I approached ending my working relationship with Geeby, I thought about how many relationships in my working career had ended seemingly sooner than they should have. This wasn't one of them. I reflected on 3rd Bass and Brand Nubian, two groups I saw break up that would have been better off if they stayed together. I thought about my career without Geeby. I pondered it long and hard and realized it would be for the best regardless of potentially damaging our friendship. I hoped we could get past it and remain friends. I mean, for a long period of time, we were like brothers as much as partners. I considered him family. He was the definition of cool to me. I struggled with doing what I knew was right for both of us. When we finished *Ism & Blues*, the time had come to end our partnership.

What happened next was a year-long ordeal in terms of studio time, and Gamble, being the engineer of the crew, was unfortunately stuck in the middle. He wanted to remain working with both of us, which seemed ideal at the time, but turned out to be fruitless in the long run. After a long period of this, Gamble decided he didn't want to be involved with either of us and retired for a while—one of his several retirements during our working relationship.

I remember saying to myself, "Can I still make music?"

I mean, although I loved music, I was not a musician. I plugged away on my MPC and SP1200, respectively, and didn't make one record for almost an entire year, though I managed to make a bunch of beats. Gamble had a similar experience. He too didn't make any records for more than a year and I guess was frustrated creatively. One day, he called me out of the blue. We hadn't spoken much that entire year. He asked me if I wanted to make music with him again. I said I did. He explained that he missed being creative, that he wished it would have worked splitting time between us. He told me he "never doubted my focus, just my attitude." I remember being adamant that if we worked together again, he would only receive writer's credit on things if the basis of the idea was brought to the table by him. He agreed, and to this day I am not sure if my decision was absolutely fair, but after a period of un-productivity, I was not going to give anyone anything I didn't think they earned.

Suffice it to say, me and Gamble did resume our working relationship. Up to that point, I had never been as close with him as I was with Geeby. Our relationship was more of a working one that would evolve into an important and intense friendship. Geeby and me had a bond based on each other's overall sensibilities. We hung out a lot outside of work whereas Gamble and I rarely did. The worst thing about the whole ordeal was that Geeby and I never did resume our friendship completely. For me, the end of our working relationship was as painful as any breakup I have ever had with a woman. It was agonizing, in all honesty, and in the wake of it, I made a huge mistake and discredited him publicly a few times.

Things were always murky when it came to credits, and at times, my ego led me to undervalue his contributions. My ego has never been my friend, and my catering to it hurt him. I alienated him, and for close to a decade we simply didn't speak.

In 2016, I reached out to him. He was extremely gracious and accepted my amends with some kind words for me as well as some harsh truths. Still, our friendship never returned to its prior incarnation as I had hoped it would. Four months before he passed, I had heard from mutual friends he was having health problems and was urged to contact him. We traded texts a few times, but he never let me know the gravity of his situation. Like always, he played it close to the vest to the end. Our last conversation is best left between me, God, and Geeby, who left the Earth on December 21, 2019, after succumbing to ALS.

If there is one big lesson in this, it is to proceed with grace and humility. I lost close to a decade of laughs and adventures with my big homie. He was a great man—selfless, funny, loving, and as solid as they come. He was, and will always be, my moral better. I regret losing that time. Losing someone and having that amount of regret has never happened to me before. I was at peace with my parents when they passed. But while I was at peace with Geeby, it was on his terms, and he deserved that. I wanted a deeper connection, to revisit the friendship of our youth. That wasn't meant to be, and I have to accept that.

I truly loved my friend Najeeb "Geeby" Dajani. I will always treasure the times we had running the streets, digging for records, making music, playing ball, and most of all, snapping on each other. We spent countless hours together enjoying each other's company while pursuing our creative dreams with no endgame in sight other than good vibes. The time I spent with him and John Gamble in our cramped basement studio are some of the most hilarious, enjoyable, and important times of my entire adult life. I, and many others, miss his spirit immensely.

As the fourth quarter of the year wound down, I felt like I was in somewhat of a career slump for maybe the first time. I would over the course of my career suffer a bunch of these. What I didn't know was this slump was due to timing as much as anything. I simply had most of my groups working on new projects and didn't have a lot of music being released. It was out of my control, more or less—something I have never been good at dealing with.

Simply put, I am a control freak.

Unfortunately, 1994 was shaping up to be a bad year for Bob Krasnow. He had caught the ire of corporate and his getting fired was an emotional moment for me. When he got the axe, I got the personal call to his office where he told me not to trust X, Y, and Z, and to keep my head up. He knew I was upset and even though he was the one who had been fired, he still did his best to comfort me. "You're talented, Dante," he said. "You're going to be fine."

I remember holding back tears that day.

I genuinely loved Krasnow, and to this day, I contend he was the best boss I ever had. He believed in me and my vision as purely as one in his position could. He gave me freedom, respect, and direction when I needed it. He was not only my boss but also my mentor and protector.

Sadly, I only saw him a few more times before he passed. One of my fondest moments with him was when we flew to LA on the Warners' jet to see James Brown after he was released from prison. We smoked a joint at 20,000 feet, which was the first and only time for me, and I have to admit, it was a thrilling high. The show itself was less than spectacular, but it was a complete spectacle—Bobby Brown and MC Hammer performed with the Godfather of Soul, and I am still baffled at the mere thought of that show.

Kras's demise closed a chapter in my life. I had to prepare now for Ms. Sylvia Rhone, and I doubted very much that I was going to smoke pot on the Warners' jet with her. I was just hoping she would let me stay and work with my artists. I'd heard she was excited I was working with Ol' Dirty Bastard, whom I had signed under Krasnow.

I took that as a good sign, because so was I.

SD50 PLAYLIST

Grand Puba—"Lickshot"

Grand Puba—"360 (What Goes Around) [SD50 Remix]"

The Sons of Champlin—"You Can Fly"

Grand Puba—"Honey Don't Front"

Del the Funky Homosapien—"Hoodz Come in Dozens [SD50 Remix]"

Junior Parker—"Taxman"

Del the Funky Homosapien—"Boo Boo Heads"

Hard 2 Obtain—"L.I. Groove"

Melvin Sparks—"If You Want My Love"

Hard 2 Obtain—"Street Dwellers"

Alphonse Mouzon—"Happiness is Loving You"

3rd Bass—"Pop Goes the Weasel"

3rd Bass—"Kick Em in the Grill"

Kurious—"Leave Ya' With This"

14

BROOKLYN ZOO

From 1990 to 1999, *The Stretch Armstrong and Bobbito Show* aired on Columbia University's community radio station WKCR, a listener supported station, meaning it was commercial-free. It was hosted by a DJ named Adrian Bartos, a.k.a. Stretch Armstrong, and my boy, Bobbito Garcia. The show was an organic, free-form platform for 1990s rappers, which ran the gamut talent-wise from Biggie Smalls to Hieroglyphics, and everyone imaginable in between. Future superstars Jay-Z, Big Pun, and Nasty Nas all made their way to "89 Tech Nine," as the show was known.

The show was a major outlet for my artists, as well as a great place to spot emerging talent—not to mention my favorite place to hang late night on a Thursday eve. They came on the air at 1:00 p.m. and rocked until five in the morn. I rarely missed a show. The amazing thing is that, for all the history that came through its doors, KCR was a dumpy little studio with a broadcast board on the way out. There were a few bummy couches and a low ceiling and some charming florescent lights to add to the character. To enter the studio, you walked up several flights of stairs and passed through a labyrinth-like record library that I boosted a few joints from over the years. The whole place had a funky ambience to it. It was not lush in any sense of the word. It was, however, historic, and it had vibes. Heavy vibes. The show was where you needed to be if you were an MC and serious about your spit game in the early nineties. There were no other proving grounds like it.

I was home listening one spring night in 1993 when I heard Bobbito say that one of that evening's guests was going to be Ol' Dirty Bastard. Being a Wu-Tang fan already and thinking that ODB was one of the crew's potential breakout stars, I listened intently. I was aware that he was available for a solo deal, since Steve Rifkind, the president of Loud Records, had apparently agreed to a deal with the Wu that allowed all of its individual members to pursue solo careers. My friend Matty C, a future A&R legend (who at the time worked at *The Source* magazine and would later work at Loud Records) had let me in on the info. I was intrigued with the idea of signing one of the crew's breakout stars.

Over the air, I could hear that the tiny studio was crammed with Dirty, RZA, and a few other members of the mighty Wu-Tang Clan. The energy was pure hip-hop, reminiscent of a basement cipher, as often was the case on the show. The Wu had a beyond healthy buzz. They also cultivated a real sense of danger that made them all the more exciting. The music was lo-fi and off-kilter. To me it felt very punk rock, and this is why I believe they eventually connected deeply with white alt rock audiences.

I listened closely as I heard Dirty rock over the "Protect Ya Neck" beat for an ungodly number of bars. It was a spectacular performance. I can't believe there wasn't a herd of A&R cats headed up there to try to sign him. I realized later on that many of the lyrics he kicked that night would end up on various Wu and Dirty solo cuts, including a scorching verse from "Shimmy Shimmy Ya" and some of "Brooklyn Zoo," unbeknownst to me at the time.

His "freestyle" was amazing, as was "Protect Ya Neck," a song that rewrote all the rules of what a hit song should be. The song contains no chorus to speak of—just a posse cut of unknown rappers, who happened to be some of the best in the game, spitting a verse each. Couple that with the Kung Fu–friendly name and sound effects, and it was something unique, creative, and visionary. I was jumping out of my skin, so I called the station and asked if I could come through. Luckily, I had carte blanche to pop in anytime.

Fifteen minutes later, I entered the studio to see Dirty, RZA, and a few other Wu-Tang members. The Wu posse were dressed in the soon to be infamous Wu Army fatigue-style gear. They were, for the most part, sans jewelry, which I found interesting since that was the prevalent style in hip-hop at the time. They sounded and looked unique. I was impressed.

I quickly introduced myself to RZA.

"What up, I'm Dante Ross, I been digging what you're doing for a second now. What's going on, G?"

"Peace," he said. "I know who you are."

I was a little surprised and somewhat happy to be honest.

"I met you with the God Melquan, when I was making that other shit," RZA said.

Melquan was someone I knew from the Latin Quarters days. It was the first time I connected that RZA, the abbot of the Wu, was formerly Rakeem, who had released an ode to the ladies on Tommy Boy titled, awkwardly enough, "We Love You Rakeem." Let's just say some reinvention had happened. Or better yet, a de-evolution of sorts had occurred. RZA was no longer trying to fit in a box. Rather, he was giving the world an honest, raw, and uncut vision of who he really was.

We both chuckled, and the ice had been broken. RZA is a funny cat, very charming, and extremely sharp. He had a wise calm about him and a disarming sense of humor. He oozed charisma. I liked the guy immediately. I started to hit him up about signing Dirty and Meth as a duo. I thought they would be the new Run-DMC or some crazy shit. Where I got the balls to pitch this idea, I'll never know. RZA, however, already had a game plan firmly in place and slowed me down—politely, I might add.

"Yo, let's get up tomorrow at your office and build, son," he said.

He missed the meeting the next day but build we would. He did come see me that following week, actually showing up with several Wu members, including Dirty, Mookie, and Inspectah Deck, but not Meth. This was concerning for me, as I hadn't given up on my master plan to sign Meth and Dirty. I explained my idea to RZA again, but in a matter of seconds he shot me down.

"Your thought's ill, but that's not the science," he said. "Meth is going to be with Russell and them at Def Jam." He explained to me the Wu-Tang Clan was going to sign to Loud, which I thought was already done. Apparently it wasn't, though RZA told me he had committed verbally to Steve Rifkind, hence why I never had a shot at signing the Wu-Tang Clan, though technically I did sign ODB before the Wu-Tang Clan officially closed their deal.

RZA noted that my roster of acts was "dusted," the street slang for forward thinking, dysfunctional, creative, and well…dusted. Dirty being a part of my team made perfect sense since I had the "Gods" on my roster. Several of my acts, including Brand Nubian and Busta Rhymes, were also Five Percenters, just like RZA and ODB. I was open to the idea because I knew I was going to get at least one of the brightest stars in the Wu-Tang Clan. That day, RZA told me that Dirty would be the first gold rap record on Elektra. This was a testament to his confidence. Little did I know how important Raekwon and Ghostface would be down the line, or I would have tried to sign them as well.

I have to say, if I hadn't run up to the station that day, I don't think I would have gotten Dirty. The rap game has always been all about relationships, and the fact that I'd always supported my brothers Stretch and Bobbito to the fullest opened the door to my relationship with Dirty and blessed me with hundreds of memories with the man. During our working relationship, Dirty and I developed an unusually close friendship. It would be an understatement to say it was a wild ride.

While I was signing ODB, I was juggling Grand Puba and Brand Nubian's forthcoming projects. The Nubians were self-sufficient on most levels, so I didn't need to babysit them. They showed up at the studio and had a game plan. Unfortunately, the musical direction was off base for them. They were strong-willed cats, and I couldn't really influence them. They marched to their own drum. I didn't think a confrontational approach would help matters. How would I steer them away from a West Coast–centric sound and tell them they were heading down the wrong musical path after the success of *In God We Trust*?

Puba, on the other hand, was impossible. When it came time to make his second solo record, *2000*, he was in a downward spiral. He was perpetually trying to hustle me. He was lazy in the studio and, worst of all, the songs weren't that good. I felt he was burned out and only in it for the money, not the art of rapping anymore, which was a real shame. There was a moment when he was in everyone's top ten list. He influenced most of the top MCs at one point in his career. It was impossible to get him to act responsible while making *2000*. He was drinking heavily, and I would often track him down by calling his favorite watering hole, Caliente Cab Co in the Village, in hopes of finding him.

He missed session after session. It was infuriating, and my new boss, Sylvia Rhone, was not having it. I was in the hot seat. She was intrigued by Busta going solo. That she was enamored with Chris Lighty, Busta's manager, helped my cause. However, she was not, in any sense of the word, enamored with me, and the chatter was starting. I did have the crown jewel in my back pocket and that was one Russell Jones, better known as Ol' Dirty Bastard. Make no mistake, before the drugs got my man, ODB was without a doubt one of the most creative artists I've ever worked with.

His vision for his first record cover was an example of this.

"D, I got thoughts, crazy thoughts for the record cover," he said in his Dirt McGirt speak.

I listened intently as he explained.

"My welfare card should be the cover, son."

I thought for a second and remembered that UB40 had done the same a good ten years plus prior on a record called *Signing Off*. There was a precedent for it, so I figured maybe we could do it, too. I marched Dirty upstairs to the art department and found my groovy coworker, Ali Truch.

"Can I use the color copy machine for a few?" I asked her. This was before the days when scanners were commonplace in offices.

"What are you working on?" she asked.

Dirty quickly blurted out his entire record cover plot. Ali, being a rap enthusiast, laughed and helped us blow up his welfare card using her color

Xerox machine. The image itself was super-pixilated, but the idea clearly came across in full. She then suggested we turn the New York State logos into Wu-Tang "W"s, which we added later. She thought the record cover would fly, as did I. She asked to borrow his card for a few hours, and she quickly mocked up a little something for us. When she came down to my office with the prototype, we were immediately blown away. She then offered to show it to the record company higher ups, which she did.

A few days later, we got the seal of approval to roll with Dirty's welfare card record cover concept. This was a prime example of Dirty's focused vision. He was a performer who had one of the most astute understandings of his own career path I'd ever witnessed. Another example of his genius was the photo shoot for *Return to the 36 Chambers*. When it came time to shoot the photos for the record, we basically had no idea what we were going to do outside of capturing an image for the mock welfare card. I hired Danny Clinch, an old pro and all-around great guy, who had also shot record covers for the likes of both Pete Rock and Nas. Danny shot Dirty in the studio for an hour or so capturing the needed image. He had the location van outside ready to go. We knew we would need shots for the LP package, but we didn't really have a concept in mind. Danny wisely asked Dirty if he had any thoughts. Dirty took that as a signal to go for it creatively and suggested we roll to his old stomping grounds in Bed Stuy, Brooklyn, and specifically, the house of his cousin, 60 Second Assassin.

"His rest looks fucked up," Dirty said.

After Dirty told his cousin we were en route, we headed out to Bed Stuy. Today it looks like a hipster carnival, but back then it was one of the most dangerous hoods in all of Brooklyn. Upon arrival, the location driver was so shook that he threatened to leave. Now, you have to understand the lay of the land. We were in the cut—on a block that housed two chop shops, a weed spot, and God knows what else. Add a crack spot around the corner, and you get the picture. We were in the heart of the Stuy. Shit was no joke, and we were a crew of white people led by ODB. It was a pretty comical, yet a legitimately treacherous scene. ODB quickly solved the problem by getting two of his neighborhood cohorts to guard the van and make the driver feel a bit safer.

We proceeded to 60 Second Assassin's humble abode on the fifth floor of a godforsaken tenement. I had grown up around shit like this, so I was used to it. I suspected Danny was not, but he didn't skip a beat when it came time to get busy. He was a trooper. When we entered the apartment, Dirty went into art director mode.

"This crib ain't fucked up enough," he said.

He sent Danny's assistant to the store to get ten blunts, some 40s, and some hood snacks. When she returned, Dirty proceeded to guzzle down a 40, empty the blunt guts onto the floor, and open the snacks and carefully arrange them around the pad. Next, he stacked two broken radios on top of each other and took off his shirt.

"Let's do this," he said.

Danny snapped off a few test shots then dove in headfirst, creating one of the most definitive rap music images of all time. That same day, after the shoot, Dirty walked me to the weed spot down the block. When we walked in, the hustlers who ran the spot looked at me suspiciously.

"He's not a cop," Dirty said. "It's all good. Sell him a few bags."

And so they did, chuckling at Dirty's antics the whole time. I copped two bags of Brooklyn Brown, a.k.a. dirt weed, and proceeded to smoke a blunt in the location van. Dirty, Danny, and his assistant joined in. It was the sweet smell of victory, if you will.

"And they thought you was a DT (detective)," Dirty said, laughing.

That was typical Dirty—always into something, talking trash, and, usually, making people laugh with some type of off-the-wall behavior. A week or so later, as we looked over the photos from that day, Danny Clinch, Elektra's art director, Ali, Dirty, and I marveled at the contact sheets from the session. We just knew we had something special, the perfect visual equivalent of the record. That was totally due to our trust in Dirty's vision and unique thought process.

Dirty was, after all, in his own way, brilliant.

Throughout my entire life as an A&R man and record producer, rappers have always been trying to borrow money from me. One thing, though, when a rapper asks for a loan, he isn't really borrowing money, he is simply jerking you. I got got a few times by the likes of Grand Puba and Charlie Brown, and I'd learned the hard way: *Do not lend an artist money.* You will not get it back. In fact, only two rappers have ever paid me back: Everlast (my best friend, no less), and of all people, ODB.

Of course, Dirty's motives for paying me back weren't quite as pure as Everlast's had been.

On a Sunday afternoon, I was at my pad in Greenwich Village watching the NBA finals with a few of my old graffiti writing crew. There was Wolf, my big homie Team, and my ace Paul Moore, a Black kid from BK who Dirty knew, as he'd been in LA with me when ODB threw craze on a West Coast promo tour a few months earlier. Mid-game, Dirty hit me up by phone. "Yo, D, I got that hundred dollars I owe you," he said. "I'm a swing by and give you that."

I told my boys Dirty was going to stop by, and they were understandably excited by the prospect. Sometime around the end of the third quarter, Dirty rang my bell. As soon as I answered, he charged up my stairs. Upon seeing my boys on the couch, Dirty stopped short.

"That's the most white boys I ever seen you with, n*****," he said, using the word he called me constantly. I'm not a fan of the word, but coming from Dirty, I felt oddly honored.

I pointed out Paul.

"Yeah, that's what I mean. I never seen you with so many white boys before," Dirt cracked.

My friends all started laughing their asses off, Paul included.

Dirty pulled out five crisp twenty-dollar bills and asked me where the bathroom was. I pointed toward the shitter. He charged toward the bathroom with a wide grin on his face. I knew I was in for it, and so did my boys, who started with the snaps instantly.

Dirty shut himself up in the bathroom, and several minutes passed.

"Man, I think he's melting porcelain in there," Team said.

"D, you're gonna have to get a new throne when he's done," Wolf chimed in.

We all laughed at this. A few minutes passed, and Dirty still hadn't emerged.

"We need to get some crime scene tape around the door, 'cause that shit's definitely a felony," my man Paul said.

Wolf took some gaffers tape I had laying on my coffee table and put it across the door. Dirty heard us laughing and started cracking wise while on the toilet.

"Y'all know I saved this one up for ya, right?" he said through the door.

This just made us all start cracking up even more.

"I can smell it through the door," I said.

Though not true, it seemed possible.

"The air freshener's under the sink," I yelled to no avail.

Several more moments passed. Dirty finally opened the door. Upon seeing the mock crime scene, complete with tape, he started rolling.

"Y'all some funny motherfuckers," he said with a huge ODB smile.

By this point, he had us all doubled over. He then proceeded to spray about half a can of air freshener all over the bathroom, living room, and kitchen, grinning the whole time. Even so, the stench wafting out of the bathroom was putrid.

"That's it, my bathroom's officially out of service," I declared, causing more laughter, and prompting Wolf to make a "Condemned by the ODB" sign for my bathroom door later that day.

Dirty said his goodbyes and gave me a super warm hug before he left. His appearance at my apartment that day has become legendary amongst that group of friends, and this is the Dirty I always keep close to my heart.

That day, not only had my friends touched greatness, but they had smelled it as well.

Amid the shenanigans with Dirty, I was having a rough time at Elektra. I had a new boss and had caught a bad one with the second Pete and CL album, *The Main Ingredient*, though I still believe that record is amazing.

There was no "They Reminisce Over You" on it, and Sylvia was not a big fan of the record. She didn't hear a hit, and she might have been right.

As for Brand Nubian, let's say it got intricate. The record was not great. It was way too influenced by West Coast rap, a.k.a. G-Funk. It was an awkward record. This was a New York landmark group and they were trying to get West Coast paper from the sounds of it. It was a reach. Sylvia was skeptical of the project, and she told me as much. They did, however, have a banging single, "Word is Bond," which used a great Average White Band sample of "I'm the One," which sounded in line with the group's music legacy. It had a shot. I was nervous, and I walked it into Hot 97 very early without Sylvia Rhone's blessings. I was pretty sure she was going to tank the record; she told me point blank that it wasn't up to par, which is the reason why I backdoored it before it could get squashed.

I had Flex premier the record. He ran with it, and it reacted. It was in rotation at Hot 97, but the Sylvia Rhone–led Elektra promo staff didn't prioritize it. The Pete Rock & CL Smooth record was released at virtually the same time. They kind of canceled each other out. Instead of "Word is Bond" winning, both Pete Rock and CL's "I Got a Love" and "Word is Bond" took a beating. Sylvia told me I was undermining her game plan and had no business taking records directly to Hot 97. She may have been right. All I know is she handed me my ass and I didn't dig it one bit. Add the fact that Puba was going way over budget and the heat I was feeling wasn't going anywhere. Chris Lighty and Lyor Cohen knew this and started whispering in my ear.

I should have never listened and rode it out. Sylvia was tough but fair. No, she didn't really care for me, but she was a good leader and I could have navigated the playing field. She respected my ears. Even if she didn't like me personally, she did respect me. I chose my immediate battles wisely for the time being and let it go, knowing I had little control over what was coming next.

While on a promo tour in San Francisco with Pete Rock & CL Smooth and Brand Nubian, I got a call from her. Thirty people had been laid off. I was told I was still good and to keep my head up. This was daunting news considering I was on a promo tour and some of the promo team had been fired. Still, I had my own game plan, and that was to finish Grand Puba's forthcoming fiasco, tend to Busta's impending solo launch, and get Dirty to the finish line, which was not an easy task.

I clearly recall being at the Gavin Convention in New Orleans early in '95, previewing the "Brooklyn Zoo" video during our label presentation. It blew people's minds; we knew we had one and we celebrated all week long. One of the highlights was watching ODB and Busta kick rhymes in the convention center together, sealing their friendship and foretelling the future, as later on down the road Dirty hopped on the "Woo Ha" remix. It was amazing to see two of my shining stars put on an MCing clinic. Hard to say who bested whom—they weren't really battling like that. I'm not sure what was written and what wasn't, but for me to be in that moment and to witness these two going at, it was what hip-hop is and will always truly be about. Bars, styles, flows, and skills—these two had it in abundance. Add overwhelming charisma to the equation and it's no wonder these two are considered legends to this day. The fact that my ears were part of the connecting thread made me proud, then and now. Little did I know this impromptu cipher would be the thing that myths are made of. It's on YouTube for those of you who have never seen it.

Late in the spring of 1995, I had just left Elektra and was in the process of starting my own label to be distributed by Def Jam. My office at Def Jam was, conveniently, right next door to my friend Chris Lighty. While shooting the shit one afternoon, he mentioned trying to get ODB to guest on an LL Cool J song, asking me if I could make it happen. At the time, Chris was the head of A&R at Def Jam, and LL was in the process of yet another reinvention after the mixed response to his last album, *14 Shots to the Dome*. Chris and I had broken a lot of bread over the years, dating back to my early days in the game when he was better known as "Baby Chris" of the Violators. Chris and his crew were a wild bunch of street cats from the Bronx known for being able to handle their biz. He'd since become a huge force in the rap game. The irony of it all was that Chris managed Busta and Brand Nubian. He also had a close relationship with Sylvia Rhone and was privy to the tension between us. Needless to say, there was a lot of intrigue going on behind the scenes in our working relationship. That aside, Chris was above and beyond a real friend, a rarity in this business.

I put Chris directly in touch with Dirty, who was pistol-hot and riding the wave of his first solo record's immediate success. Everything seemed fine, that is until Dirty showed up at Chung King Studios wasted with a deranged sidekick, Crazy Sam, a wild hoodlum of a man who'd somehow ended up on a local TV show called *Video Music Box* and had made himself into a celebrity of sorts. Sam was a total nut bag, and you never knew what might jump off when he was in the mix. He and Dirty together were a volatile combo. On top of that, Sam and Chris had some kind of long-simmering beef, and the bad vibes quickly engulfed the room.

LL was not at the session, a fact that Dirty did not fail to notice.

"Fuck LL Cool J, n**** ain't even here to rock with a n****," Dirty said. "He ain't a real mutherfucker. He doesn't even wanna chill with Dirt McGirt, do he? He just wants the God's vibes, but he can't come and fuck with the God?"

Needless to say, Chris was not thrilled.

Dirty was doing a bunch of angel dust around this time, so I think he was probably on that, but it could have easily been booze or something worse. Things escalated to the point where Chris was ready to get into it with Dirty and Crazy Sam. When Sam made the mistake of acting like he had a biscuit on him, Chris let it be known he was actually packing. It was a tough spot for me. I had respect and love for Chris and Dirty as well, even if Dirty was being a complete asshole. At this point, I literally put my ass on the line and got between them.

Sam motioned for something, and Chris broke it down for him. "You pull anything out, it'd better be a sandwich, cause you gonna eat it, my man," he said.

This slowed Sam down a notch. I think he realized he was very close to getting shot. I certainly knew it.

Dirty, who had been paid several thousand dollars, made it known he wasn't giving any money back to anyone, which only increased tensions. The look on Chris's face said it all. To this day, I am still surprised nobody got shot. Chris and his people were serious cats, and I honestly think if I hadn't been there, violence would have erupted. I told Sam in no uncertain terms to chill and ushered Chris out of the studio and over to the elevator.

"I'll get Dirty out of the studio, and I swear the studio time won't get charged to LL," I said, even though it later was. Shit happens.

Chris let it be known he was going to see Crazy Sam one day.

"You mutherfuckers best never come to the Tunnel," he said. At the time, Sunday night at the Tunnel was the most important night in hip-hop nightlife, and Chris ran it.

When Chris finally left the building, I breathed a deep sigh of relief, only to turn around and see Dirty grab an LL plaque off the wall.

"LL, fuck a LL, I'll piss on a LL," he said to nobody in particular. "N*****
won't even hang out with Dirty but wants to do songs with Dirty. Fuck that mutherfucker."

Dirty then whipped out his dick and without hesitation preceded to piss on the plaque. I scolded him midstream, but he just laughed it off in true ODB fashion. I hit the office, spoke to the terrified studio manager—who at this point was in tears—and ended the session. A few minutes later, I somehow got Dirty and Crazy Sam out of there.

One evening, I accompanied Dirty, his brother 12 O'clock, his cousin 60 Second Assassin, and my coworker Mike Jones for a meal before Dirty was scheduled to perform at the Palladium after cohosting the countdown on Hot 97 with Funkmaster Flex. We decided to eat at the Coffee Shop, a trendy eatery off Union Square that was close to the venue. As we approached the restaurant, we were stopped at the door by security who asked us for ID. I found this weird. Then again, I was in the company of some pretty rugged looking characters. The white "doorman" flanked by his two Black security guards was giving us a hard time. Ironically, we had reservations that had been made by my then-girlfriend, who also worked there.

As things got tense, multiple TVs behind the doorman started playing the "C.R.E.A.M" music video. Dirty, who could not find his ID, pointed and said, "There's my fucking ID."

The security did a double take just as Dirty appeared on the screen, and he started laughing. The doorman still held his ground, that is until Dirt Dog pulled out his just-released album, cover and all. The security guards who had been standing outside in the bitter cold when we pulled up started cracking up. One of them asked for an autograph, and Dirty obliged.

The doorman was baffled by what was going on, but still he changed his tune realizing he was being a dick to someone potentially famous. He opened the inside door for us, but not before Dirty could have a word with the security guards. Dirty looked the two security cats dead in the grill and shot them the God's honest truth and asked 'em "You ever wonder why you're outside in the cold when there's devils inside all warm and shit?"

That day was sort of a microcosm of my whole time working with Dirty. I never knew what was coming next, and whatever was coming was usually crazy, but our interactions were also always filled with laughter and what I can only call some perverse form of innocence that Dirty possessed, if that makes any sense.

As great as it all was in hindsight, there was as much crazy danger as there was just plain crazy behavior. On the crazy side, there was the time in the spring of 1995 when Dirty received public fellatio in front of several hundred people at the How Can I Be Down? Music Conference in Miami. Prior to ruining the Def Jam showcase, he found a young white groupie chick and proceeded to have her give him a very public blowjob.

"You wanna see me get it Elektra style?" he asked.

This cracked me up and disgusted me at the same time. Why he decided to refer to this public sex act as "Elektra style" only Dirty knows. Not yet having created the maximum amount of drama, Dirty ended his evening by bum-rushing the dancehall star and newly signed Def Jam artist Capleton's show and ruining his performance. A melee erupted onstage between several of Dirty's people and Capleton's yardman posse. Somehow, Dirty emerged unscathed. That wouldn't always be the case.

Of course, it wouldn't be the last time he bum-rushed the stage either. Right around the time "Brooklyn Zoo" dropped and was really gathering steam, he did it to the Lost Boyz at the Palladium in New York City. After they performed their debut hit "Lifestyles of the Rich and Shameless," he strolled out onto the stage right in the middle of their set and intimidated the sound man into putting on his DAT tape, so he could drop the brand new "Brooklyn Zoo," plus his then as-yet-unreleased anthem, "Shimmy Shimmy Ya." He turned and addressed the thousand-plus people in the crowd, yelling at them. "Make some motherfucking noise if you love the Wu," he shouted.

They did as instructed.

"Do you want me to give it to you raw?" he called out. "Are you fucking with that Brooklyn Zoo?"

The crowd was going nuts, and the tension between Dirty and the Lost Boyz, whose show he was ruining, was growing by the second. Dirty did both "Brooklyn Zoo" and "Shimmy Shimmy Ya" and absolutely destroyed it. The crowd erupted, furthering the Lost Boyz' anger.

Sure enough, after Dirty was finished, while still on stage, the Lost Boyz surrounded us. But just as soon as they did, Dirty's gang of ten plus Brooklyn Zoo cats stepped up, creating a Mexican standoff of sorts that looked like it might end in mass mayhem. If it had jumped off, I'm sure someone would have gotten shot—most likely me. Thankfully, lead Lost Boy, Mr. Cheeks, calmed down his boys, while I, with the help of 60 Second Assassin, cooled out the Brooklyn Zoo. It didn't go down, but I was scared shitless nonetheless. I also feared that the next time I ran into the Lost Boyz, I was going to get a beating. If the evening's master of ceremonies, Big Kap, hadn't been on stage to mediate, I am positive something ugly would have happened. After the performance, Dirty and his crew were quickly escorted out of the venue for obvious reasons.

Rest in peace, Big Kap. You saved my ass that night.

My gig at the label was strained; Puba was massively over budget and blowing off sessions like he was Sly Stone. Sylvia had dug into him in a face-to-face meeting I was at. It was getting ugly. Busta was just getting underway on his solo stuff. Impending success looked good and Sylvia was supportive of him, if not undermining to me in lieu of her support. Sylvia would dote on Chris like he was a visiting family member then speak to me like I was a schmuck in front of him. It was uncomfortable.

I remember Sylvia doing a little roster review with me around this time. The subject of Del came up and she said she was on the fence about him. She suggested he work with Battle Cat or Jermaine Dupri on his next record—that was, if we were even going to keep him on the label. I almost choked. I could just see selling this to Del. Though I respected these two producers, I just didn't see them being the right fit for Del. I was thinking more along the lines of Q-Tip, or possibly Prince Paul. That was what a typical interaction between us was like, though. We just looked at things differently. We rarely agreed. I was more of a purist, and she was someone who had an outsider's knowledge yet understood commerciality, which was never my strong suit. Can't say who was right and who was wrong, just that there was a big disconnection between us. Still, I forged on.

Things got so crazy with ODB that it almost seemed normal. For instance, over the course of just one month: He was arrested and hospitalized for jumping out of a second-story window in Queens after being attacked by a dog in a stranger's house he had randomly invaded. I suspected substances were the reason he'd run into a neighbor's house, as substances were usually involved with Dirty. He also got shot on a corner in Bed Stuy for refusing to run his jewels. I remember finding it really odd that when he got shot, he didn't want to let anyone know where he was, not even his cousin, Buddha Monk, who was his right-hand man. After this incident, the *New York Post* somehow tracked me down to ask me questions about Dirty, but I didn't tell them shit.

The media continuously tried to portray him as the poster child for what was wrong with hip-hop. They dismissed him as some kind of ghetto clown, and it pissed me off because there was more to him than that. I was there the time he called his mom to play "Sweet Sugar Pie" over the phone for her.

"Mama, I made that song for you," he said, erupting into tears.

I couldn't tell what she said on the other end of the call, but whatever it was, it made him break down even harder.

"I'm gonna make you proud, mama," he said.

It was an awkward sight, seeing the craziest cat I've ever worked with getting real with his mom. But Dirty was a multifaceted person and much deeper than most thought.

When he unwisely trusted the renowned journalist Touré, it led to the now-infamous welfare check-cashing fiasco on MTV. Dirty called me sobbing. He'd agreed to allow MTV to film him arriving in a limo to cash his welfare check for the segment. How the publicists at Elektra allowed him to do such a thing is beyond me, but I wasn't informed of it at the time. If I had been, it never would have gone down.

As it was, an intoxicated ODB allowed MTV to follow him as he got out of a limo, cashed his welfare check, and took a piss on the Brooklyn promenade, all while his family waited on him in the ride. Maybe he should have known better. I always felt he got set up to look like an idiot in front of the whole world, but who knows. It almost cost him his kids, as they came close to being made wards of the state behind that bullshit. How he was allowed to be involved in that form of buffoonery still bothers me to this day.

I will say this, no matter how much this segment portrayed him as a freeloading goof, it also lent to his legend. I can't blame Touré for this entirely, as we have spoken on this and I believe he actually loved Dirty as an artist. I believe if Dirty had an involved manager, this shit never would have gone down, though. He simply wasn't protected, and journalists always want a juicy story. Today we call it click bait. The repercussions are seemingly never their concern.

While this incident propelled his legend, I also feel it lent to the thought that he was a buffoon—an image that a segment of white America has held on to. I find it offensive, and I think it speaks to a bigger, thinly veiled notion of racism. It is easier for white America to celebrate a Black man as a buffoon rather than an important artist. It's that ironic hipster nonsense that made white people celebrate Gucci Mane's public dysfunction as well as Flavor Flav, DMX, and countless other rappers. I personally find that kind of bullshit offensive. Dirty was never a clown to me; he was a great artist, and that is how I choose to remember my friend.

I was in LA working at the time the MTV segment aired, and I remember Dirty calling me about the incident. I could hear the pain in his voice as he expressed how much he felt like he'd been played. He was worried he was going to lose his "seeds" to the state and said that felt he had been set up by "devils." He was scared that his bullshit was going to catch up with him. It was one of the only times I heard remorse in his voice. I felt for the man. He loved his kids above and beyond everything, and he realized MTV made him out to be a drunken fool.

"I ain't a motherfuckin joke," he said.

To me, ODB was never a joke, just an eccentric, misguided bug-out who'd been raised in group homes, on the street, and in juvie halls. He wasn't built for the success the world gave him. He was a wild cat, but not the buffoon he's often made out to be. Yes, I saw him attempt to ruin the Grammy Awards with a drunk diatribe when the Wu didn't win the Best Rap Grammy, stating, "Wu-Tang's for the children."

But he was much more than that guy.

And fuck it, that guy was awesome, too.

Over the years, I also had the pleasure of helping him get the Mariah Carey "Fantasy" remix gig after a phone call from Steve Rifkind. I saw him conceive most of his own videos, rap to every chick he ever came across, love his kids and then-wife, Icelene, and routinely eat a box of a dozen Entenmann's chocolate doughnuts for breakfast and wash it down with a bottle of Cisco. On one trip to LA, I took him to get a penicillin shot after he told me green stuff was coming out of his Johnson, and then helped teach him the wonders of eating sushi.

Much to my chagrin, he liked to scarf down sashimi while proclaiming, "Baby, I like it raw."

While in the midst of working on Dirty's record, I clearly remember thinking: *I have to get this one to the finish line. It may never happen again.* I somehow knew it would be an important moment in time, one that had to be captured for the world to absorb and then have forever. I knew it would be a crucial part of his legacy, and selfishly, my legacy. I was right on both accounts. Despite Sylvia Rhone's perpetually disparaging words about his behavior, I forged on. I felt like there was a potential self-destruct button on Dirty and the record, and that at any time, it could go off the rails, and something tragic could happen. RZA, for reasons only he can explain, was largely absent during the mixing process, and it was often Dirty, his cousin Buddha Monk, the engineer Jack Hersca, and me, trying to get this record to the goal line, inch by inch.

I took it upon myself—along with my engineer, Jack Hersca, and my assistant, Rick Posada—to start to mix the record. RZA was not particularly present during the mixing of *Return to the 36 Chambers*. His sporadic appearances made it difficult to get the mixes right since at the end of the day they would all need his approval. He was busy crafting albums for Method Man, GZA, and Raekwon, as well as dealing with the success of *Enter the Wu-Tang.* (I would find out many years later that his studio in Staten Island had been flooded, causing him to lose two vital works in progress—GZA's *Liquid Swords* and Raekwon's epic *Only Built 4 Cuban Linx*—hence his focus was on literally recreating these records.)

RZA had his own complex science to making records, and I did not possess his manual, which left me in a lurch several times. There were a few songs I had to mix multiple times. I just couldn't get them to sound right, specifically "Brooklyn Zoo." I was having a miserable time trying to get the kick and snare to pop. After mixing it and failing three times, me and Rick decided to chop up a break to back up the kick and the snare already in the track. This fourth mix worked and became the version you know. The funniest thing is RZA and True Master, who I only encountered once or twice, never seemed to notice or care. We added the break only because we didn't know what else to do. I would mention it in passing to RZA later, at mastering, but I'm still not clear if he's aware of it or not, since he paid it no mind that day. Thank God it worked, though. I did not want to mix that song and fail again.

One thing people don't know is that Dirty did not write a lot of rhymes. In fact, 12 O'clock, GZA, and others all had a hand in helping him craft his lyrics—not that it really matters. Dirty delivered them in a style that has never been replicated. His unbridled, no-holds-bar delivery remains unique. It's the reason that, despite all the antics, he remains an icon. If he didn't make great records, the antics wouldn't have had an audience—something that is overlooked way too often for my liking.

I remember pleading with Dirty to give me a second verse on "Shimmy Shimmy Ya" and showing up to the studio and him playing me his backward verse and laughing his ass off. I was tight, and he nonchalantly told me, "Your man Q-Tip used the same verse on 'Sucker N****s' and that was ill, right?"

I had very little argument for him that day.

And you know what? Nobody ever seemed to care except me!

One of the things people don't know is that RZA delivered every song on the album, except "Sweet Sugar Pie" and "Stomp," to me on five two-inch reels once the deal was completed. Dirty's vocals were already on at least ten of the songs on the reels. They were: "Shimmy Shimmy Ya," "Brooklyn Zoo," "Damage," "Hippa to da Hoppa," "Raw Hide" (minus Method Man's verse), "Dirty Dancin'," "Snakes," "Don't U Know," "Goin' Down," and "Cuttin' Headz." All the other beats that made the album were on the two-inch reels he delivered to me at the start of the album. It literally took me a year to finish the record in part due to Dirty's antics. He didn't do a lot of vocals during that time, though when he did, they were amazing.

Dirty redid vocals on a few existing songs during the course of making the record, like on "Raw Hide," feeling that his performance didn't match his brother Meths. He also touched up his vocals on "Proteck Ya Neck 2 (The Zoo)," "Brooklyn Zoo 2 (Tiger Crane)," "Stomp," and most memorably on "Sweet Sugar Pie," where he did the vocals for the first time at Chung King. It was the only song we tracked from scratch on the whole album. In terms of Dirty's vocals, when we mixed, we had to compress the hell out of them in order to get them to sound more audible. Somehow, this all added to the charm of the record. We collectively dug in, trying to make it work, and the end result I believe speaks for itself. Making this record took more than a little babysitting, and it was a ton of work. Honestly, there were times I wasn't sure if I was going to finish before he self-destructed. When it was finally finished, I emphatically knew we had the goods. RZA did, too. I mean, he had crafted the record from scratch, right?

Thank God I had done a lot of different mixes. I believe Dirty used all the bass up passes, if memory serves me right. To be clear, the genius of this record was all RZA and Dirty. They thought this record out for a long time. As the legend goes, some of Dirty's verse went all the way back to the days of his neophyte rap crew with RZA and GZA, All in Together Now.

I loved Dirty, but unfortunately, I only got to make that one record with him. By the time he was ready to make N**** Please, I was already writing the next chapter of my own musical career. I will say this: Dirty is absolutely the biggest character I ever had the pleasure to work with, and for that and all of the memories, one of my proudest achievements as an A&R person. As hectic as the making of this record was, and how taxing '94 and '95 had been mentally and professionally, I delivered it to the finish line. I had caught lightning in a bottle, so to speak. It was a great record, and one that, for the time being, made my life with Sylvia Rhone less nervous, though I will say she was always highly critical of the record, specifically of RZA's production, which to me made no sense. I thank RZA for believing in me enough to put Dirty on Elektra. That experience changed my life immeasurably. I owe this all to the strength of this record, to the RZA, and to something bigger than me that allowed this testament to the man's life to see the light of day.

15

SLOW DOWN

Kids on the half-pipe will start banging their skateboards on the top of the ramp, which only happens when someone nails a trick. The problem is we weren't in a skate park; we were in a packed nightclub filled with fashionistas, industry folks, thugs, and scenesters. The crowd mistook the banging for gunshots, and pandemonium broke out. People started stampeding.

Minutes later, my crew and I roamed the now empty club looking for our prey. Out of nowhere they appeared, running down the stairs and almost ran me over. Within seconds, I was trading punches with one of the most important men in hip-hop, the man who discovered the greatest rapper of all time.

I had just turned thirty years old, and I was out of control.

While I was making *Return to the 36 Chambers,* I also made one of the worst choices in my life. I left my long-time girlfriend and a wonderful woman, Jill Revson, to hang out with a hot Filipino lady named Leah Panlillio. Leah worked at the Coffee Shop in Union Square, a trendy restaurant whose main draw was its waitresses/models. I had lusted after her for some time, and when the door opened for me to make my move, I did. I didn't even hesitate, not caring whether or not I would hurt or ultimately lose one of the loves of my life.

Leah was exciting, gorgeous, sexy, and my immoral equal. I'm not going to pretend I was an angel. They say you are the company you keep, right? I caught her cheating with a guy I knew and a whole bunch of drama ensued. Yes, the experience made me stronger, and yes, it probably even made me a better person, but none of that shit mattered when I was going through it. Many years later, post-motherhood, Leah became a very different person—as have I. She has become a close friend.

Funny how things end up sometimes.

Suffice it to say, self-reflection wasn't a priority for me back then. Instead, I drank like a fish, smoked Cypress Hill–levels of pot, and got into fights constantly. I made multiple bad career decisions. My ego and emotions ruled my actions, and that's not the move.

Sylvia Rhone didn't fire me, nor did she take away my artists. She gave me a chance. That doesn't mean she was a fan of mine. Even though ODB's record succeeded commercially and critically, it was a difficult and trying journey. I always felt that she was appalled by Dirty's behavior and only begrudgingly celebrated his success at the time. I know some of the insanity that had transpired outside of the office got back to the new president, and she wasn't particularly happy.

Grand Puba's *2000*, which I had executive production credit on, wound up costing $700,000 to make, which was a staggering figure at the time. The album was a subpar effort for the most part, but it had a great lead single on it, "I Like It (I Wanna Be Where You Are)," which sampled Cal Tjader's cover of "Never My Love" for the musical bed and the DeBarge classic "I Like It" for the hook. The single worked, but the album did not. Sylvia wasn't happy about this. To make matters worse, Sylvia let me know that Del was on the ropes. Pete Rock & CL Smooth's sophomore effort, *The Main Ingredient,* had also tanked. I was 0-3 in '94, and if you counted my idiotic love life, I was 0-4.

My boozing was escalating, and this caused me a lot of hassles. This period was also the most violent period in my entire life. Once again, my madness spilled over into my professional career, but this time it was with one of the most recognizable faces in hip-hop.

I ran with a wild-style PR cat named Rene, who was a tattoo artist/street entrepreneur. He was also a chick magnet, and this could lead to complications. Rene was shacked up with a sexy supermodel, Beverly Peele. The relationship was always hectic. To make matters worse, Beverly got caught laid up with a cat named D-Mac when Rene returned early from a business trip of sorts. Rene relieved D-Mac of a Rolex and few other items. The Rolex apparently was a gift from Sean "Puffy" Combs. This led to a myriad of situations, with Rene being threatened by Puff and cohorts of his in an effort to get the Rollie returned. Rene had no intention of returning the watch, which he looked at as a payback of sorts.

This led to a slew of bad vibes that came to a head one night at a club called, ironically, Mac Daddies, which was at Irving Plaza, the location of De La Soul's first show. I was with my crew of dirt bags; Rene had rolled in a little after us with his lady. Stretch Armstrong was killing it on the ones and twos, and the night was dope right up to the moment someone picked up the mic and announced, "Puff Daddy's in the house!"

I looked over and noticed Rene tensing up. Then Puffy, D-Mac, and his huge bodyguard walked into frame. Immediately, Rene peeled off his jacket. My boys and I circled around to make sure Rene didn't get chumped by D-Mac, Puff, or his crew. Puff took note and started barking at me in particular. One of my friends, Vel (who would end up managing Ghostface Killah), took offense and hurled a chair at Puff.

It was on.

Rene grabbed D-Mac and started pummeling him, pulling his shirt over his head and hitting him with some serious shots. Puff and his bodyguard made a move and my crew descended like wolves.

Meanwhile, the kids that were skating the ramp, including the late Harold Hunter (RIP), started banging their skateboards against the ramp. The crowd mistook this for gunshots and started stampeding toward the exits. The bouncers descended onto the dance floor and did their best to break it up. They carted Puff and his crew upstairs onto the balcony momentarily.

We regrouped. Vel had been knocked in the head with a foreign object and was bleeding a bit. Now we were out for blood, roaming the now-empty club. Out of nowhere, the three of them came tearing down the stairs and almost ran me over. All of a sudden, Puff and I were standing face to face hurling threats at each other. Before I knew it, we were throwing punches. I honestly don't remember exactly what transpired—suffice it to say, I threw several shots and was unscathed at the end of it. Rumor also has it that Puff and his bouncer, gun in hand, ran out of the club.

Like a lot of things that night, I cannot verify it.

One thing I do recall is that they left D-Mac behind, which was *no bueno* for him. When the crew caught up to him, he was holding a bottle of grenadine, which he splashed all over the place. Some of it got on my white sweatshirt, which was mistaken for blood. I guess he realized he wasn't getting any wins that night, so he began to retreat. In my warped wisdom, I picked up a stanchion and hurled a perfect spiral that hit him in his back and leveled him. My boys descended on him like white on rice. It was ugly. At the end, all he was left wearing were his pants and one shoe. Being the most recognizable person involved other than Puffy, I was held to blame.

The next afternoon I reached out to Puff through Chris Lighty and Jessica Rosenblum, who were mutual friends. I extended an olive branch of sorts, and to his credit, Puff accepted. He also went to speak to Rene personally and made peace with him. In a sign of good faith, we went to Jessica and Chris's Sunday night party at the Tunnel. We shared a drink and a laugh and buried the hatchet, so to speak. In some weird way, I believe this incident increased his respect for me and my crew. Sometimes things are just like that.

A week later, I was suit shopping at Armani when who walks in but Puff and his bodyguard, Paulie. Thank God we had made peace or I might have been wearing that suit at my own funeral. To this day, I have the utmost respect for Puff, or should I say Diddy. He handled his business that night, and, in the aftermath, he never held a grudge or let it escalate into something stupid. And for the record, Sean Combs is one of the greatest A&R men in the history of hip-hop. From Biggie to Mary J. Blige, Mount Vernon's Bad Boy had a hand in some of my favorite music ever. He is one of the smartest businesspeople I have ever known. If I knew half of what he did, I would be a multi-millionaire.

I got a formidable offer from Def Jam and started to think very seriously about what it would be like to work with my old friends Russell Simmons and Lyor Cohen. Chris Lighty had joined the fray and he was gung-ho about me working with them.

I held out and stayed put, mostly so I could get Busta Rhymes' record going at Elektra. I started it, but I never did finish that record as the pressure became too much for me and I did eventually leave. I left Busta in the hands of my former assistant, Rick Posada, who in turn did a few questionable things, including trying to rewrite history. I remember bumping into him late one night outside of work and him talking down to me about Sadat X's recent release, *Wild Cowboys*. He went from being my protégé to kissing up to Sylvia Rhone. A lot of good it did him. He was fired after Busta's hit record. Served him right, as he unceremoniously dropped Del with a registered letter in the mail, chumped Brand Nubian, and tried to lay claim to the work I had done at Elektra. It was one of the first times an underling had taken a stab at me. It wouldn't be the last.

The biz can make people ugly like that.

Leaving Elektra was probably not the smartest thing I've ever done. During my final days at Elektra, I was knee deep in talks with Lyor Cohen and Russell Simmons about a label deal at the newly formed RAL, a.k.a. Rush Associated Labels, a subdivision under Def Jam. I wondered what it would be like to bring those guys artists instead of sandwiches.

I stalled them. *Return to the 36 Chambers* dropped on March 28, 1995. By the time it went gold, less than three months later, I had already left Elektra. I missed the celebration and the accolades. In fact, it wasn't until writing this book that I remembered it had been nominated for a Grammy Award for Best Rap Album.

I was able to get Busta his deal and get him started working on *The Coming*. As I said, I never got to enjoy the fruits of my labor with Busta.

I remember being bummed out when he got his first of eleven Grammy nominations for the first single, "Woo Hah!! Got You All in Check" and *The Coming* ended up going platinum. It was hard knowing I wasn't a part of that celebration. Had I stayed at Elektra, the sky would have been the limit. Instead, I jumped over to Def Jam way too soon, my ego and emotions once again proving they were not my friends.

Elektra Playlist 2

Brand Nubian—"Punks Jump Up to Get Beat Down"
Brand Nubian—"Steal Ya 'Ho"
Del The Funky Homosapien—"Catch a Bad One"
Del The Funky Homosapien—"No Need for Alarm"
Pete Rock & CL Smooth—"They Reminisce Over You (T.R.O.Y.)"
Pete Rock & CL Smooth—"Straighten it Out"
Brand Nubian—"Word is Bond"
Grand Puba—"I Like It (I Wanna Be Where You Are)"
Ol' Dirty Bastard—"Brooklyn Zoo"
Ol' Dirty Bastard—"Shimmy Shimmy Ya"
Busta Rhymes feat. Ol' Dirty Bastard—"Woo-Hah!! Got You All in Check"

I entered Def Jam with high expectations and was met with a lot of bad vibes. I signed Trigger tha Gambler, who was riding the wave of a hit song he made with his brother, Smoothe da Hustler, called "Broken Language." I had big problems trying to get their record, *Life is a 50-50 Gamble,* together. The record we made simply wasn't good enough. They did, however, have a minor hit with the tune "My Crew Can't Go for That," a Hall & Oates–inspired ditty that made its way onto the *Nutty Professor* soundtrack.

That my first artist with Def Jam was a dud did not bode well for me. The vibes were bad from the jump. Julie Greenwald and I bumped heads, and I lost. In hindsight, I should have played it differently. This was her show, and I didn't bow down to these facts. She helped build the machine, and

I didn't give her the respect she deserved. Humility was not my strong suit, then or now. I kept the doors open to my office but rarely went to work.

This was about the time I caught my girlfriend, Leah, cheating on me. I went to Cali for a few, saw my dad, and got some decent advice from him on how to handle my losing situation at Def Jam. He suggested I stay positive and find a project that was important to me to offset all the bad energy I was experiencing.

I regrouped for most of '95, trying to wait out my Def Jam deal, which wasn't fun in the least bit. As a way to rekindle my love for music, I started logging some serious studio hours. I was in the lab with Gamble again on the regular, something that made me feel better about what I was making and working toward creatively. The year flew by, and I was in a good place with my dad and my younger sister, who was talking about moving to New York—absolute music to my ears. I wasn't the pistol-hot A&R kid anymore for a change, and that was okay. I had other plans, and they involved making music.

I started the year trying to figure out my groove. I started buying a lot of records again, dedicating myself to digging—an invaluable part of sample-based beat making back then. I told myself, *I WILL BE A SUCCESSFUL RECORD PRODUCER.* I may have been bugging a little with that one. I made records with Casual, Del, and others that remain largely unheard to this day. I also worked on projects with a host of other up-and-coming rappers, many of which were fruitless, but fun nonetheless. I got a few remix gigs. I still had a check coming from my deal at Def Jam, but to Lyor and Russell, I was now an afterthought. Our love affair was over. I got Sadat X signed to Loud, which pissed Lyor off. He wanted to sign X at Chris Lighty's urging, but I took him to my pal Steve Rifkind instead. I helped make his record and started managing him, which was me not putting all my eggs in one basket. I may be emotional, but I'm no idiot (though I was a Stimulated Dummy).

I signed an ill-fated West Coast MC to Def Jam named NME in an act of desperation. He was raw as hell, and unfortunately the project never got off the ground. He had a knucklehead of a manager I'll leave nameless, who hasn't been heard from since. NME never came out, and that was a shame because that dude could really rap. His career, or lack thereof, was another example of a street cat thinking he knew it all and ruining his artist's shot at making it. Couple that with my dysfunctional relationship at Def Jam and he never had a chance.

That year was also full of soul-searching. I was determined to rise again. A funny thing had started to happen in front of my very own eyes. Underground rap music had been invented. The backpacker had come to be, and there was a legion of young rappers and rap fans emerging from the shadows. People like Kool Keith were putting forth brilliant music like *Dr. Octagon.* My former act KMD, a.k.a. MF Doom, was on the forefront of this movement. Rock was starting to collide with rap music. Bands like Rage Against the Machine were setting the bar in rock music with a hybrid called rap/rock or as I called it rock/hop. Groups like Cake started to get popular. Beck was becoming a MTV-friendly star and the Beastie Boys had received major kudo's, having revisited their punk roots while mixing in strong hip-hop elements on *Check Your Head,* which was a huge success, and their follow-up, *Ill Communication.* Artists as diverse as Portishead and Massive Attack were emerging, and DJ Shadow's epic *Endtroducing...* record changed how I looked at beat-making as a whole. I was, for a moment in time, once again inspired by music.

This was all more enjoyable for me to listen to than most rap music. I was into Radiohead and PJ Harvey, not Ja Rule and Foxy Brown. I rediscovered my love for hardcore punk rock. For the first time in my adult life, I loathed what was happening in mainstream rap. I started to search for new music, new sounds, and new ideas. It was an essential moment of musical exploration for me, and it shaped what I would do in the next few years. The failure of the previous year or so inspired me to think outside of my box, to blaze new trails musically, and to be more open minded about what was out there. I decided to try to make some rap/rock my-damn-self.

What did I have to lose, right?

I started working with a couple of friends of mine who had a band called Roguish Armament. I wanted to make them my Beck or my version of Cake or something like that. I started making demos with them, trying to do something I had never done before. Through Roguish Armament, I linked up with a band called Dog Eat Dog, a second-rate joke core band from New Jersey. I ended up immersed in their recording process, though I ended up having a falling out with them and their manager. I never completed the record.

I had a vision. I was onto something with Roguish, but unfortunately it didn't work out. They were a weird group. They were unique and ahead of the curve, but they were also full of dysfunctional internal energy. I did the demo, shopped it around, and several labels came knocking. They had a half-assed manager, Chris Evans, who also managed Dog Eat Dog. We got offers from a few labels and went to some serious meetings. Then the shit hit the fan.

One of the kids in the band, Ill, a.k.a. Danny Ilchuk, was upset with this turn of events. Before Gamble and I stepped in, he had been the main producer and rapper, while his partner, Chippy, worked as the backup rapper and occasional singer. I liked Chippy's voice and encouraged him to sing more. I put him out front and Ilchuk couldn't deal. We had a meeting with Michael Goldstone, a.k.a. Goldie, a legendary A&R guy at the newly formed record label, DreamWorks. Goldie was a big deal—he had signed Rage Against the Machine and Pearl Jam. He was at the top of the food chain back then.

Goldie offered the group a demo deal but stipulated that they would first have to do a showcase for the label since he had "never signed a band he didn't see live." He intimated that if they nailed the showcase, he would sign them. Ilchuk, in a moment of self-destructive madness, turned to him mid-sentence and said, "We're a live organization. If you don't know that, then you shouldn't sign us."

Goldie said, "Okay. Play live for me then."

Ilchuk froze. He realized he was in over his head. He decided right then he was going to sink the ship, so he did by saying, "I don't even like the demo, to be honest. Go listen to my old shit. It's way better."

Needless to say, Goldie quickly rescinded his offer. The same thing happened at Jive, where we actually got really far along before the deal went sour after Ilchuk told the A&R guy, "My demo's wack. It's not what we really do."

The deal also fell apart while in the last draft of a contract. We threatened to sue the label and they had to pay us a small amount of money as compensation. It was a painful experience for me. I was going broke trying to help an old friend, and this was the thanks I got?

Just for the record—Ilchuk was wrong, the demo was dope.

Nonetheless, my work with them certainly helped me grow. I experimented with them, I pushed my musical boundaries, and I learned not to be afraid of trying different techniques and combining a multitude of elements. I took cues from the Beastie Boys, Massive Attack, Beck, and even Soundgarden when making their demo.

I still had a little side hustle at Loud, too. Steve was good like that. And even after Sadat X flopped commercially, he still believed in me. Over the years, Rifkind and I have had our ups and downs, but at the end of the day, he has shown more belief in me than any other person in the music biz, barring my mentor, Bob Krasnow. A few years ago, on Rifkind's dime, I traveled to Amsterdam and Paris for a wild week to try to sign a group called the Cool Kids. I also ate a lot of free food, talked a lot of shit about basketball, and was generally allowed to be myself—all while getting paid for it. The only concrete thing he ever got out of it was me bringing him David Banner a few years later. For all of these things, I have a deep love for the man despite our sometimes-turbulent relationship.

NEW INFLUENCES PLAYLIST

Portishead—"Glory Box"

DJ Shadow—"Stem"

Tricky—"Aftermath"

Massive Attack—"Hymn of the Big Wheel"

Kruder & Dorfmeister—"Deep Shit, Parts 1 & 2"

Eels—"Beautiful Freak"

Radiohead—"Fake Plastic Trees"

Sneaker Pimps—"6 Underground"

Cibo Matto—"Sugar Water"

Combustible Edison—"Theme from the Tiki Water Bar"

Rage Against the Machine—"Bulls on Parade"

Dr. Octagon—"Blue Flowers"

The Herbaliser—"A Mother (For Your Mind)"

Morcheeba—"Trigger Hippie"

16

WHAT IT'S LIKE

The year 1997 was a tense time for the hip-hop community in Los Angeles. Two of the biggest stars in rap had been gunned down and killed within six months of one another—Tupac in the fall of 1996 after a Mike Tyson fight in Las Vegas; Biggie Smalls in the spring of 1997 after the Soul Train Awards at the Peterson Automotive Museum in LA. There was speculation and theories linking the two assassinations, but nothing has ever been proven. I tried to keep my head down and stay out of the fray. I didn't have shit to do with any East Coast/West Coast beefs that were going on. I was making good music again, and even though I was technically "cold," I was proud of what I was creating.

Unfortunately, the happiness I was experiencing on a professional level was not filtering into my personal or financial life. I was still suffering from that horrible breakup with Leah—one that had me beating dudes up, getting jumped, threatening people, and eventually getting arrested for beating someone up. I started carrying guns. I wish like hell I had listened to my inner voice and embraced the evolved person who was buried somewhere underneath my twisted, tough guy façade.

Unfortunately, I wasn't ready.

I had no idea what was going to transpire in 1997, but I was beginning to get a sense that things were going to work out if I just stayed out of the way. A year or so earlier, I was doing what I did most nights back then: drinking.

One night while in LA at the Mondrian Hotel bar with Sadat X, who I was then managing, Gang Starr's Guru (RIP) happened to be at the bar. X and I joined him for a drink or three. Erik Schrody, a.k.a. Everlast, the front man of House of Pain, came a few minutes later to meet Keith. We chopped it up for a few, as we were acquaintances of sorts. I had met him many years prior at World on Wheels during one of my first trips to LA with De La Soul. I always liked him, being white and at World on Wheels in 1987 showed a lot of heart. I always thought he was a good MC since his Rhyme Syndicate days. I liked House of Pain's whole vibe. One could say I was a fan. In the midst of us hanging, Guru turned to me and blurted, "Yo, you and E need to work together. Y'all the same type of motherfuckers."

I laughed, mostly because other friends had made similar claims. That's not to say everyone thought we should link up. In fact, a few years earlier, Cypress Hill's Muggs had stated point blank that they didn't want Erik and me to hang out because they feared we'd get into too much trouble. Years later, Erik confirmed that this had been explained to him behind closed doors.

That night, Erik and I spoke about making some music together. Erik also told X he wanted him on the forthcoming House of Pain record, which he was in the process of making. Initially, I didn't pay it much mind. I was glad to hang out with Erik. We had always been cool; he was a funny cat, but I also knew that's the shit record people always say when they're out drinking. They might be sincere when they're saying it, but when they wake up the next afternoon, it's often forgotten. Nonetheless, we had good vibes and exchanged numbers.

It was an odd time for Erik. He had been publicly disowned by Cypress Hill and was steadfastly holding on to House of Pain, which seemed like a sinking ship. I respected the man and thought he was a talent, but I wasn't sure House of Pain had much life left in it. It had been a few years since "Jump Around" had dropped and subsequently became an anthem. *Same as it Ever Was*, their second album, managed to go gold even though it received virtually no airplay and didn't have a legitimate hit on it, though I thought it was actually pretty good. All the same, Erik was putting together another HOP record; he assembled some talented artists to join Lethal, Danny Boy, and himself, including Divine Styler and Cokni O'Dire. As a friend, I hoped the record was a return to their "Jump Around" success, but as a record man, I wasn't expecting it.

Erik was perceived by many as a one-hit wonder, yet he still had an inner confidence beyond the public's perception. Physically he had gained some weight and looked like a different person—he was no longer the shaved-head, Celtics-jersey-clad, skinny front man from House of Pain. He had been through some hardships with the ladies. He had seen success but was now facing financial uncertainty for the first time in many years.

X ended up going back out to Los Angles and rocking with Everlast for a week or so, making the song "Heart Full of Sorrow." After that, every time Everlast came to New York, or X or I went to LA, we would link up and run the streets. We constantly discussed making music, but more often than not, we were interrupted by mayhem.

And we attracted trouble wherever we went.

There was the time, accompanied by Sadat X, when we went down to meet my boys at our favorite strip club, New York Dolls, and Erik witnessed a major beat down delivered courtesy of my childhood friend Manny Stacks. Manny was a wild dude who ran with a serious crew. I didn't actually witness the violence that night; I was too busy getting a lap dance, but Erik did. It was serious shit that ended up with Manny catching a gun charge when, in the middle of stomping his man out, an undercover cop happened to be driving by. Fortunately, it didn't escalate into something more serious. That would come later down the road. My brother Manny Stacks is currently sitting in prison right now. He is a LES legend, and he, along with a lot of street legends I know, ended up incarcerated. It could have been worse, of course. A lot of street legends end up dead. I hope to see Stacks on the streets again someday.

It was ill hanging with Erik. At times, it was like meeting a long-lost brother, albeit one I had causally known for several years already. We vibed musically and philosophically. We had both been around the block. After a crazy weekend at the Super Bowl in Arizona, a trip that included a jerkoff pulling my Yankees hat off my head in a two-bit titty bar and things escalating into a minor fracas, along with an incident with an enraged Steeler fan who tried to sock Everlast's Range Rover, breaking his hand in the process. It was pretty much written in stone that we would be doing a project together at some point.

Truth Crushed to Earth Shall Rise Again, House of Pain's third album, dropped on October 22, 1996, the same day Erik announced he was leaving the group. The record flopped. DJ Lethal went on to work with Limp Bizkit, often covering "Jump Around" during their early concerts. Danny Boy focused on design, and Erik and I plotted. I fed him a steady supply of beats all the while.

I was in LA, watching MTV on Erik's couch, and Rage Against the Machine came on. I suggested that he might want to do something along those lines. He balked at the idea saying, "If I do that, I can't do what I do anymore."

I suggested he might want to consider that.

He just laughed.

Even though we didn't have a game plan, much less a contract, Erik came to New York in the spring of 1997, posting up on my couch for several weeks to work on music. I might add, this is the same couch ODB, Del, a young Doom, and many others had crashed on over the years. One thing I marveled at with Erik was his lack of entitlement. He lived in a mini mansion, yet here he was on my dusty couch and never once complained. I appreciated his humility; it showed his blue-collar roots and then some.

We, along with John Gamble, started out making a traditional rap record. We were moving along and had a few cool rap joints in the stash. Several of these—including my personal favorite, "Money"—ended up making *Whitey Ford Sings the Blues.*

One night after working on some idea at our cramped studio, Erik decided to take John Gamble's beat-up old Guild acoustic guitar home. Since we had started working together, my diverse pallet of non-rap music had intrigued Erik, who also had eclectic tastes, though he veered more toward nineties modern rock and seventies singer-songwriter stuff.

That night, I realized he was a decent musician and a gifted singer. I had heard him sing a few times before and was surprised at how unique, honest, and emotive his voice was. He played me a Screaming Trees tune called "Dollar Bill" and, to be honest, I think I liked his version better than the original. He had turned me on to Radiohead, and in return I hipped him to the Bad Brains catalog. We were searching for something musically; we just didn't know what.

In the back of my mind, I remembered something Gamble had said to me when I first started hanging with Erik: "If we could get Everlast on some rock/rap shit, he would kill it." Gamble, for all his idiosyncratic ways, was an insightful cat and a serious musical architect.

A few nights after borrowing the guitar, and after a long day at the studio, I had invited a lady friend over. When she arrived, Erik was sitting on my couch with the Guild on his lap, noodling around. He was surprised; she was a tall, Irish-looking girl with green eyes—not my usual style, but nonetheless still very attractive. Erik turned to me and barked, "Home Team," which I got right away and chuckled at. While in my bedroom fornicating, I heard him playing something amazing on the guitar.

Immediately, I jumped out of bed and ran into the living room in only my boxers and asked him what he was playing. He said it was something he had written. I asked him to play it for me in its entirety, vocals and all. I was knocked out by the simplicity and emotion it encompassed. I thought it was tremendous. I demanded he play it again for me and he obliged. I asked him what it was called. He stated, simply, "What it's Like." It was a chilling moment for me. I knew I had heard the future for the both of us.

When I suggested we record it, he balked. "If I do that, there's no turning back."

I remember thinking to myself, let's go forward, fuck going backward.

Over the years, I had learned a valuable rule: If you want an artist to do something more than they do, it probably isn't going to work out. So, for the time being I didn't push.

The next day, I asked him about the tune again. He just laughed. So, what did I do? Broke my rule, of course. "We need to record that," I said. "Songs like that just don't come along every day."

The next day in the studio, I asked him to play it for Gamble. He did and Gamble lit up like a Christmas tree when he heard it. We persuaded Erik to record the song the following day. I looped the drums up on the spot using a classic break beat as the foundation of the backing track, and Erik laid down his rough vocals. I then programmed the snare live down the whole track, ala "They Reminisce Over You." I could tell Erik was inspired by this turn of events. He then decided he wanted to redo his vocals and really let it all hang out in his second performance. Those are the vocals on the final record, the second take—same for the guitar track. We recorded the whole demo in a matter of hours, ending it with Erik playing bass and Gamble adding some keyboard strings, which we later replaced. I mixed the demo that night, and a few days later, we cut another singer-songwriter tune Erik had in the stash called "7 Years," which told the story of a spurned lover. The song incorporated a great drum break I will not divulge here; it also ended up making the record.

We waited about a week, then presented the two tracks to Tommy Boy along with "Money (Dollar Bill)" and "The Letter," both of which also made the final album. Tommy Boy had released the three House of Pain records, and he was technically still signed there, though we had no idea how they would react to our new stuff. We had done it without their knowledge. My old pal Monica Lynch and our boy Albee Ragusa, an A&R man for the label, called us right after they heard the songs and told us that the two singer-songwriter tunes were dynamite. This confirmed what I already knew, but more importantly, it gave Erik some confidence in my plan. We had also sent them to Erik's manager, Carl Stubner, who worked with Mick Fleetwood. A couple of days later, we got a call from Mick himself. Erik put him on speakerphone as he said, "Erik, you got a lot of grease on that one. It's fucking brilliant."

It's not every day that a rock god calls saying you've got the goods.

Then the bullshit started.

DANTE ROSS

My on-again/off-again relationship with Leah was consuming me. One night, I "caught" her on a date with a "mutual friend," which almost led to me getting my ass kicked. Of course, it wasn't really my business—we were on and off. Still, that didn't stop me from coming home and taking out my Louisville Slugger and destroying everything in my bedroom. Erik fell back—he had never seen me even close to being that pissed.

After I had smashed as much of my shit as I possibly could, I sat on the couch, huffing and puffing. Erik joined me. He didn't say anything for a while, letting me cool down. Then, like only a brother can, he laid it out for me.

"D, this is some bullshit," Erik said.

"Tell me something I don't know."

"I don't like seeing you like this, homie," he said. "I think we should go to LA and make the rest of the record. Might be good for you"

I balked at first. We were a few tunes in and work was going well. And even though SD50 was crappy and cramped, I liked working there.

That night, I thought about it, and the next morning, I asked Erik if he really thought we could get it done in LA.

"Why the fuck not?"

I explained my concerns about switching studios. He said that we could get Gamble to build a replica in his house. As I said, I have always dug Los Angeles, and I had met a cute little chica out there recently who I dug. I was pretty sure that she could get my mind off what's her name.

The next day, Erik and I talked to Gamble about it, and he said he was up for the challenge. Then we sold Tommy Boy on the dream, which to this day, I still can't believe. That night, I sat out on my stoop and thought about what was going down. In a matter of weeks, Erik, Gamble, and I would be three-thousand miles away in a Hollywood Hills house finishing the record, a record that was going to be unlike anything that any of us had ever worked on. As I watched the taxis whiz by, it just felt right.

Pauline, the LA lady I was feeling, picked me up at LAX and stayed by my side the entire time, driving me wherever I needed to go since I didn't know how to drive. We got to LA and headed right to the studio, a.k.a. Erik's house. Pauline quickly became my confidant, noting the chemistry in the studio right away.

"You're going to make something magical," she said. I never forgot her words, as she was damn-near prophetic. I cannot stress how crucial it was to have a standup girl by my side during the making of this record. Nothing will make you appreciate a good woman like having been with a bad one.

Erik's house was a trip. We're from NYC and were used to working in a basement shithole. Erik's crib was anything but. The spot was a beautiful four-bedroom house overlooking the city. It wasn't too far up on Mount Olympus, which is the first hill when you go up Laurel Canyon Drive. I had spent time there before, crashing with Erik previously while I was in LA. I dug the pad. It had high ceilings and a huge living room with a pool table. He had a big foyer and wood-beam rafters that made for great acoustics when it came to recording stuff, which we did right there.

Gamble had set up the control room in the downstairs master bedroom. We recorded the live stuff in his living room, hanging blankets over the glass doors and windows to deaden the sound. There was a lot of nice natural reverb. We often hung two stereo mics and ran one line direct to a compressor then to tape when recording guitars and backing vocals. The room had a light color shag rug, a huge TV screen, and three sets of couches, which we would move accordingly. The house itself had an unfinished feel to it, like Erik never quite got done decorating. The upstairs had three bedrooms. Erik had the master with two smaller bedrooms—one for John and me, and one for Erik's mom, who split time between there and Erik's sister's house. I often copped Zs in the living room on one of the couches. I was used to it. In my late teens, I had done a lot of couch surfing—much like Erik.

When it came time to get down to biz, we were handed a few curve balls right away. Erik's 16-track Tascam 1" tape machine was not entirely compatible with ours, so we couldn't do any overdubbing on a few tunes until we transferred all the tapes to a 2" format (and got in a real studio).

We didn't know many musicians in LA, but somehow we made it work. One night, we attended an art opening at Galaxy Café, a bong store/art gallery, and heard an amazing keyboard player in a not-so-amazing band. I immediately pounced on him after his set. His name was Keefus, and coincidently Pauline knew his girl, Jade. We exchanged numbers, and I knew I had found my keyboard player. Keefus not only became my all-around utility keyboard wizard, but he opened his Rolodex of players in LA to us. Keefus ended up playing with Erik for a few years. He was a catalyst for a lot of the magic that would become *Whitey Ford Sings the Blues*.

LA is going to be all right, I thought to myself.

Recording usually started in the afternoon and went late into the night. Erik functioned best at night, like me. Equipment-wise, we had a Tascam MS 16 track 1" tape machine and three DA-88 ADATs, low-budget recording devices that basically recorded multi tracks to VHS tapes. This was before Pro Tools, and we needed these for additional tracks. We had also brought with us a bunch of vintage and digital keyboards and several samplers, a few amps, and some outboard gear as well. We didn't have a good compressor or a decent mic pre with us, which are both vital for making a decent-sounding record, especially when it comes to recording live instruments and vocals. So we purchased an old Avalon mic pre, similar to the one we had in New York, as well as a LA 2 compressor. Erik had a Vox AC30 amp and we copped an AC 15 as well as a Fender twin. He often used his Strat for electric parts and, on occasion, a Paul Reed Smith solid body. We also made frequent trips to Black Market Music in Hollywood, looking to pick up odd keyboards and pedals to increase our arsenal of weapons. A small box called a Sans Amp became a cheap-yet-crucial piece of gear for us. We had heard the Dust Brothers used it all over Beck's *Odelay*, so we copped one. It was a worthy purchase and then some.

Erik had bought a Tascam Mackie 32/16 board exactly like the one we used at SD50. The thing basically sounded like shit. We just made do with what was available to us and within our means. John had brought his collection of microphones, which was vast, and I shipped out twelve crates of records so we could create right then and there. I believe some of our best songs came from me just grabbing a drum sample on the spot and chopping it up, inspiring him in the moment. He was good like that. This was the case on "Get Down" and "Watch Me Shine," where he played us the tunes and I rummaged through my records, found a drum loop, chopping it up in the MPC right there. We usually recorded Erik's vocals in his living room, utilizing the long snakes we had brought with us and setting up a mic right in the center of the room. We sometimes set up a Gobo to partition off the room. This is also how we recorded most of the guitars, both electric and acoustic. All in all, it was an unorthodox but pretty vibey-sounding setup. We were winging it on some DIY shit. I wouldn't have had it any other way.

Next up, I connected with my childhood friend Dagan Ryan's cousin, Merlo. He was in a band called Spain, which was signed to DreamWorks at the time. He was an amazing bassist and guitarist. He and Norwood Fisher from Fishbone and a cat named Giovanni played all the bass lines on the record. Giovanni specialized in upright bass while the two other cats played the electric on all the other tunes. Giovanni also helped us write the string arrangement on "What it's Like." We also linked up with a guy from a local LA funk band called Breakestra, Double G, who played sax and arranged the horns for us on "7 Years." Another vital component to that record was my brother, Bronx Style Bob. Without a doubt, Bob was one of the most important cogs on that record, providing background vocals, helping with vocal arrangements on several songs, and lending us a healthy dose of PMA in the studio. I am eternally indebted to Bob for all of his contributions. His energy is all over that record.

Divine Styler also came through to bless us with his mojo, as did our compadre E-Swift from the legendary Alkaholiks. Swifty, as I called him, lived up the block and was just a righteous dude from A to Z. Both of these cats, plus my former intern Sebastian Bardin, a.k.a. Siba Giba, from Paris who somehow moved to my NYC hood as a teenager, also snagged cuts on the record. Getting these guys royalty checks was one of the best feelings ever. Swifty even flew himself to New York on his own dime to mix down his song while Siba later gave me a beautiful painting as a way to show me his appreciation. Divine, who instilled belief in Erik and blessed all of us with his energy that whole record, would pull up and sit with us for hours on end. To this day, Divine is one of my favorite people in the whole world.

That brother opened my consciousness to so much in our endless dialogues about spirituality, faith, and metaphysics.

We dug in hard, but even with all the positivity that the above-mentioned dudes brought, it wasn't always fun. Erik was suffering from a halted career and excessive living. He was going broke. He owed the IRS a gang of loot and was also coming up short on car payments to the point that we had to hide his ride at his mom's house so it wouldn't be repossessed. My money was tight as well, which didn't make things any more comfortable. To make matters worse, his house was for sale and nobody was biting. Erik was also smoking a ton of stogies, drinking a bit too much, and burning down a ton of weed with me and Gamble. The vibe could get really dark.

During this time, I got to go up north a number of times to see my dad and my sister, Carla. One of the highlights was his sixtieth birthday party where Pauline and I joined my dad and his friends and ate some magic mushrooms. We went to his favorite spot, Café Barbar, and saw how many people loved my dad.

My dad and I had several special moments that weekend. I confided in him the challenges of making Erik's record, telling him that I thought we were making something special. He found a poetry in our musical journey. He dug how we were brave enough to venture into new territories. He saw what I was too close to the process to see clearly. For his insight, I was grateful. As my dad's life wound down and his compadre Oscar and I helped him organize his life in his last days, he told me, "Dante, you don't have a lot of family, so keep your friends close to you, because, at the end, it's all you really have." He added, "Fix the relationships you have broken if you can. Your peoples are your family as much as your blood is."

When he said this, I thought of Erik and how much we were down for each other regardless of how long it had been since we last spoke. I knew in my heart there was nothing we wouldn't do for each other. I thought about Geeby and the need to one day repair that relationship as well. I remember thinking when my dad told me these things that I would always hold these words close to my heart.

I returned from my dad's birthday celebration to find a fiasco of sorts awaiting me. It had been raining for days, as we were in the throes of El

Niño, a devastating storm that produced some of the worst rains in the history of LA. The ceiling above the tape machine was filled with water. Erik also had a showing of the house in the upcoming days, so we had to move fast.

Gamble and I quickly disassembled all our recording equipment and moved it out of harm's way. I then took a broom and punctured a hole in the ceiling. The water cascaded down like a motherfucker, and Erik was in a total panic. I calmed down Erik, and Gamble and I cleaned up the mess. Erik then called his pops, who was a handy man and a half. He came over and fixed the ceiling. The craziest thing is the people who came and looked at the house ended up buying it.

We still weren't out of the woods, though. Erik had hit a wall. He had writers block—the stress had gotten to him—and I felt we still needed a few more songs to make the record complete. He sat on his couch for close to two weeks telling me he was down to his last 217 bucks. I told him I would support him as best as I could, which did nada for his self-esteem and motivation. He simply wasn't functioning like himself, which led to us having a huge blow up. It came close to fisticuffs one night; poor Gamble, who was a nervous wreck himself, had to separate us.

I wasn't in the best frame of mind either. I missed New York, my apartment, my routine. I needed some space and being around these two guys day in and day out was driving me up the wall. I finally moved in with Pauline full time just so I could maintain some sanity. The only thing that kept me going was that I *knew* the record was that good.

In all the years I have been doing this, and through all the records I have had a hand in to this day, this has only happened to me a few times: Brand Nubian's debut record and ODB's *Return to the 36 Chambers* are the two other examples.

We plugged away. We only had one more tune to go, a song that was fittingly titled "Tired." On the night Erik laid down the first two verses, he complained he was feeling shitty. I thought he was just stalling on the third verse. I was tight. I actually thought this was the night we were going to finish the record. After nine grueling months in LA, I was finally getting to go home.

Erik had gotten food delivered from Damiano's, his favorite dump on Fairfax. He had one of the worst diets of anyone I had ever known. After he chowed down some grade-z Italian food—the kind only an Irishman living in LA could tolerate—he started complaining about chest pains. I thought it was an excuse not to record the third verse. Erik was always spot on in the studio, but he usually only wanted to record for a few hours at a time. This worked well for us because he usually did his vocals on the first or second takes. Then he'd chill and leave the rest up to us.

That night, Erik and I got in a little argument, which ended with him telling me he felt like shit. I wasn't completely aware that he had a defective heart valve and took Coumadin, a blood thinner to make sure his blood didn't clot. Erik never really discussed the severity of it with me, and me being the self-absorbed asshole I can be, I just didn't take it in.

"Dante, man, I feel like shit."

"You are what you eat," I said. "Stop eating that garbage and maybe you'll feel better."

"Whatever, dude. I'm going to sleep. I'll finish it tomorrow." He got up and stormed off into his room. I was going to continue to try to get him to finish until I noticed how pale he looked. Still, at worst I thought he had food poisoning.

"Gamz, make sure he keeps the door open, and keep an eye on him. He looks terrible," I said.

"Sure thing," Gamble said. Gamble usually drove me to my girl's after the session, but I figured it would be better for him to stay with Erik, so I took a cab. Pauline was in Las Vegas for a trade show, so I was home alone, which was a rare occurrence. I wasn't complaining. This was one of the few nights I had to myself in months. I was actually looking forward to getting a good night's sleep and finishing the record the next day. My phone rang at 4 a.m. I make it a practice not to pick up my phone in the middle of the night, ever. When I do, it's usually the cops or the coroner, but something told me to get it.

It was Gamble. "Gamz, what do you want?"

"Erik had a heart attack."

"No fucking way."

"I'm at Cedars-Sinai now. You need to get here. They wouldn't let me ride in the ambulance because I'm not next of kin."

I was freaked out. I couldn't really comprehend what was going on.

I hustled over to the hospital as fast as I could. I saw Gamble—he looked shell-shocked and had tears in his eyes. I had never seen him this way. He told me that right before I got there, Erik went into a full-on cardiac arrest after suffering his second heart attack of the night. He explained that the first one happened at the house and was minor. When he had his second heart attack, the EKG went off like a pinball machine. Erik went in to full-on, code-red cardiac arrest and was in desperate need of an emergency triple bypass.

Gamble had been through enough, so I took it upon myself to make the dreaded call to Erik's mother. It was without a doubt one of the hardest calls I've ever had to make. Erik's mom, Rita, and his sister rushed to the hospital. The four of us prayed for Erik for a solid eight hours, only leaving to eat. I started thinking about the wonderful record we made and that Erik might not be here to enjoy it. I also thought about all the references to death in the record, especially in songs like "Death Comes Calling," "Hot to Death," and "Painkillers." Was all this lore of death and darkness a precursor?

I'm not much for tears. The only public emotion I usually display is anger, for the most part. But after all the trials and tribulations we faced while making the record—the fact that we had both gone broke in the process; knowing that we both took the chance to recreate ourselves, veering away from the comfort of hip-hop; thinking that my brother might not be here to see it's fruits and feeling the tremendous guilt for trying to push Erik to finish the last song and not realizing the seriousness of the situation—for the first time in many moons, I cried like a baby.

The internet was in its early stages, so it took a while for the word to get out. First Divine Styler and Bilal Bashir and Erik's Iman, Abdullah Bashir, showed up. Bronx Style Bob called me and showed up. The photographer Estevan Oriol also came and lent his prayers and love. Erik's pops and ex-lady, Kim, showed up as well. I'm sure I'm forgetting some people because it's all a little blurry. By the afternoon, more folks started to roll in. Evidence somehow found out and called me, as did B-Real and several other friends, including E-Swift and J-Ro from Tha 'Liks. I avoided all calls after B-Real because I just didn't have it in me. Pauline found out about it, cut her trip short, and rushed back.

All in all, it was a thirty-six-hour ride of uncertainty and prayer. At this time in my life, I wasn't thinking about God too often, but I joined our friends and prayed. I honestly believe it helped. We all stayed sitting vigil at the hospital until we knew Erik would make it.

They don't call him Everlast for nothing, right?

Gamble and I finally went back to Erik's house. Erik's mom was already there. Immediately, she broke down in my arms, and I'd never felt so helpless in my life. I tried to assure her the best I could that Erik was going to make it. Inside I was thinking, *Yeah, he's probably going to live, but at what cost physically?*

Gamble and I had been through the ringer. Honestly, him more so than me, even.

"You saved Erik's life," I said.

"Really?"

"Yeah. If you hadn't called that ambulance, he would have died. End of story."

His eyes opened wide, and I believe that the gravity of the situation hit him at that moment for the first time. Before I went to sleep, I listened to Erik's phone messages. There were no fewer than thirty messages from people freaking out, including Muggs, (whom he was light-weight feuding with at the time) and Guru (RIP), among others who were close enough to have his private number. The Guru message, in the wake of his passing, for me, is too painful to listen to. I loved that brother.

The next morning at the hospital, Rita asked me to be in the room with them to talk to the doctors. We, along with Erik's dad, were present when Erik finally regained consciousness. He eventually told me the first image he saw was Rita and me. He said he remembered the tears running down my face, which made him realize how serious things must have been. I told him not to repeat that to anyone. That actually got a laugh out of him.

The doctors told us that Erik suffered two heart attacks due to a blood clot. The second had forced his aorta to separate and caused the second massive heart attack. He asked what Erik was involved with. Did he do drugs? Was he a heavy drinker? We both replied, "No," which was the God's honest truth. Erik's worse vice was smoking cigarettes and eating bad LA pizza. Erik dozed off and the doctor pulled us aside and explained that if there was a tangible goal, something positive to work toward, it could help give Erik some motivation to recover faster as opposed to sinking into a deep depression, which can often follow a heart attack. I explained to the doctor that we had just finished recording a record and that maybe working toward playing the record live or eventually touring might be good. The doctor gave me a dubious look and explained Erik might have a long and tough road back to full recovery. He cautioned us to take it one day at a time.

As soon as Erik became fully conscious, I had a heart-to-heart with him about the record. I knew that he was in dire straits financially—a situation only escalated by his lack of health insurance. He knew that this was his best chance of crawling out of this situation.

"I trust you, D. Finish the motherfucker."

I was finally going to be able to go home, but now I had the entire weight of not only finishing the record but also dealing with all the business that goes along with it. And I'd be doing it all without Erik. It was daunting. The weight of finishing the record, from credits to mixing, had been put on my shoulders. I'm proud to report that I stood up and took the bull by the horns, promising myself that I wouldn't let my brother down.

I was happy to be back home, but I didn't have a moment to waste. Carl Stubner immediately set up a meeting with Tommy Boy to discuss our plan of attack. Many of the staff members had expressed their personal sorrow and condolences to us. Still, I couldn't help but think about all the times Tom Silverman wouldn't return Erik's phone calls, times when we were hiding his car and scraping up money to survive. I couldn't help but think all of that stress may have contributed to Erik's heart attack. Before I got too judgmental, I thought back to all the times I had also avoided my artist's calls, like Charlie Brown.

A lot had changed since my days at Tommy Boy. Monica Lynch had left the company right before Erik had the heart attack. I really missed her and couldn't help but think she would have put together a plan quickly and effectively. Our boy, Albee, who helped sign Erik and green-lit me to produce the record, had been relieved of his duties, which was crazy. He'd helped sign Coolio, and House of Pain, which in turn made Silverman millions.

I came to the meeting with Carl Stubner, who I didn't always get along with, and his sidekick Corey, who I did. I wasn't always sure Carl gave a fuck about Erik or if he was just in it to make a buck, but I needed allies. Carl was a shrewd cat if not my favorite person. The entire staff of Tommy Boy was there to greet us, which was odd and a bit overwhelming. Before we went into the conference room, a pal from my punk rock days, Sam Crespo, told me the record was incredible and he hoped the label wouldn't blow it. Another friend and former coworker, Rod Houston echoed his sentiments. I knew we had a good record, but I also had been working in the record biz for over a decade at this point, so I didn't take anything for granted. I had seen a lot of great records die a quick death.

I took a deep breath and walked in.

Tom Silverman dove right in. "*Whitey Ford Sings the Blues* is a great record," he said. "You guys did a great job, Dante."

"Thank you," I said.

"But I have no idea what we're going to do with it."

My heart sank.

Silverman went on to explain it was an untraditional record for the label and way outside their usual box. He didn't know if House of Pain fans would buy into the *Whitey Ford* shtick. I had low expectations for the record after that meeting. I didn't trust Silverman particularly. I met Tommy Boy's new A&R guy, Max Nichols, who was the son of famed director Mike Nichols. I had even lower expectations after rapping with him. To be fair, I was so emotionally invested in the record it wouldn't have mattered who was giving me their two cents—I didn't want to hear it. I never gave the kid a chance.

Surprisingly, Silverman and team gave me the go ahead to mix the record the way I wanted to with the mixer of my choice. Mixing records is a precise science that could truly ruin your record if it ain't done right. A bad mix can kill a great record, but a good mix can help accentuate all that is there. I had been on both ends of that equation in my career. I needed it to bang like a hip-hop record—*and* sound like a radio-friendly modern rock record. It was new territory for me, but I still had a sonic vision in my head. This record was too important to screw it up due to a suspect mix. I had to get the mixes spot on. Erik's livelihood hung in the balance.

Up to this point, Gamble had mixed most of our records. He did a great job on the rough mixes we shared with Tommy Boy, but I still wanted an outside mixer to take it to the next level. He did an adequate job on our stuff for the most part over the years, but I thought we could—and should—do better. I wanted to hire Jamey Staub, who had mixed Pete Rock's records and made them sound great. Still, I had to run it past Gamble, whom I thought would be insulted. Instead, he took the news quite graciously. In an act of selflessness, and after some discussion, we agreed that Jamey was the man for the job.

When I met with Jamey, I told him I wanted our record to knock like Pete Rock's. Gamble actually did the mix on two songs on the final album, "Money" and "The Letter," at River Sound in NYC. I liked the SD demo mix of "The Letter" better, so I kept it as it was and that's the one we used on the album. Sometimes the demo is just the one.

We holed up in Sony Studios in Midtown Manhattan and started mixing. Several of the songs were two-day mixes. This was par for the course on songs with lots of tracks in those days, prior to the advent of digital recording. We had several that fit the bill. This was before Pro Tools became the standard, when every song wasn't more than sixty tracks. It was all on 2" analog tape, or what's called a "multi" for multi-track, not an external drive, and though it sounded a lot better than digital at the time, it was pretty inconvenient. We were doing 48-track mixes, more or less, and using a Sony 48-track PCM-3348 multi-track recorder. We also were running a lot of the drums virtual out of the MPC 2000 to give us more tracks for instrumentation, outboard effects, and vocals. It was a little haphazard, but it worked. We mixed it all down on a Neve 8078 console, bouncing our mixes down to ½" analog tape and backing that up to DAT.

We hit a few bumps in the road, including the time when the studio manager fucked our schedule up and didn't let us leave up the mix of "What it's Like." We had to take the mix down and basically start all over again two days later—a big hassle. We also had to finesse the strings. They were a bit wonky; someone in the string section was slightly out of tune. It took us an extra day in the studio, and an extra day is a few extra grand to get it right. It sucked, but we kept it moving. We mixed the record down in a span of three weeks, working five days a week. My focus has never been more on. I stopped smoking weed while in the studio, which has been known to affect my ears. I remained sober until the mixes were done, then would go home and puff a little weed while listening to the mixes in my pad on a shitty pair of NS10 speakers. If a mix sounds great on NS10s, then it's a great mix. The mixes were on point, and I knew we had done our thing. Jamey Staub was a beast, and that record still sounds tremendous to this day.

I was dead-up proud. When the mixes were done, I flew to LA to see Erik, who I hadn't seen in close to eight weeks. In that time, he had come home from the hospital and started his long journey to recovery. Pauline, being the angel she is, checked up on him for me regularly. I played the entire record for Erik. I knew right away that he approved of it by the big shit-eating grin on his face.

Then I moved on to the credits. I pulled them together and started inserting some of the phone messages into the record. The one from Guru is so ominous now with his passing that I can't really listen to it these days. Don't forget, he was the one who linked up Erik and me that night at the Mondrian.

Keith, we love you, my brother.

Finally, it was time to sequence the record. Sequencing a record is serious business and something I feel I'm good at. I remember the final sequencing of the record vividly. I pulled it together at the Cutting Room back in New York. My editor was an up-and-coming kid named Justin Smith. You probably know him more by his producer name, Just Blaze. This was many years before he became the famous hitmaker, but even back then he knew his stuff. He dug the record and correctly called "What it's Like" as the single.

I couldn't believe how smoothly things had gone in post-production. We had made a great record. There was only one problem: We needed to figure out a plan to sell it. I played it for my pal, Steve Rifkind, who swore up and down it was the best record I had ever made. He cautioned me that Tommy Boy would probably blow it.

Erik asked me to write a short note about the record for his fans, which he signed. It explained what had transpired and how the record came to be. The fact that Erik trusted me to write it and tell his story showed how much faith he had in me and in our shared vision.

Whitey Ford Sings the Blues was released on September 8, 1998, earning solid press. Unfortunately, it didn't move many units. The first week numbers were a paltry 4,100 copies sold. Steve Rifkind called me and put me up on the first week's numbers and my heart sank: Tommy Boy was still trying to figure out how to sell it, and they didn't have a clue. They needed radio support and didn't have it yet. Back before streaming, radio was what broke records—and Tommy Boy had never broken an alternative record on the radio. The forecast was looking bleak.

Erik also needed to get out and play the record live for people. This is of the utmost importance for any kind of rock-based music. It simply has to work live, unlike rap. With Keefus's help, John and I put together a five-piece band with Erik on vocals and guitar prior to the project's release. Gamble and I had rehearsed them for two weeks until they were solid. In fact, they were more than solid and really brought the tunes to life. I was impressed.

We now had a band that could convey the tunes in front of an audience—now we just needed an audience.

I remembered that conversation with the doctor the day after Erik's heart attack. Carl Stubner knew he had to get Erik out playing if he was going to have a shot at breaking him as an artist. Stubner is a lot of things but dumb isn't one of them. Erik's first gig was in LA at the Gaslamp. Our friends Dilated Peoples opened, performing one of their first shows. Needless to say, both acts tore shit up. Erik got a great review in the LA Weekly, one of the first of many great press mentions.

Next, the band went to New York and completely rocked Coney Island High on St. Mark's Place, a venue I hung out in a lot when I was working with Roguish

Armament, ironically. The reviews of the show were excellent. Erik's early shows, I maintain, were some of his best. Erik did indeed have something to live for, and it helped him get his health—both spiritually and physically—back in order.

I felt I had done my job as a friend and as a producer. To this day, I feel that record was the high point of my production career, though some would dispute that. I feel that it and *Eat at Whitey's,* the follow up record to *Whitey Ford Sings the Blues,* are the best records I ever produced—hands down. They changed me from a beat maker to a real producer, a transition that many beat makers never make.

After Everlast hit the road a bit, the record finally started to sell a little. The word of mouth was good. A radio station in Seattle called The End started to play "What it's Like." Then K-Rock in Los Angeles, the most important modern rock station in the country, also jumped on it. By Christmas, we were selling 70,000 copies a week. It was a sleeper hit record, something that rarely happens these days.

My one lingering regret about this period of time that I still carry is that I broke up with Pauline and she wasn't with me to enjoy the success of the record she had such a big part in making. Like I said, I have always been an idiot with women, and she was another gem I lost along the way.

WHITEY FORD PLAYLIST

Soundgarden—"Rusty Cage"

Radiohead—"Creep"

Screaming Trees—"Dollar Bill"

Gang Starr—"Take it Personal"

Collective Soul—"Shine"

Sublime—"Doin' Time"

Tha Alkaholiks—"Daaam!"

Beck—"Where It's At"

Jeff Buckley—"Last Goodbye"

Jay-Z—"A Million and One Questions"

Jay-Z—"Streets Is Watching"

Neil Young—"Old Man"

Bob Dylan with Johnny Cash—"Girl from the North Country"

Showbiz & AG—"Next Level (Nyte Time Mix)"

17

PUT YOUR LIGHTS ON

Springtime in New York can be a magical time, and there weren't many better springs for me than spring of 1998. I was back in New York and feeling pretty good about myself. Life was good.

Even though *Whitey Ford* started off slowly, within six months it was a hit both critically and commercially. The album made Billboard's top ten; "What it's Like" hit number one on the Modern Rock Tracks, bumping the mighty Metallica's "Turn the Page"; and it was certified platinum. The reviews were solid, too. Yes, life was good, and it was about to get even better.

I got a call from Pete Ganbarg, an A&R guy at Arista Records. Pete was a nice guy and an old colleague of mine. He asked if Erik and I had a song for Santana. I told him that Erik was going to be in town later that week for a TV appearance and that we had a song, which was total baloney. We had, at this point, no song for Santana.

I was obviously excited. I was a lifelong fan of Carlos Santana. I grew up with "Oye Como Va" playing in my house on the regular. *Abraxas* was one of the "rock" records I liked as a youngster. It was also going to be a trip to work with someone my folks had not only heard of but actually dug. I was even more jazzed by the prospect of working with Santana *and* Erik. I hit up Erik and asked him if he had a song. He said he had written one, his first song since the heart attack. He intimated that it was inspired by his near-death experience and wanted to record it. I set aside time to get in our studio with him for the first time since his heart attack, which felt somewhat ominous.

We proceeded to cut the demo for "Put Your Lights On" relatively quickly. I used a Latin-sounding drum loop that was in an old Casual demo I had always wanted to repurpose as the drum track. We then set Erik up, per usual, using a Royer Ribbon for his acoustic guitar and a Neumann U47 mic for the vocal. Erik then laid a simple bass line down as a guide track of sorts. We finished it in one afternoon and I quickly got it over to Pete, who hit me back the next day. He told me he loved it, as did Santana. He asked how much I wanted to produce the tune.

As much as I wanted to make the record, I also wanted to make sure I got paid top dollar. I knew that these opportunities didn't come around all the time. I was also hot as a pistol for a change. I asked for $35,000 and got it. In fact, I had actually refused to fly to the Bay to do the song until I had half the deposit in my bank account. Pete got so flustered that he paid the whole fee upfront. This was the most I was ever paid to make a single song in my entire career up to that point. As it turned out, it was a bargain for the boys over at Arista.

I'm not going to pretend I wasn't a little shook, not only by Santana but also by his band, which included a personal hero of mine, keyboardist Chester Thompson, who was in one of my favorite seventies funk bands, Tower of Power. Shit, I was even intimidated by where we were going to work—the legendary Fantasy Studios, which served a wide range of artists from Mingus to Stevie Wonder to Creedence Clearwater Revival to The Blackbyrds. Some of the greatest jazz and funk records ever recorded on the West Coast were made there.

I was super excited for my dad to come by, because some of his peers like the beat poets Lawrence Ferlinghetti and Allen Ginsberg had recorded there. So too had his hero, Lenny Bruce. My dad was impressed that I was actually producing Santana. He told me he saw Carlos play at the Fillmore in the sixties and got all teary-eyed when he told me how proud he was. My dad had always been one of my biggest supporters, but in this instance, he was extremely emotional about my success. Unfortunately, my dad never made it over to the studio when we were making the record. I guess he was even more intimidated than I was.

I grabbed Gamble and we flew to San Francisco in first class—a first for Gamble—where we linked up with Erik before heading to Fantasy the following morning to meet with Carlos and the band. Fantasy was a beautiful studio, to say the least. The room we worked in had a huge live room with lots of natural reverb. The board was a classic Neve 8078, and it sounded great. They had a ton of outboard as well. All in all, it was a top-notch spot—one that lived up to its legendary status and then some.

We set up shop relatively quickly and got crackin'. Carlos was super chill, a down-to-earth, friendly cat with a groovy cosmic swag to him. He complimented us on the song, telling us he had listened to it a bunch and that it had really moved him. He then proceeded to ask Erik what the lyrics were about. Erik explained his heart attack and the message of near death and redemption that the tune encompassed for him. Carlos was intrigued by the tune's dark intensity. Erik asked him if he was cool with the Arabic ending. Carlos asked him to explain what it meant. Erik told him that it was part of the Shahada, an Arabic prayer that simply means there is no God but Allah. Carlos smiled his big smile and told him that was beautiful and insisted he keep it in the song. The vibes were great from jump, and for me, that was the God to whom Erik was alluding.

We all clicked right away, and I thought, *Man, when I'm his age I hope I'm that groovy.* He's a complete gentleman. I was surprised that Santana gave us so much artistic freedom. He was good like that. He listened to all of our suggestions, from amp choices to guitars (a classic solid-body Paul Reed Smith through a vintage orange head and amp recorded in the big live room with a touch of reverb) to what notes and scales he played in his solo. He was a little confused by Pro Tools, which we had started using, but he rolled with it. The digital domain was new territory for Carlos (and us—we had only recently started using Pro Tools), and he was intrigued by it. He asked us all sorts of questions about sonics and such. He was concerned that the sound quality might suffer potentially, but still, he trusted our approach. By the next time I worked with him, he was fully immersed in digital recording.

The fact that this legend who had played Woodstock when I was still playing in the sandbox actually let us produce him as opposed to some rappers who fought me every step of the way confirmed a couple things for me: First, I was a decent producer, or why else would I be in the room with a legend? Second, many rappers are controlling schmucks. Santana had us there to give him our mojo, and he didn't hold us back. I was surprised that he didn't want to play rhythm guitar on the track and left that up to Erik, who nailed it right away, as per usual. We then tracked the vocals so the band could get a feel for the tune. Next, we added bass and, lastly, we added a recurring organ part that I ended up actually sampling and flying back in throughout the tune.

Next came Carlos's turn.

Santana is a beast when it comes to soloing, ranking up there with heavyweights like Jimi Hendrix and Stevie Ray Vaughan. His playing is a rare mixture of virtuosity and soul. To say I was looking forward to him digging in would be an understatement. It was evident he had listened to the demo, as it took him almost no time to dial in his lead guitar parts. First, he hit the intro and played a long, subtle line that completely worked. Then he hit the first verse, playing fills in the spaces between the vocals. All his licks fit spot on, never stepping on the vocals as he nailed a bunch of sweet and soulful leads. The song had a nontraditional arrangement, which suited Carlos's soloing wants. As he approached the bridge, which opened up being that there were no vocals there, it gave him the space he needed to shred—and shred he did. He quickly ripped a vicious solo over the scattering Timberland–inspired drums fills. It was surprisingly aggressive yet right in the pocket. I felt spirits in the room while he ripped his leads. We tracked several solos, eventually combining several of the solos in the first bridge to make one finished "comp" part. Carlos then proceeded to take the same approach during the second verse, playing subtle fills between the vocals but stepping up the intensity of the licks, playing with a bit more aggression fitting the tune and helping it build. This approach was instinctual for Santana. He is a legend for a reason.

As he approached the end of the tune, he laid out beautiful, long, fluid lines under the vocals. He increased his emotion, and thus the emotion of the song, with these lines. As he approached the outro, he played less, subtly letting the Shahada and all its beauty sit there, stunningly surrounding it with just the right licks before ending it with one last hurricane of a solo. All in all, to witness this was spine tingling for me. Carlos recorded all of these parts in less than two hours. I was blown away.

To make it feel more fluid, we then had him overdub the comped solo in one take the following day, when we also recorded Erik's final vocal and backgrounds. To this day, when I hear that solo, it makes the hair on the back of my neck stand up. We also overdubbed parts, fixing the solo in the bridge and recorded percussion with the legendary conguero Karl Perazzo, who actually had me sit in with him at percussion kit. He graciously recorded my idea for the part, wise cracking the whole time. All in all, it was a gorgeous performance by Carlos and the band. It's easily my favorite of the three tunes I have worked on with Carlos, and one I am infinitely proud of. I had a great chemistry with Carlos and his band and thoroughly enjoyed his being and talents. Not only was I pleased with the tunes, but so were Carlos and his fans. It's probably why we worked together a few more times over the next few years.

I have to say, I made a nice transition from A&R kid to real record producer. Still, I was bad at playing the game of record industry politics, and honestly, my personal taste isn't usually pop music but way more out there and ahead of the curve, so to speak. I got lucky a few times. This was one of those time periods.

I had made some bucks and was back in New York. I was a single man, and I was taking meetings with every weasel in town. I had a manager, and I had work to do. I had to follow up another Everlast record, and I had gotten my friend Chip from Roguish Armament a deal under the guise of Hesher, a name given to him by Everlast. I was up to produce records by Monster Magnet, as well as a few other acts, but passed on them to produce my friend Chip instead—a decision I question to this day.

Things were looking up, but even still, not everything was ideal. We had studio problems. Gamble and I had split the SD50 studio with Geeby and another childhood friend, Miles Kelly, our boy from the punk rock days. In our absence, Miles had decided we were hogging all the studio time and that since we were now in the big leagues, we'd have to find our own studio. I didn't dispute the fact we were holed up in the studio far more than they were, but I also didn't want to have to slow down at the apex of our careers to find a new room for us to work out of. It was an uncomfortable situation. A preproduction studio is vital to every producer. It's where we did what's called woodshedding, which is when you work out your ideas. It's the spot where we fleshed out our ideas, wrote the basis for our songs, and worked out the kinks. It's where we would record our demos, such as the ones that helped us hone *Whitey Ford Sings the Blues*. For us, it was a vital tool for our job. You throw everything up against the wall and see what sticks. It's where you practice your craft with no pressure or boundaries, if you're lucky. Woodshedding is when most musicians, producers, and engineers log those ten thousand hours needed to master a craft.

I liked the sounds we got in our soon-to-be former room. And we had two major projects coming up but no preproduction lab to work in. We had to find a room quickly, and we did, conveniently enough, right down the hall. There was one problem with it: while it was much bigger than SD50, it was raw space. Even though it was just a rental space, we still had to build a live room, a control room, and put down floors, all of which would cost a few bucks. Worst of all, it took Gamble months to get the patch bay put in and the build out completed. It took much longer than we anticipated and put us months behind in our work schedule. Tensions were running high between us. We had a lot of pressure coming at us, and we weren't handling it well.

Santana's record *Supernatural* ended up selling more than twenty million records and was nominated for nine Grammys in 2000, including Album of the Year, which it would win. When ODB's record was nominated,

I had already switched jobs and didn't get to enjoy it. This time, I promised myself I would.

After these successes, the offers started rolling in. Gamble and I remixed records for Korn, Incubus, Xzibit, Mobb Deep, and others. We produced a record for Corrosion of Conformity, which never saw the light of day. We also worked with a great Swedish group, the Getaway People, and although they didn't have any hits, I dug making that record.

With a string of credits under my belt, I had also parlayed a production deal for myself at Loud Records, which I asked Gamble to be a part of—though he turned me down. He and I had increasing problems, technology was shifting, and even though I pleaded with him to get on top of current trends in recording, he didn't take my advice. To be honest, I wasn't the most adept with the shifting technology either. I was pretty good at other things—particularly hustling for work. In retrospect, I should have gotten more on top of the changing technology. It was part of my responsibility as well, and one I did not handle properly.

In the last summer of the nineties, we started on the Hesher record. Our new studio was cold, uncomfortable, and lacked the character and vibes of our former room. A part of me still believes that when we changed rooms, we lost some of our mojo. Couple that with my weed smoking, which I'd gone ballistic with, and my drinking like a fish most nights after work, and things were getting weird.

Gamble was so caught up in his own head that he declined to come with me to the Grammy Awards, even though he had a free ticket and hotel. I, on a selfish note, was happy hanging at the Grammys without Gamble, which was often like hanging out with a mortician. He was maniac depressive, much like my mother, and that energy brought up a lot of stuff for me. I took my new girl, Mary Sanner, instead.

Shortly after working with Santana, my friends who ran the streetwear company Stussy offered me a free trip to Vegas to hang out at the Magic Fashion Trade Show. I figured it would be fun, and maybe I could enjoy my newfound success and floss a little. Little did I know I would end up meeting one of the loves of my life.

I was at a party watching Hieroglyphics perform when I saw her there. I'd had a crush on her from a distance for several years, during which time I had exchanged a total of three words with her ever. I was feeling no pain when I decided to throw caution in the wind and approached her. She didn't even know my name. Full of liquid courage, I told myself that I was gonna shoot my shot and fuck it if I went down in flames. To my surprise, I got her number and took her out a few days after we got back to New York. She was beautiful, hilarious, and soulful, and would become my lady in a matter of weeks. We had an intense relationship, and I was more than a little grateful to share the biggest night of my life with her.

The night of the Grammys started off with us making our driver stop for In-N-Out Burger on Sunset. Then we smoked a fatty for dessert in the ride. We walked into the Staples Center knowing I was going to win that night, holding hands and celebrating my impending Grammy, our love, and each other. It was as much her night as mine; I would gladly share anything with her back then. I showered her with gifts and vacations that she never asked for. She never wanted anything from me but my love and faithfulness. I failed with the latter. She could never forgive me for my infidelities as much as she tried. I don't blame her. She loved me so much, and looking back on what transpired, I am ashamed of losing her over something as insignificant as a fling. I still hate a part of myself for this.

I was living in the Meatpacking District, a short walk to work. Mary lived with me for a while. We had something special, and I blew it—another example of losing a tremendous woman I loved over dumb shit. Everyone has that one that got away, and me, I've had a few. They say these things are what make you a man. For my part, I wish I could have spared myself the heartache. Mary remains, along with Jill Revson, one of the true loves of my life.

Before I dug in and started the Hesher record, I got another call from Pete Ganbarg at Arista Records. This time he asked me if I had anything for Run-DMC's comeback record. I was a huge fan, as was Everlast, so I roped him into the picture. I asked him if he had any ideas for Run and them. He said maybe and that he would be in NY in a few days, as he had a TV appearance to do. Later that day, I hit up Erik and told him I had an idea to flip the Steve Miller classic "Take the Money and Run" for Run-DMC. Erik liked the idea and Pete connected us with Run. I threw the beat together, recreated the hook, and shot the demo to Erik, who linked with Run. We headed to Chung King Studios a few days later.

Run was a weird cat. I had known him in my younger days. I was intimidated by him dead up. He gave me the rookie treatment early on in my career; he was a real ball buster. The greatest thing, though, about working with Run-DMC was reconnecting with my old friend, Jam Master Jay. Jay was a larger-than-life personality and a really funny cat. I had great affection for the man, and he had been really cool to me when I was just getting my foot in the door. The song, though a good idea, was marginal at the end of the day, but I got to hang with Jam Master Jay for several days in a row. We smoked a gang of weed, and he made fun of how skinny and awkward I was as a youngster at Rush. Jay and I reminisced about playing hoops back in the day and argued over who schooled whom. (I got schooled, but as you know, pride is real!) I looked up to Jay like a mentor of sorts, so it surprised me when I found out he was only two years older than me.

DMC didn't show up at the studio during the three days we worked, nor did he ever show up on the song. Jay explained to me the strange dynamic that Run-DMC had become. Everlast was super disappointed with the final result, but then again Erik hadn't gotten to hang with Jay for a few days and bug out. For me it was well worth it.

Of course, Jay was taken from the earth three years later. I only saw him one other time after that; we'd exchanged hugs and numbers, but life being what it is, we never hung. Jay was a tremendous character and I feel privileged that I got to hang with the big homie—those few days are a treasured memory of mine.

It's a travesty of justice, dead up, that it took eighteen years to finally charge someone with his murder. Now that they finally found out who his killers are, let's hope they put those motherfuckers away for life.

18

EAT AT WHITEY'S

Erik had toured for more than a year and a half after *Whitey Ford* dropped. The record was a hit, so we had a lot to follow up on. I was determined to make the best record I had ever made. As we were getting ready to embark on the next chapter of our partnership, though, it was obvious our dynamic had changed. Erik's manager, Carl Stubner, was more involved than ever, and honestly, he threw me off; he just wasn't a music cat. Often, his suggestions were asinine. I ignored them as best as I could, but his interference was a real distraction. He was concerned about the amount of the influence I had over Erik, and I was hostile toward him for trying to get more involved in our recording process. I mean, musically, he had nothing to do with the first record, and I wanted to keep it that way.

Erik had empowered his keyboardist, Keefus Ciancia, more this time, writing a bunch of the tunes with him. This was not a bad thing, but they forgot one key element this time around—the rapping. What made *Whitey Ford* so great was the back and forth between rap and singer/songwriter. Erik didn't seem to be concerned about this, and I have always felt this was a miscue on our part.

To make things even harder, Gamble was at his maniac-depressive worst. He was suffering through manopause and inflicting it on all of us throughout the entire making of the record. He was miserable, and like they say, misery loves company. I tried to be compassionate, but I failed in that regard. Our livelihoods were on the line, his included, but he was too caught up to realize it. He was having trouble sleeping in his pad due to noise and continuously complained that he was in physical pain of some sort or another. The cause for all of this, I believe, was the pressure of following up a hit record. I loved John, he was my musical and business partner, but he wasn't the most important person or thing in this equation. Everlast and his record were. This is something Gamble lost sight of, and as a result, his negativity started to take a toll on all of us.

One day while tracking guitars in our new studio back in New York, it all came to a head. Gamble was complaining about his inability to sleep, blaming the people in the bar downstairs and our workload. As a way to rectify the situation, Erik offered to put him up in a hotel for as long as it took to finish tracking the record if he would stop complaining. Gamble explained he didn't need a handout and kept on whining.

Erik finally took off the kid gloves and said, "Look, man, I'm trying to help you out, because I need to make this record. You're a part of this, G, but you're acting like a bitch. This ain't about you—this is about my record."

"Fuck you!" Gamble said. "Without me, you wouldn't be making this record."

Erik, never one to take an insult lightly, stood up. I thought he was going to sock Gamble in the mouth. "Excuse me?"

"I saved your life," Gamble said. "Without me, you wouldn't even be here to make this record."

I cringed, not believing Gamble went there. Like he had an option to save or not save Erik's life that fateful night.

Erik got right in his face and said, "I'm trying to help you. I don't need you. I can do this shit without you."

Gamble knew he'd fucked up. Tears swelled in his eyes. It was tough to even look at him. What prompted him to say this to Erik, I'll never know, but it was so out of line that I was embarrassed for him.

At this point, I started to view Gamble as a potential liability. He was too emotionally soft; he wasn't built for the pressures of the music game. Erik and I were of a different breed. We didn't know how to feel sorry for ourselves. When our backs were against the wall, we never folded. Instead, we accomplished our best shit ever. We overcame pitfalls for better, not worse. The pity party has no place in the music business.

Needless to say, the rest of the record was steeped in a modicum of bad energy between Gamble and myself. I tried my best to keep Erik out of the fray. If there are bad vibes surrounding anything creative, especially a song, then it has a much harder chance of reaching its potential. If it's steeped in bad vibes, how can the song not project that bad energy? Gamble could never understand this. I tried to explain it to him, but it fell on deaf ears. We were at a point where he just couldn't hear what I was saying anymore, and I had grown tired of his emo behavior.

The saddest part is that Gamble is exceptionally gifted and far more hands-on than I am, technically speaking; however, he doesn't have the creative vision I do. This made for a successful partnership right up until it didn't.

Still, we hunkered down in the basement and made some great music despite the unnecessary stress. Since Keefus was more involved, his presence brought more soul influences to the record. His flip on the song "One in the Same" is case in point. In writing the song, he showed two different approaches to the keyboard and bass lines. One was a New Orleans–inspired Meters-type of approach, and I have to admit it floored me. We ended up recutting the whole tune for the better because of this. Lending a different perspective to a song is what great musicians do. A good producer understands this and encourages it instead of fighting it. Keefus was a great musician, and to this day he still ranks as one of my all-time favorite keyboardists. His musical choices helped make me a better producer.

Since I had a decent budget this time, we were able to bring in some renowned sidemen. We had CeeLo Green come and sing on a tune called "We're All Gonna Die." I hired Warren Haynes, the amazing guitarist from the Allman Brothers and Gov't Mule, to come and play slide on a few tunes. I also got the legendary Merry Clayton, who sang on the Rolling Stones's "Gimme Shelter," to sweeten up a few things, including "Black Coffee," which I felt turned out spectacular. On top of that, I got to work with the string arranger David Campbell, which had been a lifelong dream of mine. His arrangements and the experience of working with live string players were majestic to me. To sit in the live room and help mic the string section and to experience the beauty of a twelve-piece string section play a song I helped put together was thrilling. That experience is one of the most amazing things I have ever gotten to do in the recording studio. We added the wonderful vocalist N'Dea Davenport to the mix as well. She added some great vocals to "One and the Same," and the stunning duet, "Love for Real."

After we finished *Eat at Whitey's,* Erik confided in me that a verse in the tune "Love for Real" was about Mary and me. When we started making the record, Mary left me—she couldn't deal with my infidelities any longer. ("And for some ass, I watched it all go up in smoke.") I spent the rest of the record trying to get her back, and we tried to work it out so many times, but it just wasn't meant to be. Keep it a buck, I couldn't listen to that song for a long time. I spent a lot of hours in a lot of bars for way too many years drinking way too hard wishing I hadn't blown it with her.

The first single, which dropped the first week in October 2000, was titled "Black Jesus." I didn't have a problem with the song—in fact, I thought it was fantastic, super creative. I thought it had a shot to be a hit. There was one thing I had a problem with: the title. No white alternative radio programmer was going to feel comfortable playing a song with that title. Erik had a big Southern base, and it was not going to fly on rock stations there. Erik's manager, as well as the label, said I was overthinking it when I brought it up in meetings. I reminded anyone who would listen that the song was called "Freak of Nature" originally, and I clearly wrote the title on all the master tapes and DATS.

We also had problems with the video. Jonas Åkerlund directed an expensive video in London. I had reconciled with Mary for a few, and she joined me there, but bad vibes were everywhere on the set, and I suspected the video was going to be bad. I was wrong. It wasn't bad. It was awful. Saddest part was that Erik and I had always wanted to work with Jonas Åkerlund; we thought he was a genius, but on this one, he came up short.

Those two problems, however, paled in comparison to the main reason the record wasn't a hit. Erik had met a young Eminem in a Washington, DC, hotel. Erik felt Em had been a prick when they met, which I later heard was just Em being socially awkward when Everlast gave him props—but who knows, I wasn't there. If I were, it might have turned out differently.

Erik took offense and decided to air him out on a Dilated Peoples song called "Ear Drums Pop," ("Cock my hammer, spit a comet like Halley / I buck a .380 on ones that act shady") in which he took shots at Em's daughter, Hailie. This was a low blow to any father. As much as it hurts to admit, I believe it was just Erik's overly healthy ego that caused this situation to escalate. Often white rappers have beef with each other just to see who's "realer," which I jokingly call white-on-white crime.

When I heard about the Dilated Peoples song, my first thought was "Don't ever fuck with the dude on top, make friends with him instead." I had always heard Em was an Everlast fan, that he grew up digging House of Pain. We had several mutual friends, and I'd heard he was a good dude. I was hoping that it would pass, but then I ran into Theo Sedlmayr and Paul Rosenberg—my lawyer and Em's manager, respectively. They told me in no uncertain terms that Erik should change his verse. If not, Em was going to go for the jugular. While I respected them pulling my coat on the situation, I was also pissed at them and everyone around me for a situation I felt was avoidable. I had worked too hard resurrecting my career to have some bullshit fuck with my money, or so I thought.

Something I learned at a young age growing up on the LES is that you have to pick your battles. Erik didn't need to go at Eminem, who at the time was one of, if not the biggest star in not only hip-hop but all of music. Em also lives for this kind of shit. It adds fuel to his fire, so to speak. I brought up the option of changing the verse to Erik.

No dice.

Em proceeded to drop his first diss song, "I Remember."

As "Black Jesus" started to tank, Carl Stubner arranged a meeting with Tom Silverman at Tommy Boy that he asked me to join. I came up with a pretty good plan, or so I'd thought. I advised that we postpone the release of the record with the hope that the beef with Eminem would blow over. Silverman didn't agree. His ad buys were in place at radio and retail, and Stubner backed him up.

I couldn't believe these guys.

Em dropped "Quitter," a second diss song I believe hurt Erik's rollout even further. He demanded that his fans take up his cause, and the fact is Em had a lot of fans, many of whom were also Everlast's fans. Both of the diss songs were very personal. Word is that Erik's friend and former bandmate, Leor Dimant—better known as DJ Lethal—leaked inside info about Erik to Em, some of which landed in the lyrics. To this day, I have never forgiven Lethal for his disloyalty. It was some sucker shit, and only suckers do sucker shit. A reliable source inside of Em's camp told me that after the first diss track dropped, Lethal and Fred Durst were talking shit and told Em that they were down to appear on "Quitter," but then they chickened out. Lethal was so shook that in an interview he said that Everlast would kick Em's ass if the two fought.

Em wasn't having it, and he dropped the song "Girls," where he goes after the two of them with the same gusto he attacked Everlast with. I had to respect Em's art of war. He dropped "I Remember" a week before *Eat at Whitey's* dropped, and "Quitter" the week after. Like I said: Don't fuck with the man on top, especially if you want to play pole position. In retrospect, I probably should have gotten more involved in trying to squash the whole shit.

At first, I played it half-wrong and lost my cool. To be honest, I think Paul Rosenberg knew it was going to hurt my pockets and I don't believe he wanted that to happen, so he pulled my coat on it. I reluctantly backed Erik. I had to, right? I'm a ride-or-die cat; that's how I was raised. Wrong or right, you gotta back your boys up. To this day, I wish I could have fixed it all. At the end of the day, Em won and we lost, and in all honesty my producing career was never quite the same after the failure of *Eat at Whitey's*.

Still, I stand by the record. It's dark, honest, and full of pain and loss. Lyrically, it is astounding. I believe, to this day, it is one the best records I've ever made. It's too bad more people didn't get to hear it. The record lacked the big hit song we really needed. It also lacked the rap dynamic that many of *Whitey Ford*'s fans coveted. Eminem nailed the coffin shut. It ended up finally going gold, but it should have sold way more. We were coming off of a triple platinum album. More importantly, it should have been heard by more people. It's just that damn good.

I had finagled a label deal at Loud Records and a publishing deal at Sony. I was also coming off a flop, and work was drying up. I went back to what I knew: rap music. I started making beats again, which Gamble hated. I wanted to get out of my publishing deal. I had a payoff waiting for me if I could fulfill my song commitment, so I convinced Loud that I should make a compilation record. They were not particularly into the idea, but I had two "puts," and this was going to be one of them. (A put means you can put out whatever you want and the label can't block you.)

I knew if I produced the bulk of the record and wrote most of the music I would be able to get out of my publishing deal and cash myself out. I ran it past Gamble, who wasn't psyched on the idea. I explained I could pay him $3,000 per song, and when he heard that he could scoop up $30,000-plus, his attitude changed.

The record titled *Stimulated Volume 1* dropped on October 23, 2001. I had a lot of fun working with a bunch of rappers, including my old friends Tha 'Liks, Everlast, Dilated Peoples, and B-Real. It was a cool experience, but at this point I was much better at making singer/songwriter tunes infused with beats as opposed to making rap music. I did, however, get De La Soul on the record, as well as King T, an OG legend and one of my favorite all-time West Coast MCs. I also put Sadat X on it and my old crony, Del.

Deep down, I knew it wouldn't sell, but it got me out of my publishing deal and netted me some bucks. It was a hustle, for sure, but then again, sometimes in this game you gotta be a hustler.

The record came out and my deal at Loud came to an end shortly after, as they were on the ropes. Steve Rifkind and his partner, Rich Isaacson, had always been fair with me. In fact, Isaacson was one of most honest, straight-up people I have ever met in the music industry. He told me the label was going under and they were going to have to let my deal go. I saw it coming and was already planning my exit and next moves. I hunkered down in the studio, making beat after beat—much to Gamble's dismay. He was so obstinate it hurt. I would bring any rapper of any note I could to work. I figured a good tune or two might fix my predicament. It had always worked in the past.

About the time of the Stimulated compilation, I had linked up with a rapper from Newark named Young Zee, who was part of a crew called the Outsidaz—who were, ironically enough, connected to Eminem. Young Zee had a lot of style. He was a talented cat who never took the biz all that seriously for reasons unknown, though the rumor in the streets was that he had money. He has since had some hard times, or so I've heard, which sucks—he was a good dude.

We made a song called "That's My N***** Fo' Real." It was a bugged-out tune for me. For one, I played keys on it, and honestly, I'm not that good. Nonetheless, Gamz coached me through it, and I played most of my parts on a cheap Moog Rogue synth I got from Keefus, as well as a Fender Rhodes electric piano. The tune was cool, but I didn't think much about it after we finished it. It didn't feel like a money record. I was also going out to Los Angeles a bunch and had connected with Dom Trenier (RIP), an old friend and Mark Ronson's then-manager, who was interested in working with me. Dom and I unfortunately fell out over a girl, ending our friendship. Dom has since passed away and we never reconciled our relationship. He did, however, put me in the studio with Macy Gray in hopes of managing me. I played Macy about twenty songs, and she dug the last song I had on my CD— a tune Gamble had demanded I add—one in which I had played melodica on. She told me she had an opportunity to get the song on the *8 Mile* soundtrack. The irony of having a song on an Eminem–driven record was interesting to me. I knew it would be a seller, thus possibly getting me a nice royalty. I told her to go for it. Macy did the vocals without me and submitted the song.

At this point, I had started working without Gamble on a record for a rock band called the Fun Lovin' Criminals. They were good dudes, but the keyboard player in the band was also the main producer. He didn't want me to produce the record from the start, making it an uphill battle. I also didn't want to bring Gamble and my bad vibes to the project, so I kept him out of it. This did not help me in the studio, as Gamble was always more technically proficient than I was.

In the midst of producing the FLC record, I got an interesting call from my lawyer, Theo Sedlmayr, and an old friend, Marc LaBelle, who worked for Shady Records. He told me they wanted the Macy Gray song for the soundtrack and asked me if I could mix it in a few days. I was floored. I asked what kind of money I would get for the track and what the publishing looked like since I didn't have a deal with Macy or Shady Records.

Theo told me I wasn't a writer on the track when it was submitted. I was pissed. It felt like Macy Gray was trying to chump me on the publishing side of a song that I had written all the music for. She also only wanted to give me coproduction credit on the tune. Theo told me he would fight for me to get what I deserved, since he was my lawyer and the one doing the administrative work on the soundtrack. I was freaked. I needed the bucks, and I also knew that down the road both the publishing and the royalties were going to be worth real money. I asked Theo what I should do.

He told me he was going to put her to the test, and he did. He demanded I get half the publishing, which ended up being forty percent at the end of the day. Macy also tried to pay me five grand, which was insulting. Theo, with Paul Rosenberg's sign off, got me twelve, as she was getting somewhere around $70,000 all in, or so I was told. I was shocked that she was so cutthroat with me. Understandably, I never worked with her again. We'd had a heated conversation over the phone while trying to work out the deal, during which I told her in no uncertain terms, "Don't you ever try to take food off my table." In retrospect, this wasn't so cool. I only saw her once after the record came out, and she looked like she'd seen a ghost.

But like I said, I am a hothead, and this was also another example of me being a bad politician. I did, however, mix the song down pretty quickly only to have her shit on the mix because of one ad-lib she didn't like. She mixed it herself, and honestly her mix sounded like dog feces. I was bummed, but I got paid and I did have a song on a potentially huge record.

A few days passed and I got another interesting call. Once again it was Marc LaBelle, this time asking about a Young Zee song I had made. Again, I was totally surprised and wondered how this came to be. He had hung with them on the tour bus in Atlanta and pulled out the CD and played it for them. It turns out that Denaun Porter, who was one of Em's main producers and a member of D12, dug it. He also played it for Slim Shady himself, who liked the record and wanted it for the soundtrack.

The rest, as they, say is history.

Marc told me I had to mix it within the next two days or so if I wanted it on the record and wanted to verify it had no samples in it. Following my work with Everlast, I stopped sampling as much and started making my own music. As it happened, samples were really killing my pockets on the publishing side. I was also still making the Fun Lovin' Criminals record, which by the way, never came out. A day later, I got Gamble back in the mix and had him get up with Young Zee to fix some vocals and start to mix the record down at Platinum Island Studios.

I came directly from the Fun Lovin' Criminals session, burned out but hellbent on finishing the mix. I took a shower at the studio, drank a big pot of coffee, and stayed up all night to finish. The engineer, Bob Brockman, dipped out halfway through the mix after I deemed him useless out loud, so his assistant Bo Boddie and I finished it up. Bo ended up actually coming to work for me a while later, basically replacing Gamble as my engineer. I nailed the mix and submitted it the next day and ended up having two songs on what would be the biggest soundtrack of the year.

Don't forget, this all went down after Em threw a serious monkey wrench into *Eat at Whitey's*. The irony of this did not escape Paul Rosenberg, who at the record release party told me I was the only outside producer with two songs on the record. I believe he was genuinely happy to put some bread in my pocket after the Em/Everlast beef. Paul, being a mensch, didn't hold any of it against me. Funny to think after the beef between my best friend and Eminem I still had two songs on his soundtrack.

I saw my man Young Zee at the party, too, and we got wasted. The funny thing is I got those gigs with Gamble and they ended up being the last records I ever made with him. I never worked with Young Zee again either. As for Theo Sedlmayr, we had a big falling out down the road, but lawyers come and go. He was a total shark, like most good lawyers in the record game, but when you're his client, you're not exactly mad about it.

To this day, the only house I ever owned was in part purchased with that *8 Mile* money.

So, Marshall and Paul, from the bottom of my heart: thank you!

19

THEY REMINISCE OVER YOU

After *8 Mile,* **I hit** a cold spell, musically. I started making a third Everlast record, but there was a problem—he still had Stubner as his manager, but he didn't have a record label. Tommy Boy—or Tommy Bitch, as we had started to call it—had gone out of business. Erik was briefly on Warner Brothers, but they didn't give a shit about him. Because I love Erik and believed in his artistry, I used the juice card I had in the stash with Tom Whalley, the president of Warner at the time.

I met with Tom at his gorgeous home in Beverly Hills. While there plugging for Erik, I figured I might as well hit him up for an A&R gig. Whalley told me he thought *Eat at Whitey's* was a lazy record. I had a lot of respect for Whalley, but I didn't agree with his critique of *Eat at Whitey's* at all. Still, I held my tongue for maybe the only time in my life because I really wanted to help Erik, and I wanted a gig. I never got the job, but Whalley did agree to let Erik go a few weeks later, which was good and bad.

We hunkered down in my spot and cut the new tunes minus Keefus, who was by now burned on the whole thing. Gamble was an amazing pain in the ass this go around and was relieved of his duties after a few sessions. We were over his garbage. We completed the demos and shopped them for an entire year and got no love. I remember playing them for the powers that be at Universal and knowing they weren't into it. We were yesterday's papers, or so it seemed. I was scared about our prospects and didn't know what to do.

I continued to try to write songs. I had gotten an offer for a new publishing deal with EMI post-*8 Mile*. I remember, while waiting to finish up my paperwork on the deal, that Gamble wanted to charge me for engineering since I got publishing on stuff he didn't. I asked him to hang in for a few months, and I would break him off in full when my publishing deal went through. He told me I was full of shit, that I wasn't getting any publishing deal, that it was all a lot of hot air.

Bo Boddie became my new engineer, I got my publishing deal, and I never did make music with Gamble again. For all of our hassles, we had something special, but the dysfunction in our relationship was too much for both of us. We couldn't coexist anymore. Breaking up with Gamble as a musical partner was one of the hardest things I'd ever had to face up to. We made great music together, but the business was changing on us and we weren't on top anymore. I know I'm not an easy person to deal with, and neither was he. I'm not going to front—my music suffered without him.

One of the worst parts about the end of our working relationship is that in the years that passed, we lost touch for a long period of time. When my dad passed in 2011, Gamble called me and we had a heartfelt talk. It felt good to hear his voice. He had lost his younger brother, who had MS, in a car crash. He understood what loss was about. My relationship with Gamble was one of the more complex relationships I have ever had. We undoubtedly made history, but at the end of the day, we failed each other as musical partners and friends.

In late 2003, an A&R guy named Lewis Largent fell in love with Everlast's demos. I was shocked. Lewis was a nice dude with a lot of brains and excellent taste. He was married to my former sparring partner Julie Greenwald, who was the president of Island Def Jam and my old mentor Lyor Cohen's right hand. (Many years later, at Asylum Records, Julie would also help throw me to the wolves.) I thought we might have a real shot, though I thought the new music wasn't as good as what we had done before. We missed Keefus, and my ability to direct Erik musically had diminished. Regardless, Erik got the deal and we got to work, but things were different this time around.

Erik decided to produce half of the record himself, which was cool by me. I came in and coproduced the songs and added bells and whistles, tightened up the drums a little and crossed my fingers. I thought the first single had a shot, but right when it came out, Lyor and Julie left the company to go run Atlantic Records. This left us in the lurch. LA Reid, who took over the operation, didn't give a shit about the record. "White Trash Beautiful," the album's first single, didn't go the distance. In retrospect, it might have been a bit too derivative of "What it's Like," and in any event it failed to connect.

We had been away for almost four years and the record we made simply wasn't good enough in the public's eyes. It also met a mixed critical response. While we were making the record in LA, I was able to travel to the Bay to spend some quality time with my dad, so I'm grateful for that. I was just glad he was healthy. My mom, unfortunately, had slipped deep into Alzheimer's disease, which made seeing her extremely depressing. Thank God I was able make peace with her while she was still in control of her faculties. Watching her demise was one of the most painful things I have ever dealt with.

When my father and I had free time together, we usually walked the streets, taking in the sights and philosophizing. We would go to museums, eat Mexican food, go to see live music, sit in the park, and enjoy the sunshine—all the while talking about basketball, art, and politics. We smoked lots of weed together and visited his old friends, who were like relatives to me. He enjoyed shopping for records together. I really loved buying him clothes. He had a great fondness for graphic T-shirts with his jazz heroes on them that I would buy at this groovy store on Haight. I once took him into Supreme in NY and got the Miles Davis shirt for him. The cats working there were friends of mine and were tripping on how cool my dad was. Funny how small memories can stay etched in your mind sometimes, right?

One of my favorites among my dad's friends was his childhood running buddy and my godfather, QR Hand (RIP), a tall, handsome, light-skinned

Black man with a voice as smooth as velvet. QR was a gentleman and a great poet. He was also one of my father's best friends, and we considered him family. QR was like the uncle I never had. He struggled with me as we watched my dad's health decline, all the while QR's was doing the same. QR passed during the COVID-19 pandemic at the age of eighty-three. True to my dad's spirit, I spent a weekend with him while he was dying, listening to stories about my dad and him in their youth. I promised my dad I would stay connected to him, and I proudly honored his wish. I loved QR. He was a great man and one of the last links to my father's youth.

My dad also appreciated my friends. He loved my boy Domino and my drug-addled pal, Harry Jumonji. I liked having my dad around my friends because I wanted people to know I loved him, and I also wanted them to understand why. When you hung with my pops and me, you could see where I got a lot of my spirit from.

After the failure of *White Trash Beautiful,* I focused on trying to write songs. The one problem was that I was a limited musician and an average songwriter. I had to hire musicians on a perennial basis, which can be expensive. Bo and I hunkered down in the basement, and in the midst of it, I started to realize it was fruitless—yet I refused to throw in the towel. I was freaked out. I ended up running through close to a $100,000 without selling one song.

I saw the writing on the wall: my career as a record producer was coming to a standstill. I revisited a friendship with a young, wild, charismatic Puerto Rican rapper named Tru Life, who ended up getting locked up for five years down the road. He had a young white girl named Robyn Spree, who I swear was one of the best female rappers I ever heard. We got her a deal at Elektra Records courtesy of my old boss, Sylvia Rhone. Robyn's record never saw the light of day as Sylvia was fired six months after the deal and the new regime kicked Robyn to the curb. I swear in my heart of hearts that she was the truth. It's a damn shame the masses never got to hear her.

I also inadvertently helped Tru Life get his deal at Roc-A-Fella Records, which was a division of Def Jam, when we scoured a 9th Wonder beats CD to find Tru's underground hit, "The New New York." It was the nineteenth beat on a twenty-track beat CD given to me by my friend Kevin Mitchell. We quickly recorded the song in my studio and Tru leaked it, and then bang, all of a sudden it was getting play on Hot 97, the most listened to hip-hop station in the city at the time.

It happened so damn quick all I got was a thank you, but I was still happy for my friend. He was a wild kid, and I thought this might be his ticket out of his crazy life. I was happy to see an MC from the Lower East Side actually get to rep in the rap game. He could have been a superstar. In 2009, he was involved in an incident that started at Club Pacha and ended in a lobby of a building on East Twenty-Sixth Street that left one man stabbed to death and another injured. Tru pleaded guilty to gang assault and was sentenced to eight years; his brother caught a dime. In April 2016, Tru was released from prison. He maintains his innocence, saying he only pleaded guilty because he thought he'd probably do a lot longer stretch if convicted. He currently has a deal with Future, one of the biggest stars in all of hip-hop. I wish him the greatest of success; he deserves it. He has been to hell and back.

Even though I had depleted almost all of my savings, I was still focused on writing songs. In the midst of this frustrating endeavor, I linked up with Anthony Hamilton and wrote what could be the best song I ever helped write: a track called "Twisted." I wrote the hook and bridge, as well as the music. Anthony and I, along with a woman named Nandi Willis, wrote the verses, and Anthony sang the shit out of the song. It was about Mary, which if she didn't know then, she knows now. It was a tale of love lost, like most of my songs. For being such a harsh person, I tend to write sentimental tunes.

Go figure.

I pitched it for Santana but was told it didn't work. A year later, when Santana started another record, I resubmitted the tune again to my old friend Pete Ganbarg. This time, the song was chosen to be on the record. Shows how full of shit some A&R people can be. I suspect the cat I initially gave the demo to probably never played it for Santana. I was back in business, or so I thought.

Clive Davis, the head of the newly formed J Records, and a young A&R man named Larry Jackson, decided Joss Stone, the white neophyte English blue-eyed soul singer, should sing the song. There was only one problem—I had to transpose the tune for her natural register, and it lost some of its emotion. Another problem was that Anthony sang the shit out of the tune. Joss Stone simply didn't have the chops to sing the song like Anthony did.

I went back to the Bay Area and hung with my pops for a few before I went into the studio with Santana again. I hadn't seen him since he played on *Eat at Whitey's* and, honestly, I was never sure if I nailed it that time. This was the first time I was in this situation with a tune I wrote and produced without John or Erik. It was scary. But Carlos, being one of the coolest guys in music, made it easy. We transposed the tune, added live drums, and replaced the keys. Carlos also replayed the guitars for the most part. He kept commenting on how great Anthony Hamilton sounded on the record and wondering out loud if taking him off of it was a smart idea. I questioned it as well, but the label had its priorities, so I played along. I already had a bad reputation as being difficult and was trying to change that.

Next, I went to LA and recorded Joss Stone for two straight days, and it just didn't work. She walked in freaked by the demo vocal performance and told me "I ain't no Anthony Hamilton, but I'm gonna give it my best." Her best wasn't good enough. I worked her hard for those two days in the studio, and she was a sweet young lady, but Anthony is the truth, and this was a grown man's song. As cute and talented as Joss Stone is, she ain't a grown man, and she isn't named Anthony Hamilton. He is, hands down, the best vocalist I have ever worked with. I always wanted to hear him make a traditional soul record. I think it would alter people's perception of him as an artist. One can always hope, right?

I took the record back to J and to the golden boy A&R kid, Larry Jackson. A few days later, I got a call from Clive Davis, who told me, "This is terrible. Come to my office tomorrow."

I didn't know Clive, but of course I knew of him. Everyone in music did. A tough Jewish guy from Brooklyn who was orphaned at the age of fifteen, he managed to win a scholarship to Harvard Law School. Over his half century in the record biz, he signed such notable acts as Bruce Springsteen, Janis Joplin, Billy Joel, and Aerosmith. He backed Bad Boy Records with Puff, even though he admitted he never really understood hip-hop. To say Clive Davis is a record man would be an understatement.

I walked into a peanut gallery of A&R people, sat down, and Clive played the Joss Stone version.

"This is awful," he said. "It sounds like acid jazz. I want to put the other guy back on it."

"I told you that he nailed it the first time. Now I have to transpose it back down again and rerecord the whole tune. That's like making the song twice. I should get paid again. This is gonna be a lot of work."

Clive Davis shot me a look that could kill. I'm still injured to this day. He turned to me and said, "If I were your manager, I would tell you not to be so cheeky. You'll get paid. Who's your lawyer?"

I ignored his question. My then-lawyer, Peter Paterno, wouldn't even return my calls at that point. "Clive, I still haven't got my advance on this song yet."

He looked right through me. "You'll get paid twice, and you'll get paid by the end of the week. I want you to go back out to California and recut the music in the right register and put Anthony Hamilton back on it."

"Okay," was all I could mutter as I was ushered out of his office. I'm sure he handed someone else their ass fifteen minutes after he handed me mine.

The check came and I headed back out to the Bay a week later to recut the tune. I hung with my pops and told him the Clive Davis runnings. He laughed and told me I was lucky, and that I should go to Mary's house and serenade her with the tune until she forgave me. My dad really liked her, but it was a lost cause by this point. I returned to Fantasy Studios and hunkered down with Santana's band and recut the whole tune in the preferred register. I then added percussion and new keys to it. I also went back to New York and had Anthony add a little extra to the vocals. Santana was psyched that Anthony was back on the song. I did a decent rough mix of the tune and resubmitted it again and waited for the call from Clive.

And boy did it come.

"I hate it." That was the first thing he said.

I was baffled because I had given him what I hoped he wanted. "What's the matter with it?"

He had his assistant pull out the original demo and put it on. "I want this," he said. "I don't want any live drums. I want the demo."

I was shocked. Clive Davis, of all people, had gotten a case of demo-itis. That's when you become so used to the demo that you chase it, even though the song had evolved into something else. Almost every producer and artist has been through it at one point or another.

Clive told me to get rid of the live drums and percussion as well, but I ignored him. The live drums, played by the legendary Steve Jordan, albeit edited and blended in under the programing are included on the final mix. He also told me Anthony's vocals were now too big. He said I should keep the original Wurlitzer keyboard stuff as well.

"I feel like I'm back waiting tables again," I said. "However you want it, you'll get it."

Clive did not care for my sarcasm. He told me, "Kid, I been making records before you were born. Whitney Houston's first smash, 'You Give Good Love,' was a demo. Kashief mixed that record seven times, and at the end of the day, I put out the demo. Sometimes the demo is just the one."

I nodded and was shown my way out.

I finished the record almost exactly how he ordered. Guess what? As much as I hate to admit it, this last version was the best out of all of them. The guy had dynamite ears and vision. I learned there was a reason why he had such a long run. He knew music.

My dad loved "Twisted" and was constantly asking me to play it for him when he visited me a few months later. I have to say, I was really proud of it myself. I had made a tune for Santana and no one had a hand in producing it but me. I felt like maybe I was artistically self-sufficient. I was creatively vindicated—though that vindication wouldn't last long.

I got paid for both versions, which gave me some breathing room. I tried to write songs for almost an entire year following the release of the Santana song. I played them for everyone I could. I also tried to get my publishers to wake up and smell the coffee. They weren't having it, and the money I made was dwindling.

I was struggling both creatively and financially.

My dad came to New York for a month around this time. We spoke about my finances and how I felt the end of my music career was near. He told me that maybe it was and perhaps I should think about other things I wanted to do if that was the case.

I started dabbling with writing and ended up writing a column for a magazine called *Mass Appeal*, which was run by my former intern/assistant. I tried to start a marketing company with *Mass Appeal,* but it didn't work out. Around this time, I created a beat-making contest called *King of the Beats* for Scion, a car company owned by Toyota. The program was a success, and it opened the door for me to start doing marketing for a few brands.

This led me to leave the music business behind for a while and focus more on marketing opportunities, or as I liked to call it, "cultural multi-tasking." It was a survival tactic of sorts. I revisited my love of art and started blogging about the emerging street art wave. My blog was NYC–culture based and ended up connecting me with a lot of people, particularly younger kids on the come up. Blogging was fun. I got to share my warped downtown sensibilities with the online world, pontificate on segments of the culture, and celebrate my friends. I managed to ride the blog trend to an alternate career of sorts for a few seasons. I also got to practice writing a bit, which was a fringe benefit. I took a consulting gig with an emerging NYC brand, 10 Deep. It was a lot of fun for a few. I was running around downtown with people like Aaron Bondaroff, Kid Cudi, Plain Pat and Dash Snow, the Alife guys, and other creatives who were forging a new movement in NYC. Things were fun again for a while

From blogging, I was given an entrée to the emerging business of streetwear, a culture that revolved around apparel that was created specifically for left-of-center people (mostly kids) who didn't want to conform to what everyone else wore. It was a do-it-yourself movement at the time. It has since become a huge business and subsequently far less interesting to me.

Since I was one of the guys in the first ad for Stüssy, the godfather of all streetwear brands in the eighties, my entry was pretty easy. Funny thing: Stussy had used my image for more than twenty years and only recently paid me for my likeness. My long history in music and strong sense of personal style helped. I was generally greeted with open arms. I still made music when I could, but I had bills, and this was the easiest and least emotional way to pay them. Making music and not having success coupled with all of the unreturned phone calls had left me burned on the biz for the time being.

The youth have always been the driving force in cultural shifts and NYC was experiencing one. Labels like Fool's Gold were emerging and people like Spank Rock and Santigold were pushing musical boundaries. A new sound and scene had sprung up, several in fact. Alternative rock music had taken a new turn and bands like Yeah, Yeah, Yeahs; LCD Soundsystem; and TV on the Radio were making interesting dance-infused alternative music with a distinct NYC bend to it. Funny how so many of the people pushing this new movement weren't even from NY, yet they were contributing to what was making the city fun and vital again. Places like 205, the Alfie backyard events, and Studio B in Brooklyn were centers for the creative community taking shape. I was hanging out at gallery openings and places like Max Fish and Lit. It was an exciting time, right before the East Village was completely co-opted. I was intrigued and inspired by what was being putting forth creatively by my peers and the younger generation, and thankfully I was able to have a front row seat for a lot of it—one of the benefits to being an OG.

The break from music did me good, and marketing made me enough money to stay afloat. I still had the urge to make music, but I had been doing it nonstop for two decades at this point without a break. I tried to tell myself that I deserved one. Watching acts like The Cool Kids and Kid Cudi make their mark with DIY music took me back to the aesthetic of my punk rock days. It was inspiring.

As much as I didn't want to admit it, I knew deep down that my true musical calling was as an A&R man. I just wasn't sure if I fit in anymore. Was I just another middle-aged guy who had been made obsolete by technology? I enjoyed writing songs, but the cost had been too great. I had gone through a lot of my life savings, and cats weren't even returning my calls.

I finagled an A&R gig from Steve Rifkind after alerting him to David Banner, whom he ended up signing. Initially I was consulting for Steve, who ended up making me a VP at his company SRC. Two acts I tried to sign while at SRC were the Cool Kids and Kid Cudi. They both slipped through our fingers. Steve never got Cudi and the Cool Kids had already signed some shady paperwork. Cudi eventually got signed by Sylvia Rhone, though his success did confirm to me that I still knew what I was doing. I had helped create a project with Cudi and the brand 10 Deep and A-Trak and the Fool's Gold guys for his mixtape *A Kid Named Cudi*. It's funny how I had the honor of being part of connecting these two cultures seamlessly. These were, I believe, some of the earliest examples of streetwear and music being so connected. I always wondered if Rifkind had signed Kid Cudi what effect it would have had on my career.

After a year and change at SRC, me and eight other coworkers were shown the door, and the label soon went under. This got me down. I had been working hard. I really thought that I might be shut out of the record business at the age of forty. I thought about Howard Thompson, a great record man who was shown the door at Elektra and who never got another shot at the big leagues ever again. I felt old. I knew in my heart of hearts that I still had good ears and that I understood culture and the nuances of subcultures of such.

But if no one else knew it, what did it matter?

I returned to my marketing hustle I worked at rebuilding PRO-Keds, a brand I had worn throughout most of my childhood. Growing up, it was a real part of NYC. I had some success with the brand. I also had to deal with some questionable upper management people who said a few questionable things regarding race more than once. I had to resist the urge to choke out the dumb fuck who was my boss. I was biding my time there and was offered what I envisioned as a better job at Famous Stars and Straps, an apparel brand owned by Travis Barker, the drummer for Blink-182.

2009 was a trying year for me all around. In August of 2009, I lost my dear friend Andy Kessler. He was a great man, like my dad. He had done so much for so many and asked for nothing in return, a lot like Geeby. My pops had heard me speak of him a bunch and called me when he read about it in, of all places, *The New York Times*. Andy was a strong life force and a constant in mine. He was the godfather of New York City skateboarding and the man who brokered the city's funding of the first public skate parks in New York. He lived a sober lifestyle and was dedicated to service and the spirit of recovery, skateboarding, and surfing. He was a community activist in his own way and an extremely righteous cat. He and I spent a lot of time trying to clean up our friend Harry Jumonji to no avail. Andy was one of the most powerful men I ever knew, both spiritually and physically—a man of true conviction. He was tragically felled by a wasp sting while in Montauk, where he was with Jumonji. It was entirely unexpected and very heavy for a lot of us. His loss started my thoughts of trying to obtain sobriety, something he always thought I would benefit greatly from. In retrospect, he was not wrong.

20

GOODBYE PORK PIE HAT

I wish my dad had lived long enough to see this book come to fruition, but he will live through me always. I was fortunate to have spent a lot of time with him during the last two years of his life. After losing so much time with my mother, I was determined to see my dad as much as possible. I was with him the first time he went through chemo and it went into remission for a year.

He spent that Christmas in New York with me and a bunch of my crazy, wayward friends. He smoked joints and watched basketball with my boys while I helped prep dinner, which consisted of putting out a fire in my oven. We ate a glorious meal and my close friend and off-again on-again junkie pal, Harry Jumonji, nodded in and out of consciousness. It was frankly uncomfortable watching Jumonji nod out in the middle of Christmas dinner.

My dad, in classic form, said, "Looks like brother Harry's as high as a giraffe's pussy," and the entire dinner party exploded in laughter. Only my pops, who had struggled with drugs for large chunks of his life, could have put it all into perspective so casually.

I remember clearly that in May 2010, when he told me he felt sick again and that it could be his last go around and that we "need to write this book, mi hijo." I was scared of the task, but mentally began to put it together. Still, it took me months to really start writing. I remember when he went back for tests in July knowing he was sick before the doctors told him. He sat in my house on my couch and told me he was at the end with such nonchalance it was hard to believe.

I was living with a gorgeous girl, many years my junior, at the time, who couldn't understand what was going on. My dad and I watched basketball a lot that spring while he stayed with me, before he got really sick. I remember her yelling at me saying that all I wanted to do was sit around and watch hoops with my dad. I told her that she was right and that he was battling cancer. I explained to her that these could be his last days and that it was important we had things to talk about, but she was too young and too self-centered to understand or care.

Frankly, she was a lot like I was at her age.

In the following months, my dad's health took a turn for the worst and he was diagnosed as terminal. This coincided with me catching my girlfriend cheating on me with a rapper friend of mine. I would find out that he wasn't the only one. She was a beautiful girl and a very flawed human being. Me, I was so lost spiritually at the time that I actually took her seriously. Shit, even Stevie Wonder could have seen it would never work out. She was the type of girl you have an adventure in Vegas with, not the type you make your lady. My dad, much to his credit, never liked her much and questioned what I was doing with her long before I did. I should have listened to him.

My weakness for beauty had bitten me in the ass again.

In thinking about my dad and all the wild adventures we shared, one that stands out most vividly occurred on May 12, 2009. Much to my dad's chagrin, San Francisco's Board of Supervisors had decided to honor him for his longtime service as an activist and esteemed journalist in the city by the bay. This was spearheaded by councilman John Avalos, a fan and friend of my dad's. Councilman Avlos was also aware of my dad's health issues and in light of that wanted to honor him.

My dad and all his crazy hippie politico friends were also given the right to conduct a shaman service in the lobby of City Hall and conduct a poetry reading in the massive assembly room. My dad was already in the midst of his long battle with liver cancer, which was for the time in remission after a bout of chemo. He was in fine spirits, and he was joined by all his friends—including Diamond Dave Whitaker, QR Hand, myself, and various other freaks who were there to lend moral and comedic support.

It was quite a sight to see. I wore a sharkskin suit and a pork pie hat in honor of my dad's jazzbo leanings. He was impressed when I picked him up that morning as we headed to City Hall to stir up some shit. My dad and his gang of psychedelic warriors assembled in the waiting chambers of one of the councilmen, which prompted him and his motley crew of friends and freaks to crack jokes about waiting to be summoned to the Board of Supervisor's North County court room. My dad had already told us he was going to turn down the honor, but in a comedic, celebratory way—not a "fuck you" way. He had it all mapped out. My dad had a perverse sense of humor, and he was going to put it on display this afternoon. It would be one of his last great performances. I think, in part, it was dedicated to me.

The councilman also shared a tale of my dad being incarcerated at San Quentin for resisting service during the Vietnam War. My dad was the second American in the state of California to do so. He is partially responsible for the conscientious objector status that exists today, and for his troubles he received almost two years of hard jail time. He never returned to prison but continued to raise hell whenever he thought the cause warranted it. My dad was always proud of his accomplishments, but he was extremely proud that he could not be broken by prison.

Councilman Avalos spoke of my dad organizing a large-scale welfare strike that led to welfare reform in San Francisco, as well as his dedication to the opposition of Prop 187, which was eventually ignored by the city. He sang my dad's literary praises and highlighted his expertise on the NAFTA trade agreement, which had him speak at several senate subcommittees. Hearing the tale of his release from San Quentin read aloud with the list of his other lengthy accomplishments in San Francisco's City Hall was a triumphant moment for all of us. We all clapped and hooted and hollered at it all. It was an amazing thing to witness. Councilman Avalos then dedicated the day to my pops and offered him the floor, which my dad seized with reckless abandon.

He promptly listed all the social and economic reasons why he simply could not accept the key to the city and the declaration of this day as his. He cited gentrification, homelessness, and the overall lack of good vibes throughout the city. He spoke of his beating at the hands of the cops in 1968, which left his vision permanently impaired, and of his filing fee never being returned when he dropped out of the 1968 mayoral race. He cracked wise about how poor people could no longer afford to even be homeless in San Francisco, let alone keep a roof over their heads, and left the room laughing, including the entire city council and the audience of about thirty of his wacky friends. It was a magnificent performance. The entire room was impressed. He closed with these words: "Life, like reporting, is kind of a death sentence. Pardon me for living it so fully."

After the ceremony was over, we were ushered into Councilman Avalos's room sans Councilman Avalos. We quickly went out to the balcony and my dad sparked a pre-rolled joint only to go ahead and spark one more. We finished toking it as Councilman Avalos entered the room. Surprisingly, he laughed it off, as if he knew he had invited this madness into his office. It was cool as fuck until a county sheriff burst into the room only to find a gang of old hippies and a councilman laughing it up. He was none too thrilled at the sight and quickly escorted us out of the office, down the halls, and to the lobby, where we waited with shit-eating grins on our faces to have the shaman service conducted on my dad and his failing liver. The thought of a major city giving a bunch of old left-wing kooks access to the lobby of City Hall is a true testament to San Francisco and how cool it once was. It was a throwback to the sixties that afternoon. Unfortunately, like so many big cities—NYC included—that San Francisco no longer exists. It has been swept away with the rise of tech companies and such in the last decade.

That day for me was one of the last great moments I got to share with my dad. I was proud to be there for it. He often toiled in obscurity, writing away for peanuts while staying true to his cause. It was an honorable profession, though not necessarily prop-laden, and here he was finally getting some of his flowers while he was still alive to enjoy them.

As his dear fried Luis conducted a beautiful Native American shaman ceremony to cleanse my dad's failing liver, the crowd grew. Those who were not invited to the dedication were out in force for the liver cleansing ceremony. It was heavy stuff. I stood by my dad with my arm around him as he prepped. He smiled the whole time, deeply involved in the ritual and appreciating every minute of it. Aging activists of all shapes and sizes watched my dad have a spiritual exorcism of his torturous cancer, and I only wish that the performance would have worked. It might not have killed the cancer, but it did put a smile on everyone's faces, including that of Councilman Avalos, who stayed to watch the ceremony. I dropped a tear or two, realizing that my dad's passing was more inevitable than I had even realized. The end was upon us, and it was time to celebrate the man before it was too late—a fact that was not lost on any of us that day.

After the celebration, there was to be a long poetry reading in the adjacent assembly room. It was a huge, ornate room full of history and activism. My dad had it rigged so that he and QR could read second ("Never read first," he told me) and then quickly slip off to my hotel downtown to watch the NBA playoffs. My dad, through it all, had his eye on his prize: watching some basketball with his best friend and his son. That whole day from A to Z speaks volumes about my dad from his wacky sense of humor to his dedication to activism and truth, and his utter love of basketball as a bonding tool.

It was beautiful, just like my dad.

My dad's health deteriorated quickly. In July of 2010, he was given a year to live, but he knew he wouldn't be here that long. He was determined to leave the earth in peace with his children. Carla and I spent a lot of time with him in New York, San Francisco, and Mexico City, and it wasn't always easy. My dad was a difficult individual, often cranky and harshly judgmental. Sound like anyone?

I moved to LA in mid-August and was miserable. I was still working for Travis Barker's clothing company Famous Stars and Straps. Travis was a good enough guy, but the working environment was not for me. With a job I hated, a dying father, and a recent heartache, it's not hard to see how my life had taken a turn toward the darkness or why my boozing had gotten worse.

My main boss, a former jock from Orange County, hated me from the jump. It was a bad fit; I was a fish out of water there. One of the most frustrating things was watching Travis make his solo record and not being able to be involved on the creative side. He would play me songs and I would suggest possible collaborators or coproducers and get paid zero mind. I was treated like a schmuck by some of his underlings—guys who in my book were musical simpletons. I really felt, and still feel, that I could have been a good influence on him musically, but it wasn't meant to be. Instead, I ran the marketing arm of the company, which was hard for me since I didn't really believe in the brand. I was only in it for three things: 1) the paycheck, 2) to get as far away from NYC and its bad vibes, and 3) to be close to my pops in hopes of spending as much time with him as possible as he neared the end of his life.

I spent my forty-fourth birthday with my dad in San Francisco as opposed to partying in Los Angeles with my friends. I had a big hotel suite and we watched a lot of sports. The San Francisco Giants, my dad's favorite team, had made the playoffs and eventually went on to win the World Series. A healthy dad would have been ecstatic. Instead, he claimed that he didn't really "love these Giants," yet he still rooted for them.

The pain he was experiencing made it tough for him to find much joy, and his outbursts were tough to deal with. He was angry about dying and upset about having to rely on Oxycodone and other pain pills, having kicked hard drugs in the late seventies. He wasn't ready to say goodbye yet, and neither was I. We spent Thanksgiving in Humboldt, the magical place he took me to as a teenager when my mom couldn't keep it together.

This time around, it was also a rough little journey. Sidney, his best friend and my other spiritual uncle, for lack of a better term, suffered a massive stroke the day after he left to visit his son in Mendocino County, and this really fucked my pops up. He saw his own mortality and then some. My dad was supposed to die at Sid's house watching basketball on the fifty-inch TV he half paid for, but it wasn't meant to be.

My father decided to return to Mexico City and wait out his last days in the cramped writer's room he had kept for twenty-five years at the Hotel Isabella. I had never once in all those years ventured to Mexico City to visit him, so over Christmas I joined him there for a week and helped him take apart the last pieces of his life with the help of his friend, Oscar, a crazy sax-playing Mexican rebel.

Showing up for my dad was an honor and a challenge. As he got sicker, he verbally assaulted me a few times. They say you lash out at the ones you love at the end, and he did just that. It wasn't always easy to take, but I stood tall and gave back love as much as he would allow.

One day, his abusive behavior got so bad that I had to check out. I gave him a hug and went and got stone-cold drunk instead of spending the day with him. I can't explain how much I regret not having that one extra day with him in retrospect.

One night, he asked me to put him to bed. He had never asked me that before; I knew the end was near. We spoke like we had never spoken before and said all those things you want and need to say in these situations. We left no stone unturned and pulled no punches. He apologized for disappearing during my childhood. I told him he was forgiven many, many years ago, and he finally knew he was truly forgiven. He broke down in tears and told me he was sorry for being an asshole for so long, that he loved me more than anything. I did the same. He made me promise to keep my sister and her daughter in my life. He made me swear I wouldn't lose touch with his dear friends, QR Hand and the stroke-addled Uncle Sidney. He made me promise to stay close to Sidney's son, Zac, whom I had avoided for reasons unknown. Zac had been like a little brother to me as kids, and now he wanted me to promise to rebuild that bond, especially with Sidney being sick.

I agreed to all of it and told him he was the most important person in my entire world. It was and is the truth. I also promised to finish this book for him. I put my dad to sleep and held his hand he dozed off, as did I in a chair next to his bed. My dad awoke in the middle of the night and told me, "Dante, I have you in my hands. I'll always keep you with me."

He then fell back asleep, leaving me with those words for the rest of my years on this planet.

I asked my dad if he wanted me with him when he passed. He said he didn't want to do that to me because he didn't think I could handle it. He may have been right. I asked him what, if anything, he wanted me to tell Dylan, my estranged older sister, his stepdaughter he raised and never considered anything but his daughter. He asked me to speak to her and explain that he wasn't strong enough to undertake the task.

I told her this to the best of my abilities. In truth, it was less than she deserved. I was just trying to comply with my dad's wishes. I did the best I could. Unfortunately, I don't believe it was good enough. Our father, John Ross, passed away on January 17, 2011, twelve days after I left him in Mexico City at a hospice run by his friend, Kevin, and his wife, Arminda, in Michoacán. My dad had been there when Arminda's mom passed and remarked that it was a lovely way to make the passage to the next plane of existence. He chose to enter the next realm in the same way she did. It's hard for me to accept that he didn't want his children by his side, but those were his wishes. No matter how much it hurt me and my two sisters, we had to respect them.

The day my dad passed, I went to my sister Carla's house. I needed to hold her daughter, Zoe, who meant so much to my dad. I needed to see her face, to see my family's lineage. We looked at pictures of my father and she said, *abuelo*, the Spanish word for grandfather over and over again. It was a fitting tribute from a two-year-old child who somehow knew something had happened.

Thank you, Zoe. You comforted me more than you will ever know.

My dad was a complex man. Much like myself, he could be extremely selfish. Other times he was so compassionate it was bewildering. His rhymes and reasons were often his own and nobody else's. He danced to his own beat, and some beat it was. My dad will always be with me, and I will take him everywhere I go until the day I wither away.

I am in my fifties, and I suffer from arthritis and may develop Alzheimer's one day as it tends to be much more prominent in the children of those who suffer from it. I have no children. I have a surgically replaced hip, anger management issues, and a lifetime of self-centered dysfunction, as well as alcohol and addiction issues to contend with. I have suffered from a self-indulgent prolonged adolescence. My memory is already bad, and my heart still hurts as I write this, thinking of life without my parents. I often wonder if this book will ever be published. I wonder if I will have to read from this book somewhere and speak about my father and our bond to complete strangers.

I was not shy about my father's illness and passing. I shared it with the few thousand people who followed my daily runnings via social media. I did so because I felt as if my relationship with my dad was worth celebrating, that people should know of the love that can exist between father and son. I hoped my remembrances might ease someone else's pain.

I received words from hundreds of people—some I knew well, some I never met—all who understood the sense of loss I was experiencing. I know it is not a unique experience; most people will lose their parents someday. Still, the compassion I received in those months after my father passed helped me tremendously and helped confirm my belief in something bigger than us.

Writing about him online, and then again for this book, has been a cathartic exercise, and one that has helped me ease my personal pain. I simply loved my dad more than any person I have ever known, and that love will never fade. This book is a testament to that love, and with it I say, John, I will always treasure your memory for as long as I am breathing. I thank you, Dad, for passing on your legacy on to me and inspiring me to write.

MY FATHER'S PLAYLIST

Charles Mingus—"Goodbye Pork Pie Hat"

John Coltrane—"Giant Steps"

John Coltrane—"Naima"

Miles Davis—"So What"

Gary Bartz—"Celestial Blues"

Bobby "Blue" Bland—"I'll Take Care of You"

Dizzy Gillespie, Sonny Stitt, and Sonny Rollins—"On the Sunny Side
of the Street"

Ornette Coleman—"Peace"

Billie Holiday—"Strange Fruit"

Bill Evans—"On Green Dolphin Street"

Duke Ellington and John Coltrane—"In a Sentimental Mood"

Donald Byrd—"Cristo Redentor"

EPILOGUE

CELESTIAL BLUES

In the wake of my dad's passing, a bunch of crazy things happened to me. My sister Carla and I conducted heartfelt memorials for him in Mexico City, San Francisco, and New York. His friends threw him a great party in Humboldt County, so I was told—unfortunately neither my sister nor I could attend. The memorial in San Francisco was particularly emotional and amazing. My sister and I, along with my dad's crazy hippy friends, spread my pop's ashes down Mission Street from Twenty-Forth Street to Sixteenth Street via the Mission 16 bus. It was deeply healing.

I left my job in Los Angeles after being abused one too many times by my boss, who actually called me to berate me the day of my father's memorial. I moved back to New York and sunk into a deep depression of sorts. I was swimming in pity, drink, and dark thoughts of loss and pain. In a sense, I had hit an emotional bottom. I was reeling, and the thought of my dad's passing and the realization I would never see him again tore me up.

And then something happened that I did not expect.

I made the decision to try to get sober. For the first time since I was thirteen, I abstained from all substances. I am proud to say that more than eleven years later that still holds true, though it hasn't been easy. I took up meditation. I started to reconnect with my higher power through my Unitarian Universalist beliefs and explored a deeper sense of spirituality.

I started to develop a clarity I hadn't yet experienced in my adult life. Still, my personal relationships were hard to maintain, especially work-related ones—always a problem of mine. I am not a different person, but I'm striving to be—specifically one who handles life's issues, triumphs, and hardships with a more even hand. I'm not there yet, but maybe one day.

Buddhists say that we are each composed of three people:

The person you were.

The person you are right now.

The person you truly want to be.

I believe this sums up where I am right now.

I am still a work in progress, though, as I work diligently to deal with the loss of my father and to hopefully come to a place of internal peace, something I have never completely had in my entire life. It's said that through pain and struggle often comes growth. I believe this is one of those times. You could call my sobriety and journey of self-exploration my father's departing gift if you will. I call it my path.

My first year of getting and staying sober took every bit of energy I could muster. I was angry, sad, and lonely. I missed my dad. I kept thinking of all the women I had let slip away. That shit may have been cool when I was in my twenties, but in my forties, it played differently. No, I wasn't happy, but on a deep spiritual level I knew that the healing had begun. One morning after I meditated for the first time, I got a phone call from Lyor Cohen, who knew my father had passed.

"Where are you?" Lyor blurted at me.

"New York, why?"

"I know, but where?"

"My house. Why?"

"Because today is Thursday," he said. "You're going to start working at Warner Brothers next week."

"What's the pay look like?" I asked.

Lyor said, "Dante, be happy you will have a job." He then told me that Todd Moscowitz, my new boss, would be calling me in a few minutes and hung up on me. I started that following Monday.

This call was what we in twelve step programs refer to as a "God shot." It confirmed that my want to get sober and change my life was the right choice. Needless to say, it helped me develop a meditation practice I continue to this day. I was nervous at the prospect of starting a new gig, but I was also felt extremely grateful to be given the opportunity to do something I loved again.

My first year at the new job was relatively uneventful. I felt uninvolved, but at least I didn't have to deal with getting Lyor's breakfast order right. On my own hustle, I had started to work with Action Bronson right before I came to Warners. I tried to get him signed there but he didn't fit their bill at that time. The irony never ceases when I think about what would later transpire.

Working with Action was, at first, a seemingly a perfect fit. He had talent. He was a very good rapper, and perhaps even a great one. A real New Yorker, he had a point of view and irreverence about him I found enthralling, and I was excited about the prospect of working with an artist who reminded me of why I loved hip-hop in the first place.

Action came to me somewhat formed. I would be lying if I said I made him a success; I merely accentuated what was already there. I opened a few doors for him, introducing him to a great music-making partner named Justin Nealis, a.k.a. Party Supplies. I took him to Alchemist Studio the first time we went to LA. I road managed the early shows, as well as booked them. I got him some mainstream looks on sites like Complex and got The Fader to finally give him some light after repeatedly being dismissed by their music editor.

We went on the road. I was newly sober and Action was anything but, and that was where the problems began.

As a matter of fact, I can't think of many jobs that would be more of a challenge for a recovering weedaholic than road managing Action Bronson. I was irritable and he was a master ball buster—not a good combo. Road managing a new act, especially one as difficult and stoned as Action, was not an easy task. We did some shows in Canada that went relatively smooth, but by the time we got to California on our second run, it had started to get a bit rough. We butted heads but forged on.

As much as I tried, I couldn't get him signed, and he was getting more and more frustrated. Honestly, I wasn't sure getting signed to a major label was the way to go for an artist like him. I still don't. But Action wanted to get paid. I felt the noose around my neck tightening. We went to Europe to do five shows. The noose got tighter when we were in Amsterdam, the capital of weed and hookers. I could feel the end coming, but I stuck with it, thinking it might work out. After all, I still completely believed in him as an artist, and I still do.

But between a new live-in girlfriend and eventual wife, my newfound sobriety, my gig at Warner Brothers Records, and managing Action, I was doing too much. After the Europe run, tensions got even more strained. Some of Action's peers started getting signed. A$AP Rocky was the toast of the town. Then an artist named Mr. eXquire, another of Action's peers, got signed, which led to even more tensions. The A&R person who signed eXquire had passed on Action.

Action started blaming me. Things were getting heated between us and I didn't know how to play my hand. I tried to strategize. I wanted to team up with Chris Lighty and have him and his team help manage Action with me, thus removing me from the line of fire. Action balked.

Paul Rosenberg had an underling who was in Action's ear, which I was acutely aware of. Paul was a fan of Action, not to mention an uber manager. If I were an artist and he wanted to manage me, I would have to listen. All of these things were starting to really work against me.

I could see the writing on the wall.

In the midst of all of this, South by Southwest was on the near horizon. I had parlayed a situation with Reebok to finance the mixtape *Blue Chips*, which Action had created with my boy Party Supplies. The dichotomy of this coupling wasn't lost on me at all. Action is a five-foot-six chef who is as wide as he is tall. He looks like a human bowling ball and is a brute of a human being. He's a tough kid, an Albanian, and he comes with all of the attributes attached to Albanians. Party Supplies, on the other hand, is a small, slight-framed, ethereal pretty boy of a kid from Long Island who had reinvented himself from a rapper into a quasi-hipster eighties-influenced singer. But with his talent, somehow, I was confident they would be a good combo. They had common ground—they both were complete stoners—and I knew if they linked, the vibes would flow. I was right, apparently.

After getting Reebok to pay us $35,000 for the mixtape, samples and all, I convinced them to fly us to SXSW and pay for our hotel and lodging. They also unwittingly paid for our incidentals, and to say that Action and the entourage went above and beyond in sticking them with an outlandish bill would be an understatement. It was actually pretty funny to watch.

We had five shows to do, including one at the Fader Fort, the premier gig at SXSW every year. I had also rigged a free trip for Meyhem Lauren, Action's sidekick, so that he could run with us. Action's entire squad came down, including producer Harry Fraud, who set up a studio in Action's room as we recorded, performed, and bickered for five straight days in Austin. I didn't always exercise the most patience. Action and I got into it several times. I was pretty sure the axe would soon fall.

It all came to a head when we headed to a gig at the Fader Fort. The artist Riff Raff was with us and was going to perform "Bird on a Wire," the internet hit that he appeared on with Action. I mistakenly put Riff Raff in the sprinter van, leaving out Action's main man Big Body Bes. I always think that whoever's on stage needs to roll into the venue first. Bes wasn't performing. This move created major tensions the rest of the trip. I didn't do it on purpose. I was just doing my job. Let's just say this led to a lot of tension between Bes, Action, and me for the remainder of the trip.

When we returned to New York, Reebok had pulled the "pimp" video from the site and ran the other way from the project, realizing the samples we used were blatant and the first video was titled "Hookers at the Point." It was a recreation of the HBO documentary, albeit it with a chick pissing in the street and Action playing a sadistic pimp named Silk. It was genius, but it was also a tough sell to corporate America and probably ensured I will never do business at Reebok again. Keep it 100, I can't believe they even bankrolled the project and the video in the first place.

We came back to NYC and the blame game got serious. Action was positive I was the reason why he didn't have a deal. I pleaded with Todd Moscowitz to let me sign him at Warner Brothers before I got blown out. He advised me to take it to Vice Media, which I did. Action officially fired me two days before he and Vice were going to do a deal. Action made sure I wouldn't get paid for connecting the dots. He used our hassles as an excuse to fire me and to hire Paul Rosenberg. He should have just told me that he thought Paul was a better manager and paid me for my time and for putting the Vice deal in motion. This didn't happen, though I tried to get my commission from Goliath, Paul's company, a few times. I never did. Eventually, I gave up.

I can't say I was perfect in managing Action—far from it—but I deserved better. I also couldn't make a big stink about it. I worked at Warners and it might jeopardize my job. I will say this: Suroosh Alvi and the people at Vice have never acknowledged that I steered Action their way and that's not cool. (I was actually told all about Action from an employee there who unwittingly claimed credit for it all. To make matters worse, Suroosh tried to pick my brain later, asking me if he should sign the Flatbush Zombies. I told him he should ask his interns and left it at that.) Paul never paid me any commission, either, per Action's instructions. Of course, Paul no longer manages Action—Todd Moscowitz, my former boss who wouldn't let me sign him, does.

Crazy, right?

By this stage of my life, I had learned to pick my battles, and this was one I chose not to fight. I was taught a real lesson in humility during this time and, looking back, I believe God wanted me to learn it.

I am proud of what I helped accomplish with Action in our brief run. He did soil it a bit with some sideways words on Twitter, but that's okay. I'm happy for Action's success and feel like I am—or was, anyway—a small part of it. If nothing else, it confirmed two things for me: This is a cutthroat business of big-bank taking little-bank, and that I could still spot talent and help it grow.

Action ended up being absorbed into Atlantic. To make matters worse, the urban department at WBR folded into Atlantic when Todd Moscowitz and Lyor Cohen left WMG. Let's just say there was a lot of intrigue going on, and for my part, I was not offered a job at Atlantic but stayed put at WBR after being told I would be fine.

I stayed at Warners for a year and change after Lyor left. My gig was often frustrating. I worked for a team of people who didn't get me. They mostly just looked at me like I was Lyor's leftover friend—which was not inaccurate, mind you. I'm sure some of them also thought that I was living on my past glory and that I just didn't have it anymore. A few senior A&R guys treated me like dog shit, repeatedly. And that did hurt.

Prior to Lyor's leaving, I came across an artist I thoroughly believed in called Macklemore. I thought he had the potential to become a real star. The kid from Seattle was not necessarily an obvious artist for me to be enamored by, but nonetheless, enamored I was. Regardless of how anyone feels about his artistry, he is amazing at what he does. I fought hard to get him signed at WB. Todd Moscowitz, in front of a room full of fellow A&R people, told me point blank that we weren't going to sign him. Still, I persisted and was shot down again.

I dragged Lyor to see Macklemore after he got the *XXL* magazine freshmen cover. Lyor seemed to think he was great but told me he wasn't signing him. To this day, I have no idea why. I had forged a friendship of sorts with Macklemore and found it impossible to tell him I couldn't sign him. I was $180,000 in the hole to the IRS. I had also shacked up with a wonderful woman who couldn't work because she was not a citizen, and I was helping support her. My finances were strained. So, although the fact I couldn't sign Macklemore really hurt my pride, I kept my mouth shut. I needed the gig. I acted out in other areas of my life, yet remained sober, though my marriage suffered.

I had no business becoming deeply involved with anyone at this point in my life in the first place. I was newly sober. I was trying to find my footing emotionally and spiritually. I married the first great woman who accepted me as me. I feared it might never happen again, as I was socially awkward in my early sobriety. I took her hostage and convinced her to uproot her entire life for me. In retrospect, I should have been wiser, less self-centered. To say I blew it would be an understatement. Our relationship didn't work out at the end of the day, and eventually we went our separate ways. She was, and is, a good person, but ultimately we were not good together.

I was frustrated with my career, my place in the music business, and the fact that after all the great acts I had unearthed, I didn't have enough juice in my own company to sign Action Bronson or Macklemore. My sense of entitlement had made me resentful. To this day, I still have some negative vibes when I think about these things, but I also know that my sense of entitlement doesn't do shit for me except make me more resentful.

Macklemore eventually got signed to ADA, the distribution company owned by WMG. Lyor had suggested I bring him there. Kenny Weagly, who ran ADA, got hip to Macklemore on his own accord and knew I was a fan and had pursued signing him. He told me he was going to do a deal with him and his manager. I advised him to do it and told him I believed the kid was a superstar in the making. Kenny, to his credit, kept me abreast of all Macklemore-related info, sending me sales numbers on the preorder for several weeks. He believed in my ears and eyes more than my employers at Warner Brothers, though frankly it would have been hard to believe in me less than those guys did. Macklemore, of course, became a star. I helped Todd Moscowitz broker a deal with Kenny Weagly, ADA, and WBR that helped utilize the WBR promo staff in return for a small override. Macklemore went on to sell more than seventeen million singles, have a multi-platinum album, and won a Grammy.

What did I get out of discovering one of the highest grossing rappers of the twentieth century? Kenny Weagly, with the help of Craig Kallman, the president of Atlantic Records, created a role for me at ADA, eventually reactivating the Asylum label with me at its helm along with Kenny. I am still waiting on a platinum plaque for *The Heist* LP.

In a roundabout way, I can thank Lyor for all of this. For all of his complexities, the guy was in my corner when it counted most. I appreciate how he kept my hopes up even after he left WBR and how he let everyone in earshot know how much I had wanted to sign Macklemore. Still, the events following his departure were uncomfortable up till the end. Todd Moscowitz and Joie Manda would also leave WBR, leaving me as the one rap-friendly fool still standing. I still can't believe they kept me around.

Unfortunately, my troubles didn't stop with Macklemore. I tried to sign Chance the Rapper, but he wasn't interested in being part of Warner Brothers—or any record label, for that matter. I was scolded by Rob Cavallo, the head of A&R, for my inability to reel him in. We got into it in front of a bunch of coworkers. I thought I was getting fired that day. Chance is now a Grammy-winning superstar, and he has still never signed a traditional record deal. There is no love lost between me and Rob Cavallo. He was, in the immortal words of GZA, "a mountain climber who plays an electric guitar."

As for Lyor, my music biz Rabbi: he is a savage of a man, but also a good friend and an amazing businessperson. I believe when our mutual friend and my early mentor Sean "Captain Pissy" Carasov took his own life, Lyor was jolted deeply. It changed Lyor, in a sense, and it also led to our reconnecting. He is a controversial person, yet someone who has taught me a great deal, and for that and many other things, I will always respect and admire that man. His belief in me has helped keep me going. In fact, several years after Sean's passing, Lyor and several of Sean's closest friends, including Mike D and Ad-Rock, helped spread his ashes over the warning track at Yankee Stadium. Sean was a huge Yankee fan. How Lyor managed to make this happen is a mystery to me, but it was a beautiful thing to do for our old friend.

I also lost my friend Adam "MCA" Yauch, someone who inspired me on so many levels, as well as my brother-in-arms, Chris Lighty. Yauch fell victim to throat cancer at the age of forty-seven. It was a real loss to mankind, as he was a truly enlightened soul. Chris took his own life, which I still find very hard to believe most days, for he was one of the strongest people I had ever known.

My big-brother figure and former production partner, Geeby Dajani, passed from ALS in December of 2019. John Gamble, the third Stimulated Dummy and the man I won a Grammy with, passed a mere ten months after Geeby.

Gamble and I reconnected again in early 2014, as we had some outstanding royalty issues we needed to settle. I was a few years sober, and John seemed a bit lost. He had gone back to school and gotten his mechanical engineering degree. (Ironic, right?) He had started doing building management for the NYC public school system and was trying to find himself. At the time, I was working on the ninth step in AA, which involves confronting your past and making amends to those you have wronged. I was given the chance to make amends with John that year. It helped me put down a lot of resentments I had toward him. He was graceful and forgave me for my plentiful misdeeds. We had an intense relationship, and I wasn't always the nicest person to him. I owed him a deep personal apology and thank God I was given the chance to make one to him.

In 2016, I had the luck of running into John at an AA meeting in NY, further rekindling our friendship. I spent a bunch of time with him, going to meetings in New York, before I moved to LA in 2018. He and I sat together at Geeby's memorial in January of 2020, and communicated every few days after the service.

The evening after Geeby's memorial, John came to hear me and our friend Emz DJ. Emz and I both marveled at how good he looked and how happy he seemed. This would be the last time I saw him in the flesh. John Gamble, my friend and longtime production partner, passed on October 16, 2020, in his sleep of natural causes less than a year after Geeby passed.

His passing haunts me daily. We spoke four days before he passed when he called me to say happy birthday, albeit a day late. I busted his balls, and we commiserated about Eddie Van Halen's recent passing.

To say I miss him immensely would be an understatement. Over sixteen years, we shared highs and lows that I have not shared with anyone in my entire life. He was as much my brother as any one I have ever known.

In the wake of his passing, I'd reached out to Doom to tell him about John, not wanting him to hear it from someone else. The two of them were once close. John greatly valued Doom and Doom the same. Fourteen days later, though the world—me included—wouldn't find out about that until December 31, 2020—Doom also passed. I can't help but feel that this happening so close together is a sign of something bigger—though a sign of what I don't know.

John died sober, seemingly in a good place both mentally and physically, his unique sense of humor firmly in place as he made me laugh every time we spoke in the months prior to his passing. His death was a huge shock to me and many around him. Losing John, Geeby, and Doom so close together was and is rough for me. Thinking about them, I feel as mortal as ever. In the weeks after Gamble's death, I often couldn't sleep out of fear that I might never awake. The pandemic only added to that paranoia. I also know that I am a strong person, that everyone has a cross to bear, and for now, this is mine. I know I'm still here for a reason. I can't say I know exactly what that is, but I also don't question it—it just is.

I do my best in the wake of these tragedies to try to express gratitude for being able to live and love another day. It ain't always easy, but it is always worth it. I still have a lot of things to share with the world and apparently my higher power knows this. The fact they are all three gone and I am still here is daunting. All I can do is keep their names alive by speaking of them often and hope that, in time, it will heal my sense of loss.

I miss these people and all the people I lost along the way but have come to a place where I can celebrate their collective life forces. They all affected me deeply and the love that I have for them remains eternal. For me, that love is God.

There are days I'm not sure if I am cut out for the new record business, but I am trying my best. I feel I still have an eye for talent as esoteric as my current tastes may be. I'm in my fifties, and I don't know if I love where music, in particular rap music, is these days, but I do know that I can still smell a hit. I refuse to complain or get stuck in that "back in the day" bullshit. In fact, I'm perfectly happy to scour the internet for new talent, as opposed to risking my life in a club like the LQ.

I can't tell you I believe in the power and importance of rap music today like I once did. I try to approach it in an open-minded way and embrace what works for me and leave the rest. Many decry the lack of lyricism, but I try to think back to the early days when lyricism wasn't a big asset. I mean, was Rob Base a lyricist? The lost art of crafting an album is often singled out as another reason rap music isn't vital art anymore. I remember when this was also the case in the early days of rap, pre–Run-DMC. My defense of where rap stands is often based on artists like Kendrick Lamar, J Cole, Anderson .Paak, and the Griselda movement. All of these artists are great and could hold their own in the so-called golden age of rap

Is rap music a shell of its former self? I don't know, and honestly, it doesn't really matter what I think. Rap music is youth music. It doesn't belong to a fifty-six-year-old white man, right? Fortunately for me, I have been able to find a few things the kids relate to still. I understand the culture of music, if not the constant use of auto-tune. I can still see what's moving the youth and this allows me to embrace what goes on instead of hating.

At my new digs, I signed a guy named IAMSU! first. He hailed from the Bay and is a talented kid. We had moderate success, enough so that I kept my job. Several months after, I found a guy named Dave Burd, a.k.a. Lil Dicky, who had big numbers on YouTube. What I saw was a really good rapper with a unique perspective. Dicky is a lanky Jewish ex-marketing wiz from the suburbs of Philly, who was bitten by the rap bug in college. He is a sloppily dressed, unshaven slacker of sorts—physically unimposing, yet charismatic. To look at him, you would think he was an unemployed waiter or something. I had a feeling about him from day one and pitched him to my new boss, Kenny Weagly, who let me run with it. We signed him, and he hit a home run right away with a hilarious record called *Save Dat Money*.

I actually got to do some real A&R due to a relationship with Fetty Wap's manager, Danny Su. I had tried to sign Fetty Wap, who was bubbling with his soon-to-be huge hit "Trap Queen" but had been shot down by Kenny Weagly and my head of business affairs, the project being deemed as too expensive for a distribution deal. I still can't believe they let it slip through their fingers. Regardless, Danny and I stayed friendly and with the help of Anthony Martini—who Dicky was signed to via his production company/label, The Commission—we arranged to get Fetty Wap a brown bag filled with some bucks to do the hook on the record. That, combined with an amazing video dreamed into existence by Dicky himself, helped generate one hundred million views on YouTube, and the next thing we knew we had a platinum single and a gold album.

I found another hit song with an Atlanta artist called MadeinTYO, who had a great jam called "Uber Everywhere." TYO is typical of a lot of modern rap artists. He makes great songs but is not always recognizable. He has had several hits at this point but the title of his single "Uber Everywhere," which eventually went platinum, is often more well-known than his name as an artist. TYO has since added several more gold records under his belt and become a star in his own right.

TYO is an example of me shifting the way I look at signing acts these days. I knew "Uber" was a great song, so I signed him. I didn't have a deep emotional connection to him as a person, but it didn't matter. I have never spent any real time in the studio with him watching his creative process, but the A&R game is not the same as it was when I was in my twenties and thirties. Still, I was pretty sure the song was going to win. He made good records that moved the youth, and to me, that's all that matters when it comes to doing A&R these days.

At Asylum, I signed a young upstart from Biloxi, Mississippi, by way of Houston named Ugly God. His first single "Water" went platinum. Ugly God is not the most talented kid I ever worked with. He's a funny-looking kid, a goofy six-foot-plus former basketball player who loves Pokémon. He has a self-deprecating sense of humor, often attempting to blur the lines between sarcasm and art—which is probably the most interesting thing about him.

Working with him was a trip. He could make four to five songs in one session, all the while making fun of me while he ran around with his shirt off acting like a kook and Facetiming his girlfriend. Are any of the songs good? Well, that would depend what you determine to be good.

He often refused to cooperate with any form of marketing plan we created for him and publicly criticized the label on social media, making all of our jobs that much harder. He often denies the fact he is even signed to a label. He will mockingly make fun of great artists like Kendrick Lamar and Anderson .Paak. He once told me he didn't know who Rakim was, and I still don't know if he was being serious or just busting balls. He turned down potential collaborations with real talents like Dram and others. I have seen him scapegoat people who work hard for him while bossing his "yes man" manager (his uncle, a.k.a. "the homeboy management network") around, goading him to support his bad career decisions. His sense of entitlement is infuriating. It's also par for the course when it comes to a certain segment of today's youth. The sense of entitlement is to be expected.

Ugly God is the new breed of self-empowered artist. He produces his own music, often in his bedroom; he controls his own messaging via social media, for better or worse. He created his own video for his hit song "Water" for four-hundred dollars and then refused to create any visuals for almost two years. All of these things led to his success and ultimate demise. His rapping skills were below that of most people I've worked with who made a hit record, but I knew he had a shot at being successful. In that regard, his success was and is a double-edged sword. He simply is not an artist built for the long haul. Whatever issues developed between Action Bronson and myself, my purist notion that rapping is still important makes me far more likely to be attracted to an Action than an Ugly God. For me, signing Ugly God was simply playing the game. I don't regret it, but I'm also fully aware of where he fits in on my resume.

In a two-year span at Asylum, I had amassed seven gold or platinum singles, as well as two gold albums. I was as hot as I had ever been in my entire career. And then it all went bad. The label went cold, meaning I didn't break anything new. I chased a lot of stuff I couldn't bring in. I was being directed to bring in artists based on research, yet the research would dictate that any deal based on research would exceed my employer's financial willingness. At Asylum, and over the eight years I worked at WMG, I had brought a litany of acts to the table that I was unable to close on, including: Macklemore, Action Bronson, G-Eazy, Goldlink, Blueface, Fetty Wap, Joyner Lucas, Megan Thee Stallion, Denzel Curry, IDK, 21 Savage, NLE Choppa, Smino, Lil Nas X, and Lil Tecca. I also fought hard to keep Lil Dicky in the WMG system but was shot down for reasons still unclear to me. Often if it was an Asylum or ADA deal, it came down to money restraints. If it was an Atlantic deal, as was the case with Lil Tecca, I simply wasn't empowered enough to make it happen. To be straight about it, I think higher ups within the system just didn't believe in me. Over the course of working at WMG, I also tried to sign several acts that ended up getting signed to Atlantic by other A&R people after I was there first, such as Kyle, Joyner Lucas, and Dram.

All A&R people go through this. It's part of the game. There are no secrets anymore. We all have the same research. The days of scouring the Latin Quarters, listening to mix shows, or scooping up the hottest mixtape artist in the streets are long gone. The days of finding the next superstar on your favorite blog is going, going, gone. It's all being done via research now and it has taken a lot of critical taste out of doing A&R. These days, I think it stands for analytics and research, not artist and repertoire. This is fine for finding the Ugly Gods of the world, but will it help you find the next Kendrick Lamar?

The thing I found the most frustrating was the constant second-guessing. Megan Thee Stallion, for one, was second-guessed by everyone I worked with, including my twenty-four-year-old female assistant and a handful of under twenty-five-year-olds who sat on research calls with me every week. My former boss, Kenny Weagly, refused to spend $200,000 to sign her, which would have closed the deal. He tried to get me to lowball her manager Jay Farris, stating we were not spending more than $100,000 to sign her. To this day, I am still baffled.

The desire to keep Lil Dicky in the WMG system was also questioned and ultimately shot down by the upper management at both ADA and Atlantic Records. He would go on to sell six million singles of his first BMG release, *Freaky Friday*. I found this hard to live with, especially as he was, of all the acts I worked with at WMG, possibly my favorite based on his sense of humor and rapping ability.

They say all good things must come to an end. I think this applies to mediocre things as well, and with Asylum faltering, changes were made. I was given a new boss, Gaby Peluso. She brought in a full staff and, to her credit, there were far more people of color employed within her new team. I believe hip-hop is a Black art form and it is important to have Black people working on music made by Black people. I also think I earned my spot; my track record says so. I earned my stripes.

I am not someone who was handed a shot through nepotism. I clawed tooth and nail for everything I got. I also think there are a lot of white people who are what I call "Blackperts." They are authorities on rap music, are rarely questioned, and actually participate in the culture at large. It has just come to be accepted, for better or worse. I do not see this changing.

From day one, I knew it would not work with me and Gaby. She talked to me and everyone like it was Def Jam circa 1997. Never mind political correctness—in all honesty, I often found her insulting. She didn't like me or want me there from the jump. She thwarted several deals I put forth and, in particular, she hated on Lil Tecca to people at Atlantic. She lowballed every offer we made in our brief tenure working together, blowing any shot I had at Lil Nas X. She also refused to embrace Jack Harlow, who was offered to us by Atlantic to help incubate. She second-guessed everything I suggested. She lacked any sense of decorum. Her invasive questions about my wife's ethnicity and her homophobic statements directed at me and Teezo Touchdown, an artist I wanted to sign, were out of line. It became a pissing contest. People around me told me she was going to axe me for months, and in June of 2019, I was relived of my duties—the first time I had ever been fired in my long and winding career.

I will say that I am proud of my last two signings: Big Freedia and Sada Baby, both of whom I believe are stars in the making. Kenny Weagly, my former boss and the president of ADA, allowed all of this to happen on his watch, as did several executives within WMG (one of whom now runs Soundcloud and declined to even interview me for a job there recently). It clearly showed me the point that friends are few and far between in this business. Ironically, Kenny would also get thrown to wolves a year after I was relieved of my position. Shit happens, right?

I will admit I was not particularly politically savvy in my handling of the situation. I turned down a job within WMG eight months prior to my dismissal that might have altered the final fallout. I have to admit I was pissed off at how I was dismissed. Still to this day, I do not know what Ms. Peluso has accomplished to allow her to subject me to her nonsense. I have to think that this is an opportunity for me to get back to working on music I believe in for a change. I am looking forward to the challenge and trying my best not to look back with bitterness.

The hardest thing to accept, though, is this: As a fifty-something-year-old white male, my days of signing rappers for a major label may be behind me. I will have to operate outside of a label in order to continue my career, which is both a scary proposition and a liberating one. I have been beholden to record companies for a long time and have seen peers accomplish far more in a financial sense while working on the outside. I believe it's worth it to actively become more of an entrepreneur. Without leaving WMG, I would not have this in front of me right now and for that, on some level, I have to be thankful. Like I have said several times throughout this book, I am a masterful survivalist.

The tricky part of all of this, which I learned in sobriety, is two-fold: 1) life is a balancing act, and 2) it's progress, not perfection, that counts. I am not always emotionally sober. My ego still has way too much to do with the way I behave. This time around, I am way more philosophical about where I stand career-wise and more aware then ever where the creative and artistic bar now resides. While I strive to find the next Kendrick Lamar, I also understand where rap is right now and can spot a hit—something I may not have been as apt to understand twenty-five years ago when I signed Ol' Dirty Bastard. They don't call it the music *business* for nothing.

For me, the practice of acceptance comes into play when I approach my job these days. I accept where the music is and I see things I like and understand the way the culture surrounding it is moving. And in doing this, in not being an elitist snob, I have found a new version of success, and for that I am full of gratitude. I have learned to balance my gig with deejaying 45s, the oldest, rarest piece of music you can play. I enjoy doing this. I believe it connects me to the root note of the music I love while allowing me to further enjoy and excel at my day job signing rappers. In not being a so-called rap purist, I have found a new version of success—one I am comfortable with. I am a careerist when need be these days, something I once found offensive.

I try not to get too high off of my successes or too low off of my failures. One of the most valuable things I have learned is that shit changes. A year and a half after I lost my dad, I lost my mother to Alzheimer's. My mom had been sick for a long time. I was at peace with her passing, knowing that the last few years of her life she was a mere vessel of sorts and no longer the vibrant woman who raised me. In a strange sense, it was a relief to know she was out of pain and no longer helpless in her own body, dementia having taken most of her faculties from her a few years before she eventually left the earth. It was my newfound sobriety, my yearning to grow up spiritually and mentally, and the loss of my father that allowed me to hold it together in the wake of her passing. Somewhere my dad is proud of me and where my head is at these days. So is my mother. This allows me to carry them in my heart for the rest of my days, truly proud to be her only son.

Or so I thought.

Social media did not exist when I was growing up. I often decry it, but in 2012, it helped change my life again. In August of that year, I was first approached by a stranger named Dan Cuomo on Facebook about the possibility that he might be my brother. He then, over the next few months, supplied me with a litany of information. He unfolded his story of adoption. I discussed this with my older sister, who immediately scoffed at the idea. After all, he was born a mere eleven months after her. She had no recollection of any of it. I hemmed and hawed. I felt I owed him the right to know his own story, yet it still took me over a year to finally take the DNA test.

In late 2013, I took the test and it determined that we were indeed brothers. My sister still would not accept it, but I was intrigued. We made plans to meet in San Francisco in January of 2014. We had exchanged pictures; we did indeed resemble each other. Meeting him was mind-blowing. He was close to my height and had the same wiry build as both me and my mother. We had similar eyes and cheekbones. Our mannerisms were similar. He also shared the same warped sense of humor as my mom and me. I spent the weekend with him and his wife in the city my dad and I had spent so much time in together. This was not lost on me.

I got to answer questions about our mother for him. He wanted to know what she was like. I soft-pedaled some of her neurosis and tried my best to explain a very complicated woman. He told me about his upbringing in Long Island and his own life on the LES in the late eighties. We wondered if we had ever crossed paths and it turned out I had indeed, with his adoptive brother in my punk rock travels. It was a trip, another gift on a long journey filled with gifts. It further confirmed my belief in God. Beyond that, I really believe that if I weren't sober, I would never have had the courage to meet him, to take the DNA test, to allow us to further understand what made us and continues to make us, and who and what we are. I have come to know and love my big brother.

That my mother went through so much I never knew about and couldn't fathom—from giving up a son, losing another, the dissolution of her marriage to my father, and her battles internally with alcohol and her Catholic upbringing—has given me a lot to ponder in the wake of her passing. I now realize that she had a disease fueled by pain and guilt, and that she did the best she could. In spite of it all, she raised a creative, artistic, and spiritual man and a strong woman.

I think my mom would be proud of me. One of my fondest memories is of watching MTV one time at her house in Rhode Island many years before she passed. She was in her sixties, still wiry and feisty. Bone Thugs-N-Harmony came on and my mom started singing along. I asked her if she liked the song, and she said, "Yes! Those guys are really talented, and they loved their Uncle George."

I cracked up and said, "You're right."

She didn't skip a beat, saying, "Dante, why don't you make music like that?"

I had no answer. I just laughed and gave her a hug. This was my mother, after all, and she was amazing. Without her, I would not have my musical sensibility, my want for justice for all, or my sensitive-yet-conflicted soul.

I wish she knew how wonderful I thought she was; I am not sure if she ever did. We had an intense, often dysfunctional relationship. We also had a deep mother-and-son bond that is unlike any other love I have ever experienced in my life. To say I miss her deeply is an understatement. I know her spirit is aware of where I am now in life and is smiling upon me daily.

For this, I am blessed.

Where do I go from here? Finishing this book closes one chapter of my life, for the time being. I am currently fascinated by the written word. I have been exploring the world of screenwriting, acquiring intellectual property rights for film and television development, and I feel good about the possibilities. I am also managing a few acts I really believe in, artists that remind me of why I feel in love with hip-hop in the first place. Every day is a new chance at doing something important, and where it takes me is anyone's guess. Me, I try not to worry about it while reminding myself that wherever I am is exactly where I am supposed to be.

To my parents, I say:

Dad, thanks for the gift of higher consciousness. You are one of the greatest minds I have ever known. Mom, thanks for always doing your best to raise a wild kid like me. You both instilled a love of art and culture in me, two of the greatest gifts you could have given me. I carry a piece of both of you in my heart everywhere I go and will continue to do so till I no longer walk the earth. I have so much gratitude for both of you, mere words cannot express enough. Beyond it all, I have to say thank you to New York, the world's greatest city, for helping to make me the man I am today: a true son of the city.

ACKNOWLEDGMENTS

To the culture of hip-hop, I say thank you for accepting me and therefore altering the course of my life. I am honored to have been allowed to contribute a small piece to a much bigger picture.

To the Lower East Side, where I was raised, I thank you for the many life lessons. Being raised where I was informs my entire being.

To the New York City that shaped me, thank you. I have the highest amount of gratitude for being able to experience New York City when it was still raw, dangerous, and the greatest city on Earth.

I am forever a Son of the City.

Special thanks to Russell Lauricella, my LES brother from another; my sister, Carla Ross Murray; my brother, Dan Cuomo; mi novia, Mimi Majgaard; my editor, Guy Intoci; Peter Conti, my writing mentor; my extended family members, Zach Dominitz and Jane Rabb; Mark Pearson; Damien "Domino" Siguenza; Bill Spector; Stretch Armstrong and Bobbito Garcia for the decades of friendship and laughter; Operator Emz; my brothers, Paul and Pete Moore; and the most honest person I have ever known, Jill Revson.